Social Interaction and Professional Identity in Allied Healthcare Education

Studies in Social Interaction
Series Editors: Steve Walsh, Paul Seedhouse and Christopher Jenks

Presenting data from a range of social contexts including education, the media, the workplace, and professional development, the *Studies in Social Interaction* series uncovers, among other things, the ways in which tasks are accomplished, identities formed and communities established. Each volume in the series places social interaction at the centre of discussion and presents a clear overview of the work which has been done in a particular context. Books in the series provide examples of how data can be approached and used to uncover social-interaction themes and issues, and explore how research in social interaction can feed into a better understanding of professional practices and develop new research agendas. Through stimulating tasks and accompanying commentaries, readers are engaged and challenged to reflect on particular themes and relate the discussion to their own context.

Series Editors
Steve Walsh is Professor of Applied Linguistics at Newcastle University

Paul Seedhouse is Professor of Educational and Applied Linguistics at Newcastle University

Christopher Jenks is Professor of Intercultural Communication at Utrecht University

Titles available in the series:

Social Interaction in Second Language Chat Rooms	Christopher Jenks
Social Interaction and L2 Classroom Discourse	Olcay Sert
Social Interaction and Teacher Cognition	Li Li
Social Interaction and English Language Teacher Identity	John Gray and Tom Morton
Social Interaction in Language Teacher Education	Fiona Farr, Angela Farrell and Elaine Riordan
Intercultural Transitions in Higher Education	Alina Schartner and Tony Johnstone Young
Multimodal Participation and Engagement	Christine M. Jacknick
Human Spoken Interaction as a Complex Adaptive System	Aki Siegel and Paul Seedhouse
Social Interaction and Professional Identity in Allied Healthcare Education	Irene Walsh, Niamh Reynolds and Caroline Jagoe

Visit the Studies in Social Interaction website at www.edinburghuniversitypress.com/series/SSINT

Social Interaction and Professional Identity in Allied Healthcare Education

Irene P. Walsh, Niamh Reynolds and Caroline Jagoe

EDINBURGH
University Press

Edinburgh University Press is one of the leading university presses in the UK. We publish academic books and journals in our selected subject areas across the humanities and social sciences, combining cutting-edge scholarship with high editorial and production values to produce academic works of lasting importance. For more information visit our website: edinburghuniversitypress.com

Edinburgh University Press Ltd
13 Infirmary Street
Edinburgh EH1 1LT

First published in hardback by Edinburgh University Press 2025

Typeset in Minion Pro by
Cheshire Typesetting Ltd, Cuddington, Cheshire, and
printed and bound by CPI Group (UK) Ltd, Croydon, CR0 4YY

A CIP record for this book is available from the British Library

ISBN 978-1-4744-0315-3 (hardback)
ISBN 978-1-4744-0317-7 (paperback)
ISBN 978-1-4744-0316-0 (webready PDF)
ISBN 978-1-4744-0318-4 (epub)

CONTENTS

DEDICATIONS

To my parents, John and Joan, who lovingly imbued me with a strong sense of my own identity, aided in no small part by their steadfast support for my chosen personal and professional pathways. (IPW)

To my parents and my siblings, thank you for constant encouragement and support always. (NR)

To Maya and Lucy, may you build your identities in the mosaic of your lifeworlds. (CJ)

FIGURES AND TABLES

FIGURES

TABLES

ACKNOWLEDGEMENTS

We would like to firstly thank all the owners of the 'voices' in this book, without whom the arguments put forward would have lacked depth, richness and, most crucially, authenticity. Thanks to our survey respondents, current and past students and to our wide circle of colleagues in the educational and clinical 'wild' that is the allied healthcare professional world of teaching and learning. Gratitude must also be expressed to the Studies in Social Interaction Series Editors – especially Steve Walsh – and to all at Edinburgh University Press for their patience and expert guidance.

Finally, thanks to our supportive families and loyal friends who may well have believed – just like we did at times – that this 'never-ending story' would never get told. Well, it did...

Irene, Niamh and Caroline

1

INTRODUCTION TO THE BOOK

... who we are as human beings develops through social interaction.
Little (2016: 208)

1.1 AIM AND SCOPE

This book aims to demonstrate how social interaction is core to allied healthcare education. For students on allied healthcare programmes of study, such as physiotherapy, occupational therapy, and speech and language therapy (the three disciplines which are the focus of this book), social interaction is pivotal to their experiences of teaching and learning both within and outside the university classroom. Allied healthcare professionals (AHPs) do not operate in a vacuum; they are at the coalface of everyday clinical interactions with colleagues, patients and families. As such, their education reflects this active involvement with others as they learn together and grow to become outward-facing, caring professionals who interact with the public who seek their services. Moreover, we will show how social interaction is core to the student's developing identity as an allied healthcare provider.

The core concepts of social interaction and professional identity have become more topical than ever in recent years, given that such concepts have been talked about in more considered ways since the Covid-19 pandemic forced physical in-person social interaction into the shadows, or at best to the enforced virtual environment. The focus of this book has these concepts at its core, as reflected in the title *Social Interaction and Identity in Allied Healthcare Education*. Our book contributes to the Edinburgh University Press series entitled 'Studies in Social Interaction' and in fact fills a gap, as healthcare education is under-represented in the series thus far. This volume aims to take the reader on a journey through the nuances of social interaction in allied healthcare educational contexts, shining a light on teaching and learning practices and student experiences while exploring how professional identity grows through those experiences. Much of the data across the chapters to be presented in this book stem from the reflections of AHPs and students on issues of concern around their working lives, their roles in healthcare teams and their educational experiences in the classroom and beyond. As such, social interaction is referenced at a remove from the *in vivo* act of social interacting through spoken discourse reported in other texts in this series, where extracts of talk in interaction are examined. Our approach allows for a different lens through which to explore the role of social interaction and its key function in the developing professional's identity.

1.2 BACKGROUND

At the time of writing this book (2020–2023), the world has been experiencing a pandemic (Covid-19) affecting every level and aspect of life as we know it – from our personal to our professional lives, from how we see the world to how we interact socially in, and with, the world around us. Everything has changed, and some things will not go back to the way they were pre-pandemic.

Education may be considered a casualty of the pandemic – or is it? Higher education (or adult learning) has not escaped the impact of what we came to know as the 'lockdown' experience. Allied healthcare educational courses were badly hit, as the 'live', in-person socio-clinical interactions, so much part of training and education in healthcare areas, were compromised in many ways. These disruptions ranged from the communication barriers created by mandatory personal protective equipment (PPE) to the necessary switch to telehealth or tele-practice when patients were required to 'attend' appointments via a computer screen.

There is little doubt that the modes of how we teach and learn have changed irrevocably. In many ways for students, these changes have been for the better. Some students welcomed the opportunity to learn online, with some even expressing a preference for this mode of learning. However, this was not the case for all. The social isolation that resulted in almost exclusive online learning at times has taken its toll on students' mental health; students were left to engage in learning activities from their homes, bedsits or kitchen tables, without the proximity of other students in the classroom or the lecture theatre. Interestingly, the realisation that teaching and learning while 'face-to-face' trumps 'face-to-screen' was recognised some years ago by Kemp and Grieve (2014), long before we knew a pandemic was on the horizon that would force teaching and learning online. Surveying psychology students' experiences of both contexts, a predominant theme of 'engagement' was identified by Kemp and Grieve (2014: 8) in response analysis, most aptly summarised by one student's comment: 'I would rather be in a classroom talking to actual people and engaging more'.

The pandemic also affected teaching staff's more usual modus operandi, where taken-for-granted in-person teaching was suddenly not permissible in many educational settings, and staff, like their students, began working from home. For some teaching staff, motivation and job satisfaction suffered when trying to deliver a curriculum in adapted ways, while others welcomed the steep learning curve that came with the switch to online teaching. On the plus side, innovative ways were found to engage students to maximally optimise the experience of this different learning environment for all. Moreover, the pandemic spawned a wealth of published material on how the education sector coped with the sudden switch to online learning in university contexts across the world (e.g. Sahin and Shelley 2020).

Anecdotally, and also suggested by research findings (Gregory, Clegg and Cameron 2021), the key ingredient missing for students and instructors or teachers alike was that in-person contact, or 'social interaction' – the key concept of this book – within educational contexts. In AHP courses in particular, many students missed the 'buzz' of the interaction with others as they explored, discovered and learnt about their chosen allied healthcare discipline. Staff, likewise, missed the interactive positive dynamic that can be created by a classroom full of motivated students, or the 'water-cooler' conversations that were there for support and promotion of team building and camaraderie.

Moreover, the very nature of the clinical practicum component of healthcare educational programmes was challenged when faced with necessary adaptations due to the pandemic. Practice educators and tutors had to find ways for students to get the clinical experience they needed against a backdrop of disruption, not only to the physical infrastructure of clinical settings where repurposing of clinical spaces was often necessary but also to the changing roles and responsibilities of clinicians due to, for example, redeployment and a changing patient demographic.

Social interaction in teaching and learning contexts was not the only aspect of the educational experience that was impacted by the pandemic. Professional identity, and in particular the process of professional identity formation in allied healthcare education, was also found to be impacted, as Gregory et al. (2021: 147) comment in their paper on the subject: 'studying in uncertain times has been destabilising for students having the potential to impact on the more nuanced aspects of clinical and professional development (e.g. self-efficacy, confidence, and professional identity formation)'.

Moreover, during workplace experiences, students may have witnessed a blurring of roles or challenges to staffing provision when the hospital or clinical setting found itself under pressure due to staff illness and shortages. Such disruption may have impacted the individual's ability to maintain/preserve their profession-specific identity over a profession-generic one in the face of such challenges.

1.3 TEACHING AND LEARNING EXPERIENCES DURING THE PANDEMIC

A few studies have attempted to explore actions taken to address the impact of the pandemic on allied healthcare education, most particularly in the clinical practice domain, where the effect may have been felt more acutely. In the speech and language therapy discipline, Gregory et al. (2021) describe examples of educational practice that were implemented to address the 'uncertainty' of the teaching and learning environment because of the sudden shift to online learning and the pandemic-imposed constrained contexts of engagement. These included, for example, the establishment of 'student communities' and 'practice-based communities' to help support students, the latter giving rise to initiatives such as remote school liaison activities for pupils with communication difficulties and virtual seminars delivered by clinicians in the community. Such activities served to bring 'the outside clinical world into students' university learning environment' (Gregory et al. 2021: 152) and proved to be highly beneficial for the student learner, as reflected in the comment by one student: 'it's [school liaison] keeping me sane – I look forward to it' (Gregory et al. 2021: 152).

Rainford et al. (2021) considered the impact of the Covid-19 pandemic on radiography students within the context of their clinical placement and training experiences. They distributed an online survey across 12 countries (including, for example, Australia, Belgium, Denmark, Ireland and Singapore). Their findings, based on 1,277 responses (of which 592 students had completed placements during January to June 2020), found that those who attended placement reported experiencing challenges such as 'concern about training assessments' and 'travel to and from clinical placements', with a wealth of other concerns impacting them (e.g. financial concerns, feelings of isolation, accommodation worries). Of note is the comparison across stages of their respective courses, in that final-year students and recent graduates were less likely to be concerned about their education and training compared to second- and third-year students. Similarly, Alhasan and Al-Horani (2021) also explored radiography and medical imaging students' perceptions of learning in the online environment during the pandemic, surveying over 300 students. In general, their findings showed that although stress factors were high, some enjoyed the online teaching format and recommended its continuation for some aspects of the course. However, most of the students across the years of study did report missing and valuing the face-to-face teaching format that they were being denied due to the pandemic restrictions. Some of the comments from the students underline this need for engagement and social interaction in the teaching and learning environment. It seems that Year 1 students missed the college context and campus experience, as reflected in some of their comments, for example: 'It should be in classroom'; 'Back to campus'; 'Wish we could go back to campus, at least year one students some of us are lost and confused'. Some Year 5 students recognised the need for the clinical component of courses to be delivered in the hospital or clinic environment, as reflected in comments such as 'For clinical placement course students must go to the clinical [sic] for better learning' and 'Only for clinical placement courses must attend in the hospitals to practice well' [sic]. The authors in their conclusions recognise the shortcomings of the online teaching format for clinical courses and warn that 'poorer engagement, flexibility, analytical skills, and critical thinking training via online instruction can lead to poorer outcomes for the laboratory and online clinical training' (Alhasan and Al-Horani 2021: 76).

Moreover, the possible far-reaching impact on student personal and professional development in allied healthcare educational contexts (and most especially as related to the almost exclusive online teaching format in the early stages of the pandemic during 'lockdowns') should not be minimised. Not least among the probable effects in addition to missing out on the holistic university student experience is the impact on a nascent professional identity, where beginning (and continuing) students only got to meet their classmates, peers, and even educational clinical and academic staff, virtually. Having to operate in this virtual environment where screen-to-screen was the only medium by which to socially interact cannot be ignored as students began (or continued) their professional identity journey. Such contexts meant that communicating virtually was the only conduit, meaning that students missed out on the key foundational experiences of in-person social interaction and learning with future colleagues, mentors, (clinical) educators and even their future clients/patients as clinical practice was conducted via telehealth. The risk of 'poorer outcomes' (Alhasan and Al-Horani 2021: 76) and a potential lag in professional identity formation without the in-person educational context is not lost in the arguments put forward in this book, where social interaction in the teaching and learning environment is in focus.

It seems also that it was not only healthcare students who were negatively impacted by the effects and restrictions resulting from Covid-19. Practice educators and academics were also affected in differing ways, concurrent with the experiences of the authors of this book. However, more positive experiences during this time were also reported. Once again taking the discipline of radiography as an example, Strudwick et al. (2021) explored the lived experiences of staff who were involved in supervising and supporting final-year students who joined a temporary register early and who had begun practising during the pandemic. This study adopted a phenomenological approach to analysis of the data gathered based on in-depth interviewing of practice educators (n = 6) and academics (n = 2) (the small number of participants being consistent with such an analytic methodology). Their analysis yielded the following themes: 'Communication', 'Support mechanisms' and 'Competence and the transition to registration'. Both practice educators and academics reported that they 'observed the new registrants gaining confidence during their time on the temporary register and suggested that professional bodies could consider curriculum changes to encompass a final transitional placement similar to their experience' (Strudwick et al. 2021: 1179). The gaining of confidence while on clinical placement is a common theme that emerges from studying student engagement in teaching and learning contexts of allied healthcare education, and is one which will be revisited later in this book.

Porter and Wilton (2019) explored professional identity in healthcare staff, recognising its importance for interdisciplinary team working, and these authors also considered the threat to identity in times of organisational restructuring (Porter and Wilton 2020). One cannot ignore the impact of the role restructuring necessitated by Covid-19, which was also a threat to professional identities in the healthcare context.

It seems important then, in the opening chapter of this book, to outline our rationale for considering social interaction as an approach to understanding identity formation in the very specific context of allied healthcare education. To appreciate what this professional identity work might look like in such healthcare educational fora, it may help to briefly contrast such identity work in other contexts of interaction.

1.4 IDENTITY FORMATION EXPLORED IN DIFFERING CONTEXTS OF TEACHING AND LEARNING

Much work has focused on the meaning of identity and how it may be formed in teaching and learning contexts and across differing stages of a student's educational journey. Identity has also been explored using differing data sets, from survey responses to in-depth interviews and, most commonly, in talk-in-interaction contexts.

Although our primary focus in this book is on undergraduate (or pre-registration) students, following some consideration of professional identity among qualified practitioners, identity development has also garnered some attention in relation to doctoral students. Kovalcikiene and Buksnyte-Marmiene (2015) investigated identity among doctoral students across the following areas of study: social sciences, biomedical sciences, technology, humanities and agriculture. In their study, Kovalcikiene and Buksnyte-Marmiene analysed responses to a 27-item Likert-scale survey where students responded to statements within three categories or scales pertaining to (i) researcher professional role identity, (ii) teacher professional role identity and (iii) practitioner professional role identity. Their findings suggest that doctoral students in general align themselves more readily to the practitioner's professional role identity than to a teacher or researcher's identity, suggesting that most doctoral students in their cohort perhaps did not consider themselves as remaining in academia or instructional contexts, but more in terms of their profession of origin as practitioners. Kovalcikiene and Buksnyte-Marmiene (2015) observed slight variations in these findings according to the student's year of study but did not follow the participating students' identity trajectories over time to discern the possible changes in their identity perceptions on the educational journey towards achievement of their doctoral degree. Of interest to the focus of this book, however, is not only the survey-style data collection method but also the researchers' conclusion that 'introspection and self-discovery are important tools for professional development' (Kovalcikiene and Buksnyte-Marmiene 2015: 2697), a consideration that is echoed throughout the following chapters. The use of reflection and reflective practice are the conduits for such 'introspection and self-discovery' and shall be revisited more specifically in Chapter 6 (as core to the data collection methods referenced in this book), with further discussion in the final chapters to reinforce the value of reflective practice in allied healthcare.

Surveys are not the only means, however, to 'get at' such introspective reflections on identity or to reveal identity work in action. Identity has been considered through the analysis of everyday talk (e.g. Tracy and Robles 2013) and general workplace talk (e.g. Sarangi and Roberts 1999), as well as through reflections on working life and clients that professionals have met, as we shall see in Chapters 4 and 5 of this book. Additionally, the nature of identity work, and indeed the tools to analyse it, can be accessed through various research methodologies and forms of data collection, such as the (discourse) analysis of spoken data from bespoke focus groups or topic-led in-depth research interviews. Social interaction may or may not be explicitly considered as a factor in these differing contexts, but forms of data collection such as focus groups and interviews, by their very nature, can only be achieved through social interaction. Although social interaction is not always named as a key player in identity work, it is ubiquitous to many such research contexts by virtue of researchers and research participants coming together to explore a phenomenon of common or mutual interest. Moreover, it is often the case that reflections on social interactions are voiced as key moments in identity development by many practitioners as they consider pivotal moments in their careers or during their education. While social interaction may not also be explicitly a named player in identity research, establishing the centrality of social interaction to identity is made easiest perhaps when we examine the corollary, which is when one's identity is 'robbed', as in the experience of a disability (see Table 1.1).

Table 1.1 Social interaction and identity: Examining the relationship through a corollary

Disruptions in social interaction underscore its centrality to identity, arguably most clearly illustrated in the body of research addressing identity in people with aphasia – a communication disability that commonly occurs after a stroke. The nature of aphasia causes a sudden disruption in social interaction, and renegotiation of identity can be seen as the 'greatest challenge' (Shadden and Agan 2004: 174). Indeed, research suggests that 'identity-enhancing interactions', such as that which occurs in the context of support groups, are important to support such identity work (Simmons-Mackie and Elman 2011: 312), both in online and offline interactions (Taubner, Hallén and Wengelin 2020). In the seminal paper 'Aphasia as identity theft', Barbara Shadden (Shadden 2005) expresses the importance of the 'mediation of identity through social interaction'.

It seems then that social interaction is undoubtedly a central concern for identity, providing a context in which identity can be renegotiated after an acquired disability or, as is the focus of this text, a context in which professional identity is developed.

However, as the title of this book series suggests, our text is not the first to consider social interaction in order to explore and better understand identity development in professional contexts. For example, Gray and Morton (2018: 5), in their text *Social Interaction and English Language Teacher Identity*, build on previous work around teachers' professional identity 'by addressing interaction explicitly and consistently across the data chapters'. We too foreground social interaction throughout our text – it is key to the claims we make in our discussions of professional identity as viewed through a healthcare lens. In contrast to other books in the series, rather than examining talk in interaction as an area for the excavation of identity work, we endeavour to consider social interaction as a salient theme or issue relevant to the student educational experience as indirectly considered within reflections on identity formation. Considering the AHP perspective and given our belief that education in this area is highly nuanced and necessarily multidimensional in its scope, we adopt an implicit focus whereby we examine where social interaction was made relevant in teaching and learning experiential reflective accounts in both classroom and clinical contexts.

Being of central concern to allied healthcare delivery in general, it comes as no surprise that social interaction is at the core of the education of healthcare professionals. Unlike teacher identity (or indeed language learner identity), which is perhaps predominantly shaped in the dynamic context of the teacher–pupil relationship within classroom interactions, AHP students face social interaction at every turn in their educational experience. Social interaction is a pervasive and necessary activity (or process) which the student engages in as they participate in university-based classroom instruction, small group tutorials and group work with peers. Thomas, McGarty and Mavor's (2016: 137) assertion that group interaction may be considered 'the crucible of social identity formation' resonates strongly with the treatise under discussion in this text and could be extended to professional identity in a similar way. Likewise, in the context of talk in interaction in research interviews with

English language teachers, Gray and Morton (2018: 24) describe social interaction 'as a primordial site where identities are produced and made relevant'.

Moreover, for healthcare students, social interaction is core to the learners' ongoing exposure to those they will be working with and alongside in their chosen profession through their experiences of clinical practice placements (i.e. interacting with clients and their families, along with colleagues from their own and other professional groups). Stokes and McCormick (2015: 10) further underscore this idea when they state: 'Through participation in placement, professional identity is largely socially constructed. It changes over time and develops with further and deeper exposure to a community of practice'. Social interaction, then, would be hard to avoid in healthcare education and as such provides a rich forum to examine how it influences identity formation. It seems apt then to focus on student professionals' teaching and learning contexts as they prepare to become members of public-facing healthcare profession(s) within and across communities of practice (e.g. speech and language therapy, physiotherapy and occupational therapy, which are the subject of this book). A critical focus must interrogate the role social interaction plays in identity formation. Such an interrogation is relevant not least because social interaction with others is both the conduit for learning and also the means of practice for the healthcare professional in the workplace.

Finally, to conclude this section, McHale and Cecil (2021: 356) consider the relationship between identity and (inter)action as follows: 'Although professional identity is itself an individuals' cognitive internalisation of values and beliefs, it is expressed through actions, behaviours and practices that exhibit these values and beliefs'. Hence, what we are aiming to do in this book is to take the consideration of this 'expression' of values and beliefs in the pursuance of a professional identity a step further. The AHP student brings their own beliefs and values to the educational experience, only for such beliefs and values to be honed, moulded and even nurtured by engagement in social interaction. We will argue that social interaction is the bedrock on which professional identity flourishes in allied healthcare education.

1.5 SOCIAL INTERACTION AND ALLIED HEALTHCARE PROFESSIONAL CONTEXTS: THE DATA SETS

The data sets examined in this book represent, to varying extents, the voices of three main groups within allied healthcare professions: members of multidisciplinary teams, qualified practitioners within a single discipline and student professionals. Data have been drawn from a number of studies to access these voices, including those collected (i) via in-depth interviews to explore individuals' experiences of working in a multidisciplinary team; (ii) via focus groups of single-discipline practitioners and their experiences of working with clients; and (iii) through the analysis of survey data from student-focused questionnaires on their experiences of teaching and learning practices during their education. All data have been analysed qualitatively and are presented in a descriptive manner through the analytic methodology of interpretative phenomenology. We have used these data sources to view social interaction as a core common concern among AHPs, not least because of the central role it plays in professional practice but also because of its pivotal role in a diverse range of teaching and learning contexts, all of which have a bearing on professional identity formation.

1.6 CONTENT AND STRUCTURE OF THIS BOOK

Chapter 1 introduces this book to you the reader, sharing our backgrounds and motivations as authors for writing this text, while at the same time contextualising the topic and its significance within the current global context of a pandemic. Chapter 2 considers the main concepts which are the focus of this book. Prior to presenting our own beliefs of what we understand by 'identity' and 'professional identity', we outline the typical teaching and learning environments for AHP students on professional courses. The student contexts of teaching and learning see *social interaction* and *socialisation* as key concepts to be defined in this chapter, while we also refer to our own socio-cultural stance in approaching this book. Chapter 3 focuses on how professional identity and professional identity formation has been discussed in the literature across the educational contexts of AHP students, including disciplines such as medicine, nursing and pharmacy, in addition to physiotherapy, occupational therapy and speech and language therapy – the three disciplines which are the focus of this book. This chapter lays the groundwork for the data-driven chapters to follow.

The data-driven chapters begin with Chapter 4, entitled 'Negotiating workplace identity through social interaction: An end goal or work in progress for the student professional?'. This chapter continues our focus on identity and provides an opportunity to look back before looking forward, that is, to explore qualified healthcare professionals' perspectives on their professional identity formation as honed within the workplace and as part of a multidisciplinary team. In this chapter, we draw on research that shines a light on workplace identity, which in this case is a child and adolescent mental health clinical setting. Exploring AHPs' accounts of their own identity formation (via analysis of data collected from in-depth interviews) offers a chance to consider professional identity formation as a negotiation of sorts in the real world of the workplace as one socially interacts with colleagues, clients and families. Chapter 5 continues the focus on the qualified practitioner, in this case speech and language therapists, and how the clients that speech and language therapists interact with may impact how they see themselves as professionals, increasing their awareness of what kind of therapist they are or have become. Drawing on focus group data and analysed through an interpretative phenomenological analysis (IPA) lens, the themes identified reveal some interesting insights into the impact of social interaction on professional identity and sense of self. Chapter 6 introduces the data that are discussed in the remaining chapters of this book and how we as authors went about collecting and analysing the material. Having given a brief overview of how social interaction and professional identity have been investigated in specific educational contexts, we focus on IPA methods, which we believe honour the nature and nuances of the data collected. We also consider the use of reflection and the value of reflective practice in this chapter, given that it is students' written reflections we turn our attention to in the remaining chapters of this book.

Chapters 7 to 10 deal exclusively with the AHP student voice, presenting key arguments for the place of social interaction in their teaching and learning experiences and their developing professional identity. The data to access the student voice were derived from a survey adapted for use from the original by Sharpless et al. (2015). A short, focused online anonymous survey was conducted pre-pandemic, which gathered the thoughts and reflections of students emanating from a relatively small but diverse selection of countries, including Ireland, Malta, South Africa, India and the USA. We focused on the allied healthcare disciplines of occupational therapy, physiotherapy (termed 'physical therapy' in the USA) and speech and language therapy. The student responses (n=45) came from final- and pre-final-year students, who all had – at their stage of education – experience of both college life and the clinical world they would hope to inhabit on qualification. We acknowledge that this sample of data collection sites may be small and somewhat biased towards the familiar in terms of similar educational healthcare programmes to that which the authors are directly involved in. However, we believe that some familiarity with course formats crossing international boundaries may be a strength as it meant that (i) there was some awareness of the nature and format of teaching and learning experiences on such courses, which enabled an accurate interpretation of the survey responses, and (ii) we were keen to attend to the quality of responses from a discrete set of educational contexts. This focus allowed us to dig a bit deeper into the lived experiences and reflections of students as they participated in the many social interactions that made up their respective undergraduate programmes. The use of a reflective tool (such as a written survey in this instance) has been found to be beneficial in exploring topics such as professional identity formation in medical education fields in general (see e.g. Bouayed, Dost and Hussian 2018; Wald et al. 2018).

We were keen, therefore, to hear the collective voice of AHP students as they experienced their college and clinical education. To honour their voices, we adopted a qualitive analytic methodology –IPA (Smith, Flowers and Larkin 2022), described in detail in Chapter 6 of this book (a methodology also used to analyse the focus group data in Chapter 5). Most usually used in the analysis of interview or focus group data, we used it in this instance to analyse the written responses of students to our survey. The attraction of an IPA methodology is captured in the preface to the latest edition of Smith et al.'s book, where the authors comment that they 'think of IPA's core interest group as people concerned with the human predicament; this clearly takes us to a focus of people engaging with the world' (Smith et al. 2022: 4).

The findings from the student data are presented thematically from Chapters 7 to 10. Chapter 7 considers pretending and 'imposter syndrome', a phenomenon not unique to AHP students, who are required to socially interact with their lecturers, practice educators, clients and families as part of their education. Discussing student experiences of formal and informal contexts of learning in interaction as they relate to identity formation is the focus of Chapter 8, while Chapter 9 considers the notion of 'owning' professional identity as a student learner. The final chapter (Chapter 10) looks to the future and pays continued attention to the collective student voice as we explore ways that educators can consider professional identity formation as intrinsically related to opportunities for learning through social interaction in academic and clinical contexts.

1.7 THE SIGNIFICANCE OF THIS BOOK

We believe that the significance of this book lies in its origins, that is, from the rich and diverse nature of the data drawn from within allied healthcare professions (i.e. from accounts of multidisciplinary team members and those of single-discipline practitioners, as well as from student professionals), their accounts allowing social interaction to come into focus as a core concern for their developing and evolving professional identity. The book's significance is also supported by the experiences and professional profiles of its authors as AHPs themselves with clinical and teaching and learning experiences. As a rough estimate, the authors of this book collectively have approximately 60 years' experience in clinical work and in teaching and learning contexts. The authors are all qualified speech and language therapists and are at very different career stages (i.e. early, middle and late stage). As such, they have differing levels of clinical and teaching experiences. Their experiences also differ in quality, as their work spans many years, witnessing changes and significant developments in healthcare practices, not just within their own discipline of speech and language therapy but among professionals from other disciplines as they worked together in healthcare and educational settings. There is, therefore, a wealth of knowledge, experience and critical thinking brought to bear in the writing of this book. Both personal and professional experiences have influenced how we have approached this book and the analysis of the data set discussed.

Despite the differing levels and nature of experience, however, we do have one clear commonality: we were all students once, and we are now the professionals we were educated to be. This commonality brings with it a desire to hear the student and professional voice in the current context of healthcare professional education and practice. We are concerned with giving the student voice a podium from which students can express their thoughts, ideas and reflections on their experiences of healthcare education, both in the clinical and academic domains of teaching and learning; we strive to hear the qualified practitioners' voice as they hone their practice and their professional identity. Our focus is one of social interaction, a highly relevant concept to discuss within healthcare as so much of that education centres on just that: how we socially interact with others as we experience education or how we are educated through our social interactions. Developing a professional identity through the social interaction of educational and clinical contexts is also our concern here. There is little doubt that our own professional self-identities, as therapists and educators, along with our personal self-identities all have a bearing on how we approached the story told in this book. The arguments are ours, informed by our life and professional experiences, as well as that of the student and professional voices we have honoured.

We hope there is something in this book for AHPs and students alike, along with their educators. We aim to offer some insights into the nature and nuances of social interaction and how it helps to hone a professional identity that students and professionals enact in the care of those they serve and as they set about their daily lives in the workplace and beyond.

2

CONTEXTS AND CONSTRUCTS OF IDENTITY NEGOTIATED IN SOCIAL INTERACTION IN ALLIED HEALTHCARE EDUCATION

I am part of all that I have met.
Alfred Tennyson

2.1 INTRODUCTION

We begin this chapter with a short, simple narrative describing a 'first day at college' which hints at a few points that are relevant to the ideas described in this chapter and indeed in this book – the social interaction that occurs when people come together with a common cause, goal or simply because of circumstance:

> *A: tell me about your first day at college*
>
> *B: well, it started one bright morning and ahm we'd just been to our introductory lecture in the Anatomy Department*
>
> *A: OK*
>
> *B: and everyone was looking around kind of nervously and kind of giggling nervously*
>
> *A: sure*
>
> *B: pretending like that you know maybe recognising a familiar face and ahm then after that was over our class kind of got together and said maybe we should go for a cup of tea and get to know each other so we were all walking along*
>
> *A: real 'speech therapy' style*
>
> *B: yeah, walking along by the college and then we said 'Where will we go?' and everyone was chatting. And then Kay and I were walking ahead and realised that we'd separated from the entire class, and it was just me, Kay and Clare and we thought 'This is a sign of things to come', that the others would think we were a bit strange, and they were all going to hate us. And so, we went along to the café, and we had a cup of tea and we bonded because we realised we liked our tea the same way and then we were talking about boys and Kay was just chatting and chatting and chatting - you couldn't get a word in edgeways! And I was just thinking, the innocence! I was just seventeen, very innocent, and Kay, twenty, told me things I needed to know, and we bonded and then lost the rest of the class.*

`And then for the rest of the week we were - we spent lots of time together and then we've been best friends ever since.`

In this narrative, the reference to being part of a 'class' and becoming 'separated' from others into a sub-unit, with a premonition of 'things to come' in becoming long-term friends, suggests belonging to a collective of sorts. This collective is even named by the listener here, who comments that the description of them all walking together was 'real speech therapy style'. There is a hint of a co-construction of identity here, that is, the 'in-group' of a certain professional discipline, in this case the speech and language therapy community, one that is often characterised as predominantly female and socialising together in groups.

In this chapter we will give an overview of our beliefs on identity as a construct. We will also seek to explore how the processes of social interaction and socialisation contribute and give meaning to that construct, defining what we mean by these terms in this context. Considering identity within the context of social interaction allows for consideration of how identity is (co-)constructed in interaction. Professional identity, with its focus here on allied healthcare professions, is also discussed. What is of central concern in this book is how social interaction and identity formation and awareness act in a bidirectional nature as students and other healthcare professionals experience teaching and learning during their education and practice. The resultant process of socialisation, or being socialised into a profession, is also in focus here. In this way, we hope to understand how identity – or indeed identities – are played out across teaching and learning activities in professional courses. There is room, therefore, for consideration of profession-specific and profession-generic considerations, both of which will be explored accordingly.

Being human means that social interaction is what we do; we are social beings, and many activities have social interaction at their core, be they in-person face-to-face or online. Education is no exception. Little (2016: 708) defines education as a 'social institution' where individuals are taught 'academic knowledge, learning skills, and cultural norms'. It is a 'given' that skills and knowledge are central to what most forms of general education should achieve, but the added dimension of 'cultural norms' speaks to the social dimension of education. Considering learning about cultural norms is also of particular interest in the context of allied healthcare education, not least because learners are aspiring to become part of a profession with its own cultural complexion and unique practices. Furthermore, during education, and perhaps most especially in allied healthcare professional (AHP) courses, social interaction is a conduit for that learning. Teachers and learners interact, learners and learners interact, and learners learn to interact with others, including their potential 'public', that is, the clients or service users they will serve as professionals. Learners also interact with healthcare professionals within their own and other healthcare disciplines as they undertake clinical placements and training as part of their qualifying programmes. These interactions happen in differing ways depending upon the context of the learning activity. Take, for example, interactions that unfold in group work, tutorials, class presentations or student clinical practicum. All such activities involve social interaction to greater or lesser extents. Social interaction in these contexts is both verbal and non-verbal; it can be passive or active, in-person face-to-face or online. Identity work is often played out in these contexts, perhaps both consciously and unconsciously, and explicitly and implicitly. The tacit socialisation that results contributes to this identity work and hence is important to include in any discussion of identity formation.

Analysing oral or written accounts is a means to 'get at' or access identity work. Mining descriptive accounts from professionals and the teaching and learning experiences of undergraduate students is one way of casting a spotlight on the dynamics of interaction where a professional identity grows. Through our interactions and our communication(s), be they verbal, non-verbal or written, we say more about ourselves than we think or, in Goffman's (1959) words, we 'give off' meta-messages, which in turn can inform how we negotiate our identities while interacting with others. However, before exploring the concepts of identity and professional identity, social interaction and socialisation, it is necessary to consider the contexts of teaching and learning that underpin AHP education.

2.2 THE EDUCATION OF ALLIED HEALTHCARE PROFESSIONALS

The term allied healthcare professionals (AHPs) will be used throughout this book to refer to the professional disciplines under discussion. The definition of allied healthcare professions is: 'any of a wide range of professions related to healthcare other than nursing and medicine, for example physiotherapy, dietetics, or radiography' (Collins Dictionary 2023). Included in this category are professions such as occupational therapy, speech and language therapy, music therapy, drama therapy and emergency medicine, to name but a few. What is considered 'allied healthcare' can vary from country to country. For example, other similar but perhaps more inclusive terms used are 'Health and Social Care Professions' (HSCPs) (i.e. as used by the Health Services Executive (HSE) in the Irish context; National HSCP Office 2019) and includes professions as diverse as clinical engineering, clinical biochemistry, counselling and psychotherapy, podiatry, orthoptics, audiology, phlebotomy, psychology and play therapy. Like those practitioners classed more generically under 'allied healthcare', these professionals 'work in all settings including acute, community, disability, specialist, mental health, primary care and residential services. HSCPs are highly qualified and skilled and play a significant role in the health, wellbeing and quality of life of the population' (HSE 2019: 6). Despite medicine and nursing generally being considered outside of these categorisations, we reference these professions in our discussions here, as a wealth of literature has been published within these domains of practice in relation to professional identity formation.

The education of AHPs is now predominantly a third-level educational experience. Most AHPs have completed a three- or four-year university degree programme, while others take the programme at postgraduate level. Within that time, students experience learning both in the classroom and 'in the wild' (to borrow a term coined by Hutchins (1995) from his treatise on 'cognition in the wild') – that is, in clinical/work experience contexts, referred to more generally as clinical practicum. Learning in both contexts brings with it challenges and opportunities, not least the need for social interaction in its many forms.

Almost all AHPs have social interaction at the core of their professional life. Their duties bring them into close contact with people, and by the very nature of their profession they must be social in nature and in practice. However, prior to defining what we mean by social interaction in this context, it would be useful to give a background not only to 'what' contexts students are expected to interact within, but crucially 'who' these students are and 'who' they are interacting with. We will see in Chapters 7 to 10 that the discussions therein are informed by online survey responses from an international group of student AHPs, hailing from Europe, the USA and South Africa. We did not, however, collect data on race or ethnicity from these informants. Ethnicity interacts with professional identity development (Coster et al. 2008), and therefore it is necessary to consider below how diversity is (mis-) represented in AHPs in general to further contextualise the dynamics at play in allied healthcare education practice. We will revisit this area in the final chapter of this book as we look to the way forward in AHP education and training.

2.2.1 WHO ARE WE? STUDENT AND PRACTITIONER PROFILES IN ALLIED HEALTHCARE PROFESSIONS

It has been our own direct experience as the authors of this book, across our multiple roles as educators, clinicians, researchers and past students, that our own discipline of speech and language therapy, particularly in the 'Global North', is populated and dominated by white females largely from middle socio-economic classes. This skewed representation is evident in speech and language therapy (Malik 2023) but is far from unique to the profession. It has been well recognised that the same ethnic and demographic profiles are similarly experienced in the disciplines of physiotherapy (Yeowell 2013) and occupational therapy (Banks 2022; Colaianni et al. 2022).

Despite growing recognition of diversity and inclusion, and some concerted efforts from healthcare educators and providers to address these key issues across the allied healthcare professions as a whole (see e.g. Baldwin, Woods and Copeland Simmons 2006; Snyder, Frogner and Skillman 2018; Wilbur et al. 2020; Knettle et al. 2021), there remains a lot of work to be done. In discussing the challenge of racial inequities that persist in the allied healthcare professions, Nancarrow and Borthwick (2021: 57) reference the 'contemporary context', stating that:

> In many ways, the world has moved on but the professions (particularly the highly structured and gendered health professions) are relics of their post-industrial era formation. At the start of the 21st century, the stereotypical allied health profession is still predominantly female, middle-class and white.

Of crucial importance here – and for any discussion related to issues of diversity and inclusion – is the central tenet of 'who' we are as AHPs. Moreover, the following question must be posed: do we resemble or even begin to mirror the increasingly diverse populations we purport to serve in delivering a racially informed, culturally sensitive and respectful service? This is not a question we can hope to address in this volume. However, it is of great concern that we recognise this trend and the limitations and restrictions that can result. We should not assume that the collective populations involved in both education and healthcare services (i.e. students, educators, clinicians and patients/clients) are adequately served when diverse ethnic origins, beliefs and practices fail to be embedded, respected and accounted for in day-to-day social interactions. It is to the contexts of these social interactions in AHP education that we now turn to further explain the teaching and learning environments of healthcare students.

2.2.2 CONTEXTS OF INTERACTION IN ALLIED HEALTHCARE PROFESSIONAL EDUCATION

From our own experience in teaching and learning contexts, we have observed what seem to be the challenges to identity that college education brings. Some students will recall the 'shock' of the new college or university world, the awkward navigation of people, places, times and contexts, hinted at in the opening narrative to this chapter. For undergraduates entering the AHP programmes of study, they are entering that world from the moment they join their class, their peers, who will become their future AHP colleagues. Many of them are already thinking themselves into the 'space' of becoming an AHP. They have entered that AHP environment, albeit not in the real-world clinical context yet, but in their thinking and being. They have become part of that community as students and prospective clinicians. Becoming part of this community is then reinforced in the many contexts of interaction, both physical and what we term social-structural spaces, they find themselves in.

There are many contexts of interaction experienced by students entering AHP programmes. Figure 2.1 depicts the physical contexts that students must navigate, that is, the spaces they occupy with others.

The classroom, lecture theatre or clinic/laboratory is most obviously the first physical space the student experiences as part of a group of AHP students. The students will soon find out that they are part of a 'department' or 'academic unit', most usually defined by their discipline, and will form a discrete cohort within that named department. The department may occupy a physical space where students gather. In turn, that department is part of a 'faculty' or group of departments, units or centres, variously named. Most AHP courses are housed within a health sciences faculty. However, some sit within other faculties, for example, arts and humanities, depending on their makeup, ethos and pedagogical orientation. Which faculty a programme is aligned to may have implications for that department or discipline's identity. Finally, faculties are positioned within universities, and particular universities may be known or recognised for their concentration of health science-based or arts-based programmes. Students need to navigate these physical/structural spaces from the outset and occupy them throughout their education.

However, these departments and faculties are not solely the physical or structural spaces occupied by prospective AHPs while they experience and participate in their

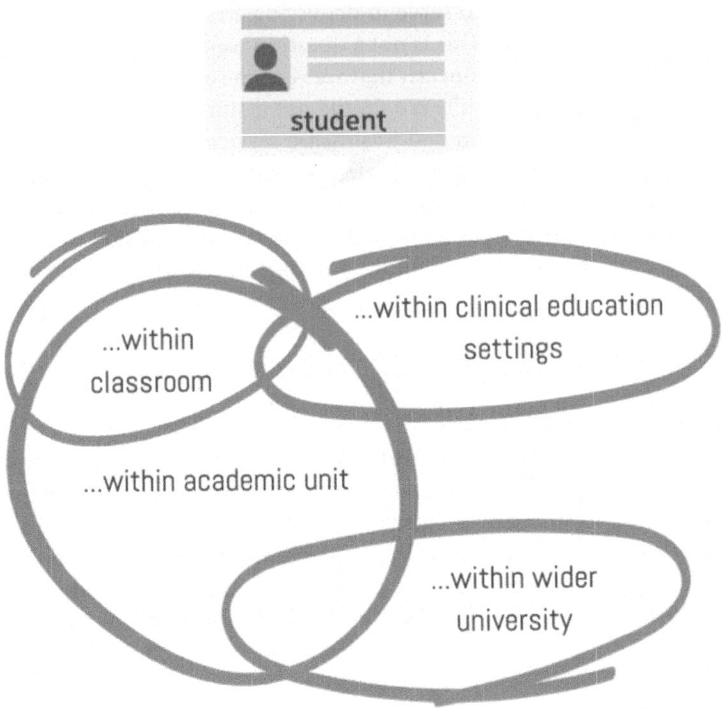

Figure 2.1 Physical/structural spaces that students must navigate in AHP education

education. Of importance also is the 'class' or 'year group', that is, a social grouping occupying a social-structural space where students find themselves joining others and together beginning the shared journey of AHP education through social interactions. These interactions are essentially 'social' as students congregate, mix and learn together. In this book, having considered social interaction as a conduit for the continuing honing of professional identity among qualified practitioners, we are proposing that it is the social interactions that take place among AHP students in education which interact with professional identity formation and where identity and identities are forged and negotiated. Figure 2.2 depicts the gradually increasing contexts of social interaction that the AHP student finds themselves in as they make progress in their academic and clinical learning. We also provide a brief description of the social levels of interaction concerned, taking the speech and language therapy student as an illustrative example.

The first context of social interaction (Context I) the student finds themselves in is their class group, having entered this group unit by choice. Students come together with shared interests and goals (to become a member of a specific healthcare discipline). In this initial context of interaction, the students are 'all in this together', eventually becoming the 'class of [date of graduation]'. The student is part of a class within the larger context of their chosen programme in allied healthcare.

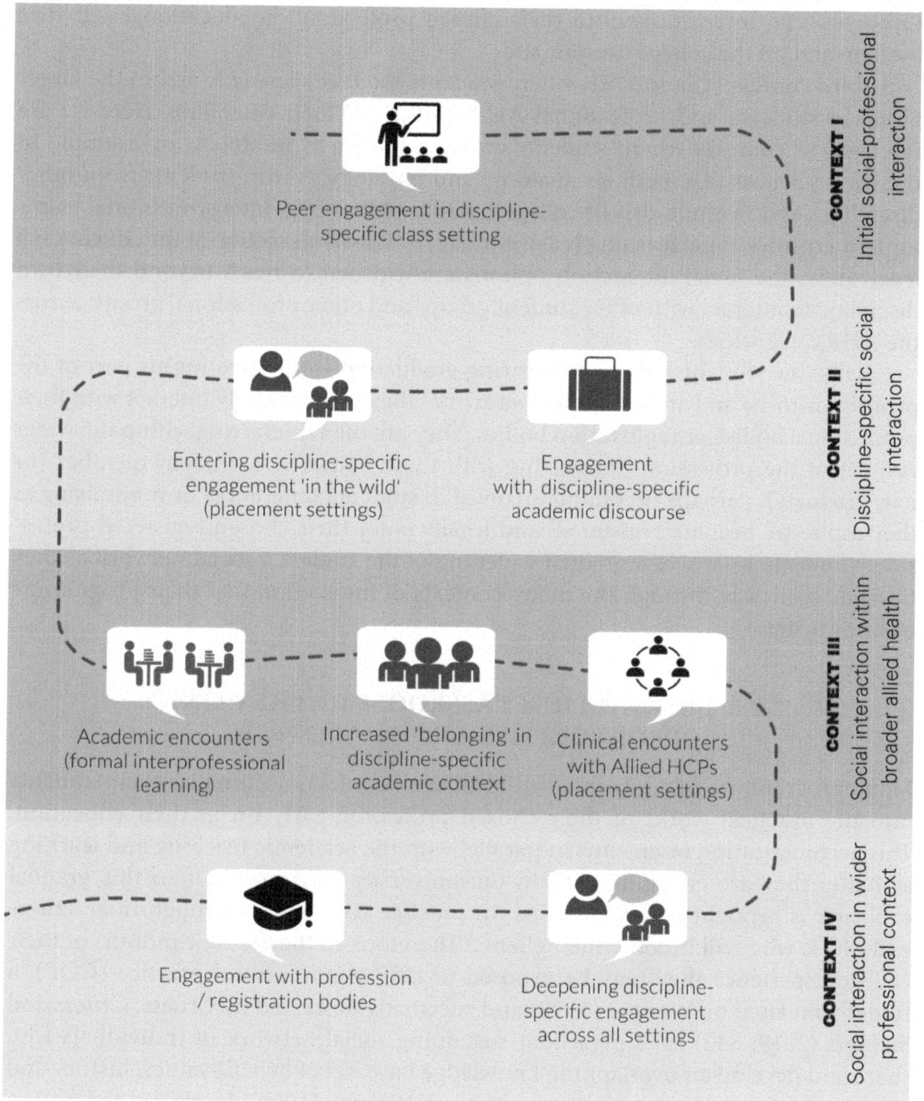

Figure 2.2 Contexts of social interaction between a student (e.g. SLT) and others, suggesting sites for professional identity formation

Throughout their education, the student also gets to socially interact with professionals within their own discipline, 'in the wild' (clinical) and in academic environments (university/college) (Context II). Here, the student is part of a larger context of their chosen professional discipline, gradually becoming aware of what is expected of them and catching a glimpse of what they are to become. They are still part of their group, as in Context I, but now in Context II, they are gradually being inducted through social interactions into their chosen profession via educational activities both on and off the college campus site.

A third context (Context III) where students interact socially is within the larger group of students and professional AHPs *outside* of their discipline. Here we are referring to contexts where students co-learn in shared modules, for example in the basic sciences (e.g. perhaps anatomy and physiology) with students from other disciplines and in clinic-driven college-based activities (e.g. interprofessional learning). Interprofessional learning is a prime site for social interaction at the educational level. Here, the social interaction options are widened to reach beyond their own discipline to interact with other student groups and other professional groups across the AHP categories.

Finally, the student as they are nearing graduation (or graduating) is part of the profession-to-be and at this level (Context IV) they get to socially interact with their professional bodies or registration bodies. They are then interacting within the wider context of the profession, interacting with these bodies as a student member (or new graduate), perhaps becoming involved in student conferences or fundraising as they aspire to 'become registered' and legally enter their chosen registered profession. Contexts I–IV sees a gradual widening of the student's social network as they navigate their way through the many contexts of interaction that their programme of study brings.

2.2.3 BEYOND THE CLASSROOM TO THE CLINIC: OPPORTUNITIES AND CHALLENGES

Many programmes of study in allied healthcare contexts acclimatise their students into the practical world of their chosen profession early on in their education. This acclimatisation often runs in parallel with the academic teaching and learning activities they are engaging with in the university classroom. Often this gradual exposure is brought about by 'visits' to practice contexts or through interactions with those who will become their clients. Therefore, in the first few months of their college experience they may be exposed to that community of practice (COP), a term formulated by Wenger (1998) and succinctly described by Cruess, Cruess and Steinert (2019: 642) as 'a persistent sustaining social network of individuals who share and develop an overlapping knowledge base, set of beliefs, values, history and experiences focused on a common practice'. Wenger (1998) developed the notion further to include 'landscapes of practice' (LOPs). As their education progresses, students are increasingly exposed to contexts where their profession is relevant, such as in schools, community clinics, hospitals, rehabilitation centres and the like. AHP students, then, get to mix with members of their own community of practice and across landscapes of practice, each having its own identity and influence. It is this social interaction that brings with it identity work, which is a work in progress throughout the students' education and beyond. As such then, we see students getting to interact and learn across these landscapes of practice, further described in an edited text by Wenger-Trayner et al. (2014) and described more recently in the context of organisational structures by Pyrko, Dörfler and Eden (2019: 482) as 'multilevel, including local situated practices, generic practices, and cultural fields'.

AHP students, then, are required to enter and navigate these communities and landscapes of practice. Although most students cope well with support as they are inducted into their community (and communities) of practice, others struggle. Such struggles can result when their aspirations of 'who they think they want to become' in their professional career is at odds with their initial or subsequent learning experiences in college or in clinical sites (see the reference to Higgins' (1987) theory of self-discrepancy in Section 2.2.3). These experiences can cause distress, disappointment and, if such feelings go unaddressed or unresolved, can result in students exiting their course of study prematurely. Quite often their struggles may be related to the demands of what they perceive to be a requisite 'different kind' of social interaction, one that becomes intimately identity related, and something that will be explored elsewhere in this book.

As highlighted in Chapter 1, for some AHP education programmes during the Covid-19 pandemic beginning in 2020, providing students with the necessary clinical practicum for qualification necessitated an abrupt move to the online environment, where telehealth practice was introduced. This shift to telehealth of course was a new and unique experience for many, but it too had social interaction at the core, albeit in a virtual medium. Students and clients reported having to work a lot harder to engage or remain engaged, underpinning the centrality of social interaction to teaching and learning in health professions (Gregory, Clegg and Cameron 2021).

It has long been the belief of the authors of this book that AHP courses catapult students into the spotlight of exposure and scrutiny, that is, being observed or watched in their learning in both clinical and non-clinical contexts – a necessary and crucial component of clinical supervision. Students are required to behave, communicate and relate in certain ways, some of which are profession specific (i.e. 'like a speech and language therapist, or physiotherapist', etc.), while other ways are more generic (i.e. 'like a healthcare professional'). We are arguing in this book that all this work happens through social interaction for both novices and qualified practitioners, and it is to definitions of 'social interaction' and the associated process or outcome of 'socialisation' that we now turn.

2.3 SOCIAL INTERACTION, SOCIALISATION AND IDENTITY WITHIN THE CONTEXT OF ALLIED HEALTHCARE PROFESSIONAL EDUCATION

2.3.1 SOCIAL INTERACTION

Social interaction is at the core of education in allied healthcare disciplines, as both the process and the product of AHP education. Social interaction is the conduit for AHP students to grow and learn during their education. As outlined in Figure 2.2, once a student enters AHP education, they immediately become part of a group, that group being their 'class' initially, only to trigger many more contexts of social interaction within and across groups. For the qualified professional they will become, social interaction becomes the modus operandi as they set about their daily professional duties, working with other professionals, their clients and their families in delivering healthcare services.

Social interaction can be defined very narrowly or very broadly. For example, Hoppler, Segerer and Nikitin (2022) define 'social interaction' in a comprehensive and detailed way, considering no less than six intrinsic components: ***A**ctor*, ***P**artner*, ***R**elation*, ***A**ctivities*, ***C**ontext* and ***E**valuation*. Their developed taxonomy, referred to by the acronym APRACE, is the result of an analysis of over 700 responses across a wide age demographic of participants (18–83 years). The descriptions of social interaction were drawn from a pre-existing database (Nikitin and Freund 2018) made up of subjects' descriptions of experience of both positive and negative social interactions. Based on their analysis, incorporating grounded theory and other qualitative analytic methods, Hoppler et al. (2022) propose that in using APRACE, a social situation can be described according to these combined components and their features. They discuss the future application of the APRACE taxonomy as one that can be applied to many fields of research, including organisational psychology, psychotherapy and even artificial intelligence. (The reader is referred to Hoppler et al.'s (2022) full paper for further discussion of the origins of the APRACE taxonomy and its potential uses in research and practical domains.)

However, less detailed descriptions of social interaction are also worth considering and are perhaps more easily applicable to the examination of social interaction in this book. Little (2016: 914) defines social interaction as:

> the process of reciprocal influence exercised by individuals over one another during social encounters. Usually, it refers to face-to-face encounters in which people are physically present with one another for a specified duration. However, in contemporary society we can also think of social encounters that are technologically mediated like texting, skyping, or messaging. In terms of the different levels of analysis in sociology – micro, meso, macro, and global – social interaction is generally approached at the micro-level where the structures and social scripts, the pre-established patterns of behaviour that people are expected to follow in specific social situations, that govern the relationship between particular individuals can be examined.

We welcome this definition of social interaction. The definition fits with the stance we are taking in this book, that is, considering social interaction as relevant to Little's idea of 'the pre-established patterns of behaviour that people are expected to follow in specific social situations, that govern the relationship between particular individuals', and as a key process in healthcare education and practice. In the chapters to follow, we consider social interaction as one step removed from 'live' interaction, that is, through AHPs and students' reflections on the same, providing a unique take on the process as we also consider the development of a professional identity.

In the context of allied healthcare practice and educational contexts, there are quite specific 'pre-established patterns of behaviour' that AHPs are 'expected' to follow, tied to the institutional norms of the relevant establishment (e.g. university, classroom, clinical context, workplace). Social interaction in educational and clinical practice contexts can refer to in-person, face-to-face interactions, where AHPs and students mingle and where a physical presence is relevant to the context.

Most common forms of social interactions in this sense of allied healthcare education are classroom-based teaching and learning (be it in small or large groups), tutorials and that which occurs in laboratory or clinical placement contexts. Sert (2015: 9; emphasis in the original text) argues that 'classroom interaction *is* social interaction, or at least one type of it', and we concur with this belief as we discuss classroom interaction as one of the contexts of social interaction among healthcare students in the chapters to follow. For qualified professionals, social interaction is often the means by which they carry out their work, with clients, patients, family members and their colleagues in multidisciplinary teams, both within and outside the workplace (e.g. the wider community).

Moreover, Little's (2016) notion of 'reciprocal influence' is also key here, as interactants (i.e. clients and professionals and teachers and learners) are 'in this together', where each exerts influence over the other in these contexts. Social interaction can also refer to online communication or, as Little suggests, it is 'technologically mediated', such as how students engage in teaching and learning activities via computer-mediated contexts. Such computer-mediated contexts can include, for example, email, virtual learning environments (VLE), and recording reflections on that learning in structured or unstructured ways. VLE were used and evaluated in educational contexts (O'Rourke, Rooney and Boylan 2015) before their use became ubiquitous during the recent Covid-19 pandemic in many healthcare educational programmes (e.g. MacRae et al. 2021; Nikas et al. 2022). Clinical sites also saw increasing moves to online media to work with students and patients via telehealth or telemedicine, with varying degrees of success and satisfaction reported by users (Gregory et al. 2021; Holtz 2021; Kyle et al. 2021; Shaver 2022).

In the context of English language teacher training, and the achievement of professional development goals, Liu et al. (2023: 1158) position social interaction as central to what they call a 'mobile team-based competition approach', in addressing apparent student reluctance to engage with teachers and fellow learners. This team-based competition approach is based on the premise that:

> Scholars have indicated that many students do not like to present their thoughts in class; that is, they have low motivation to share ideas or to take part in discussions, Therefore, it is necessary to adopt a learning approach which facilitates students' social interaction, in order to help them fully participate in classroom learning tasks, and solve problems they encounter during the learning process. (Liu et al. 2023: 1159)

It is interesting note here the explicit need to target 'social interaction' in this form of pedagogy, contrasted with most AHP programmes of learning which assume social interaction as core or at least central to many teaching and learning activities in both academic and clinical contexts. In Liu et al.'s study, however, they found that in contrast to individual modes of learning, the team-based approach with social interaction at the core improved the students' attitudes to learning and tendencies for learning collaboratively, with a greater positive impact on their professional identity as future language teachers.

For the purposes of this book, we are concerned with social interaction as a process both as reflected upon by the qualified professionals and students and where and how they reference it as salient to their learning and identity during their AHP education. Therefore, social interaction here is viewed through two lenses, at least:

(i) that which the practitioners and students have experienced in their teaching and learning contexts (see Figure 2.2), both within formal academic contexts and contexts of interaction in their clinical practicum experiences and working lives and how their social interactions outside of these contexts are also made salient in their responses to the data.
(ii) that reflective activity in which the practitioners and students are engaged while discussing their experiences (Chapter 4 via interviews and Chapter 5 via focus groups) or when completing the survey (Chapters 7–10).

2.3.2 SOCIALISATION

Socialisation is often discussed alongside concepts within the broader notion of 'social interaction'. The term may suggest an end product to some, that is, being 'socialised' into a community or an identified group, for example. However, socialisation may be better understood as a process. Turning to Little (2016: 205; emphasis in the original text) once again for a clear definition, 'socialisation' is defined as:

> the process through which people are taught to be proficient members of a society. It describes the ways that people come to understand societal norms and expectations, to accept society's beliefs, and to be aware of societal values. It also describes the way people come to be aware of themselves and to reflect on the suitability of their behaviour in their interactions with others. Socialisation occurs as people engage and disengage in a series of roles throughout life. Each **role**, like the role of son or daughter, student, friend, employee, etc., is defined by the behaviour expected of a person who occupies a particular position. ... Socialisation is not the same as socialising (interacting with others, like family, friends, and co-workers); to be precise, it is a sociological process that occurs through socialising.

That socialisation is a 'process' is further underpinned by Cruess et al. (2019: 641), who state that learners must 'understand the process of socialisation through which an identity is formed'. Socialisation, then, is an ongoing process, and one which is a necessary part of any AHP's education. Moreover, 'communities of practice'

(Brown and Duguid 1991; Wenger 1998), within which socialisation takes place, are not just discipline specific as referred to above. Clinical work, educational practices and research activities, all within or across disciplines, can constitute communities within which students and practitioners of allied healthcare can interact (see, for example, Figure 2.2.). During their education, students traverse these communities and assimilate characteristics of their profession-specific discipline and profession-generic identities.

2.3.3 IDENTITY

Identity is also a concept which has undergone many attempts at definition depending on the orientation of the context under study. One of the questions posed by Ellis and Hogard (2021: 1) in their introduction to their edited volume on *Professional Identity in the Caring Professions* is: 'How do we describe identity at the interface of an individual and a profession?' This question is relevant to the subject of this book. As referred to above, we consider social interaction to be a component of that interface, a dynamic that helps the student learner to hone that identity (or identities), at the level of the individual and their chosen profession. Thomas et al. (2016) discuss group interaction as the 'crucible' of social identity formation. Such social identity formation must be part of the professional identity formation that students in AHP education experience.

We are also concerned with what can be considered the 'generic' professional identity and the 'specific' professional identity, as will be discussed later in this book. Richards (2006: 4) contends that 'more than one person can work together over extended interactional space to construct a shared identity', which is as relevant to specific and generic professional identities as it is to student professional identities. Sharing the interactional space of education through interaction is one such context relevant to identity work.

For now, however, definitions and descriptions of identity both outside and within the professional context also need to be considered. We would like to explore identity according to some of our own beliefs and premises on which our understanding of identity is based and therefore echoed throughout this book. These beliefs are as follows:

- Identity as dynamic
- Identity as a social interactional resource (see Richards 2006)
- Identity as enacted

The following sections will outline our understanding of these premises, illustrated with examples as relevant.

Identity as dynamic

Of relevance to the arguments developed in this book is the premise that identity is a dynamic entity. As illustrated in Figure 2.3, we believe that identity is not stagnant or static but is affected or moulded by various contexts, for example, *contexts of being*

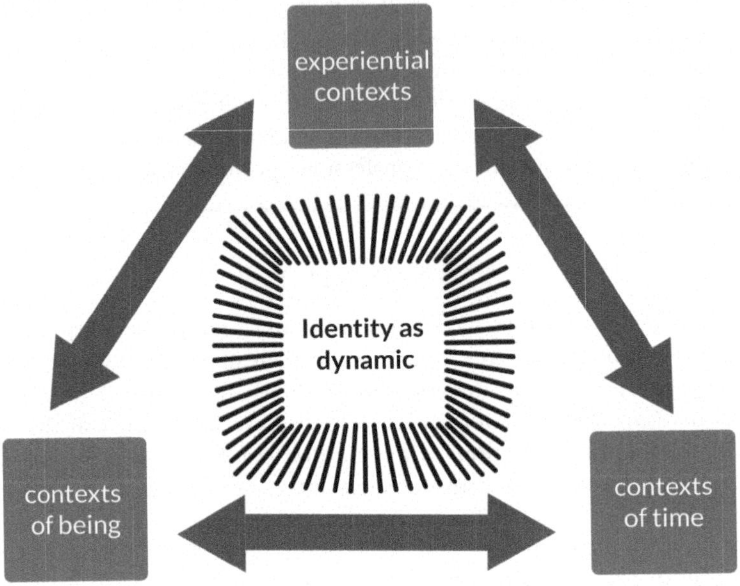

Figure 2.3 *Identity as dynamic*

(who we are, or who we think we are), *contexts of time* (where we are in our lifetime trajectory) and *experiential contexts* (what we have experienced). As such, then, identity interacts in a dynamic fashion with these contextual variables and is subject to adaptation and change.

Identity as a socio-interactional resource

Identity can be considered as a socio-interactional resource. Richards (2006: 7) states that 'sensitivity to the ways in which different identities might be constructed, invoked, exploited, or otherwise made relevant develops from a perspective that sees identity as an interactional resource rather than a category in search of a name'. Being 'formed and shaped through action' (Richards 2006: 3), we believe, then, that identity is in a reciprocal, bidirectional relationship with social interaction. Through social interaction we become socialised into our communities of being, be they communities of family, friends, college peers, workplace colleagues or other communities of relevance to our everyday lives. These communities of being impact our sense of identity, honing and shaping that identity through our interactions. Likewise, our sense of identity also impacts how we socially interact in formative ways. We believe it is difficult to reflect on identity in the absence of a consideration of social interaction.

Identity as enactment

Interacting with others has an impact on how we present ourselves or 'see' ourselves, which is akin to the notion of our public 'face' developed by Goffman (1967). In other words, how we want to be seen may be important to us, and we therefore enact identity (or identities) in certain ways. We enact our identity (or identities) in contexts of interaction which allow that identity (or identities) to be reinforced, foregrounded or backgrounded as relevant to the interaction(s) taking place.

Let us consider a hypothetical case vignette to illustrate or operationalise these premises. To maintain the relevance to the subject of this book, we present the case of a healthcare professional (in this case an occupational therapist):

> Ruth is a senior occupational therapist, a profession she long wanted to enter since her school days. At work, she supervises those less experienced than her within her own profession, and contributes to multidisciplinary team meetings on a regular basis at the health centre she works in. At the end of the working day, she goes home to her partner and baby son, where she relieves her own mother of the childcare duty Ruth's mother carries out while living with the family. Outside of work and home, Ruth is a keen tennis player having won many competitions and enjoys the outdoors and time to herself when she can get it.

For the sake of explication of the above premises, let us assume that Ruth (when asked) identifies primarily as a mother to her child, the marker of a major milestone in her life trajectory. This identity is important to her and is enacted (e.g. identity as enactment) not just in the more obvious context of home but also in conversations and discussions at work with clients and colleagues, where motherhood and the caring role become salient to the business of the day – be that sharing the experience of sleepless nights or empathising with a parent who is worried about her child's development in the areas of motor skills or sensory needs (e.g. identity as a social interactional resource). Ruth's identity as a mother, then, may be enacted in varying social interactions and to greater or lesser extents as the context shifts.

A professional identity is also important to Ruth, marked (in her own words) by her 'hard-earned' seniority and played out and foregrounded in supervision with more junior colleagues, as well as during multidisciplinary meetings where her opinion is sought on case management issues, for example. A blurring or an overlap of identities often occurs when Ruth's tennis friends, through their social interactions at the club, consult her on their own children's development, or in her childcare arrangements involving her mother, where issues relevant to her profession and daughterhood may become more or less salient (e.g. identity as dynamic). Birney (2023: 23) exemplifies a similar vignette of a female professor with children (i.e. a mother and an academic), concluding that she may be 'undoubtedly aware of the assumptions that others have about her as she navigates these two parts of herself. They are also likely to shape which attributes she emphasises (i.e. intellectual or nurturing) depending on who is around her'.

It seems, then, that what we can describe as a 'dance of identities' may occur every day, which, if applied to the above vignette, contribute to making Ruth 'who she is' (or who she thinks she is, while never really knowing how others view her). Ruth's ongoing identity journey is such that she was once that student of an AHP educational programme, gradually developing her professional identity while navigating the twists and turns of teaching and learning contexts against a backdrop of her own developing personal identity.

Giddens (1991: 186) explains these ideas well, stating that 'a self-identity has to be created and more or less continually reordered against the backdrop of shifting experiences of day-to-day life and the fragmenting tendencies of modern institutions', with one such institution in this context being that of professional education. The navigation of one's developing and shifting identity through the journey of education is challenging for the student learner. As referred to earlier in this chapter, education to become an AHP necessitates the close consideration of identity, as it is challenged and honed by new experiences of learning and caring in instances of illness or disability. The altruism of the healthcare professional requires one 'to give', and that social role of 'giver' has its impact on a developing personal and professional identity. Many students and new graduates struggle with this burgeoning identity development in the face of new clinical experiences in practice contexts, such as hospitals, schools, clinics or specialist medical settings. Not only are students faced with the environmental 'newness', but they are also required to interact with many different medical and educational multidisciplinary teams, as well as a vast array of clients and families within the clinical populations they are working with. Such 'newness' brings with it its own demands and reflections. Stillman, Snow and Warren (1999) discuss this issue, captured most aptly by a comment made by a new graduate, 'I used to be good with kids', bemoaning the perceived 'loss' of a skill they believed they had when faced with children who challenge them because of interpersonal communication difficulties intrinsic to their neurodevelopmental profile or clinical presentation.

Higgins' (1987: 319) theory of self-discrepancy is also of some relevance here. Higgins explores 'how different types of discrepancies between self-state representations are related to different kinds of emotional vulnerabilities'. Essentially it seems that the premise of this theory is that how one views oneself – and the discrepancies therein – has direct consequences for how one feels about oneself. In healthcare educational contexts, experience tells us as educators that students are often 'disappointed' with themselves as novices in their clinical practice interactions as they struggle with possible discrepancies between (in Higgins' terms) their *actual self* (who they currently are), their *ideal self* (who they'd like to be) and their *ought self* (who they think they should become). We shall see how semblances of both 'the ideal' and 'the ought' self resonate throughout the data to be presented later in this text. Such selves become particularly relevant to the student learner as they aspire to meet their own and others' expectations to become a skilled healthcare practitioner. At the same time, their identity work is happening within a developing 'group identity' of, for example, their 'year group' (e.g. first, second, third, fourth year), their chosen discipline/profession (e.g. physiotherapy, occupational therapy, speech and language therapy) and as a student body in their host university. Tajfel and Turner's (1979) social identity theory allows for an appreciation of how such a group identity is integrated into our self-identity over time through social interaction. Furthermore, the key role of reflective practice to build that awareness of self and group identity is also highly relevant to a developing sense of self, a topic which is revisited in later chapters of this text.

2.4 A SOCIO-CULTURAL STANCE

It would be remiss of us in this early chapter to ignore the theoretical stance of how we are approaching the understanding of social interaction in AHP identity formation. Given the authors' respective backgrounds and experiences, a socio-cultural stance fits with our arguments and assertions in this text. In the first instance, we see the interactions of healthcare professionals, whether at student or qualified clinician levels, to be characterised by social interaction. Social interaction with clients and their families, and fellow and other professionals, is integral to allied healthcare practice and cannot be divorced from the day-to-day work in the clinical or hospital environments in which AHPs find themselves. Therefore, the '*socio*' prefix is key to any stance adopted here through the arguments presented. Secondly, we perceive healthcare interactions and practices in this context as *culturally bound*, that is, there are characteristics and features of an institutional nature that define clinical interactions, differing only in limited ways from one healthcare discipline to the next, despite the varying foci of discipline-specific targeted interventions (e.g. occupational therapy, physiotherapy, speech and language therapy). There is a healthcare culture that pervades. In fact, one need only ask a 'patient' what they expect or how they are expected to behave in medical contexts to begin to see the characteristics of such cultures. There are key players (e.g. professional, patient, healthcare assistants) all playing their respective parts in pre-defined roles of interaction, where power is also a consideration. Only when such a culture is challenged does one appreciate the rules and rigidities of interactions within the culture of the healthcare context. Walsh et al. (2018) consider the benefits of such a disrupted culture of a typical speech and language therapy intervention, revealing the more familiar modus operandi of more traditional clinical cultures. Our concern here in this book, however, is that typical clinical culture that students become aware of as they experience their clinical placements. Hence our 'socio-cultural' view is just that, a stance that is influenced by the social and cultural dimensions of allied healthcare education.

2.5 SUMMARY

In this chapter, consideration of key concepts relevant to the arguments to be discussed in this book were defined and discussed. The chapter started out with an outline of contexts of interactions that AHP students find themselves in as they navigate the journey of their education and eventual induction into their chosen profession. These contexts were discussed with reference to key sites for professional identity formation. Definitions of social interaction and socialisation were then presented and considered within the educational context of teaching and learning. Our own understandings and beliefs around identity were presented, while the rationale for adopting a 'socio-cultural stance', while considering the nuanced experiences of AHP education, were explained.

Finally, as Berger and Luckmann (1967: 195) propose, if 'identity remains unintelligible unless it is located in a world', it is the world of the AHP student and professional that we must look to in order to understand and map professional identity formation. This, we would argue, characterises both the richness and complexity of identity, considered within the ongoing and fluid milieu of social interaction core to our ordinary everyday life and experiences. In particular, the AHP student's world is challenging, as many learning contexts are, and yet it provides fertile ground for the exploration of professional identity formation.

3

PROFESSIONAL IDENTITY FORMATION THROUGH SOCIAL INTERACTION IN ALLIED HEALTHCARE EDUCATION CONTEXTS

Education is not preparation for life; education is life itself.
John Dewey

3.1 INTRODUCTION

Professional identity formation has been considered in the healthcare education literature but most especially with regard to the education and training of medical doctors or physicians. Less attention has been paid to this aspect of development across allied healthcare contexts, although this is gradually changing as educational programmes are further developed in line with advances in pedagogy and clinical teaching. Furthermore, the increasing interest in interprofessional learning has also brought with it a closer examination of identity formation across disciplines as they interact, such as occupational therapy, physiotherapy and speech and language therapy, among others.

This chapter will firstly set out an overview of professional identity in medical education as a backdrop to the discussion of professional identity formation in other allied healthcare disciplines. The review will keep an eye on the role – if any – that social interaction has played in the reporting of this research from the various disciplines. The chapter will close with a consideration of how interprofessional learning has begun to inform the literature in this area.

3.2 PROFESSIONAL IDENTITY IN HEALTHCARE EDUCATION

Across healthcare education contexts, specific attention to the development of a professional identity is gaining traction as part of undergraduate curricula, to greater or lesser extents. Snell et al. (2020) published a scoping review on the development of professional identity and professional socialisation among allied healthcare professional (AHP) students. This review was in a response to the predominant literature coming from medicine and nursing, with less research emanating from allied healthcare disciplines. The authors state that:

> The purpose and focus of this review is the development of professional identity by allied health students, with studies excluded if students were from nursing, medicine or dentistry as a single profession. While the body of work from these

professions and lessons for allied health are acknowledged, we believe there is sufficient difference in professional roles to warrant specific attention on students enrolled in programs for allied health professions. (Snell et al. 2020: 45)

More and more papers are being published in this area in discipline-specific journals (e.g. see Whalen et al. (2018) for research in emergency medicine, specifically on paramedics) and in more general education journals relevant to teaching and learning contexts in the health sciences (e.g. Guinan et al. 2018). In this section, we first consider medical education before outlining some of the identity research covered across a variety of healthcare disciplines (i.e. nursing, pharmacy, physiotherapy, occupational therapy and speech and language therapy). The final section of this chapter looks briefly at interprofessional learning as a site for professional identity exploration and development.

3.2.1 EDUCATION OF MEDICAL STUDENTS AND DEVELOPING PROFESSIONAL IDENTITY

The education of medical students and consideration of their developing sense of identity formation have received considerable attention in the literature, especially when compared to other areas of healthcare education. Identity formation considerations in the medical education context have helped to fuel and progress the development of ideas being discussed in other areas of allied healthcare, both in terms of theoretical constructs and practical applications. The work of Cruess et al. (2019) reflects upon the extensive research currently being conducted in medical education in the context of professional identity formation, viewing it as a fundamental pillar of medical education. They discuss the link between professional identity and socialisation in everyday practice while also emphasising professionals, role models and mentors as powerful influences impacting the professional identity of medical students, thereby helping them to achieve a deeper understanding and establishment of their professional identity formation.

Theoretical constructs that help to inform 'professional identity construction' are discussed in detail by Pratt, Rockmann and Kaufmann (2006). Their theory development is based on a six-year qualitative study of medical residents, and their findings present a rich array of perspectives and perceptions from an analysis of semi-structured interviews. Among their considerations, they discuss: (i) how different bodies of knowledge (including *socialisation*) can influence construction of identity, (ii) how work and identity are intimately linked, one informing the other in a dynamic ongoing way, as opposed to a static 'work-identity fit' (p. 259), (iii) how the timing of identifying with a professional organisation may have an impact on identity, and finally, (iv) how important 'the understanding [of] "what they do" in order to gain a richer understanding of "who they are" is to professional identity construction' (p. 259). Pratt et al. conclude that an organisational culture that includes feedback and role model provision is key to supporting identity work – two key aspects of student learning and development that are echoed in the chapters to follow in this book.

Linked to what students' understanding of 'what they do' helps inform 'what they are' or become is the increasing use of reflective study tools in education. The use of online media is growing in healthcare education, both as a pedagogical tool and a site for students to record their reflections. The data which inform discussions in later chapters of this book (i.e. Chapters 7 to 10) were collected from AHP student reflections in response to questions posed in an online survey. In these chapters, we will show that student engagement with online media can facilitate reflection on learning as professional identity develops. In medical education, Hsieh, Kuo and Wang (2019: 1) developed what they called 'a clerkship programme to teach professionalism with the support of social media'. They required medical students in their first year of clinical training to post comments on a popular social media site on the positive behaviours they had witnessed or observed while on clinical placement. Instructors and fellow students responded to, or commented upon, such posts. These data, collected over two years, comprised 435 records. The data were then analysed, using appreciative inquiry as a framework, and the findings demonstrated that most students referred to the passion of their teachers or clinical instructors as an important attribute of professionalism. Other attributes they referred to from their observations were *compassion*, *competence* and *openness*. A high percentage of the students (90%) were positively disposed to this online method of teaching and learning as they recorded their observations – observations of attributes that they found desirable and were eager to incorporate into their own future behaviour or identity as a medical professional.

Using the online social media platform, then, in Hsieh et al.'s study (2019) seemed to allow the students to identify explicitly – or name – the positive behaviours observed in a safe and communal way, and via a method familiar to most (i.e. posting comments on social media). In so doing, they were reflecting on desirable attributes to help inform their own professional identity formation. Also of interest here is the nuanced potential of any consideration of what 'social interaction' means. Here, as in other data sets discussed in this book, we can appreciate at least two differing but important discursive dimensions of social interaction, that is: (i) social interaction as observed and engaged in by the students that led them to comment on the compassion and openness of their clinical teachers, and (ii) social interaction as they virtually 'interacted' with their peers and instructors online, recording their reflections. In the data discussed in this book, we consider both dimensions of social interaction identified here. In Chapters 4 and 5, we discuss data from qualified clinicians as they reflect on their interactions with colleagues and clients, respectively. Chapters 7 to 10 consider the data collected from students by virtue of completing an online survey, where participants are given the opportunity to reflect on and record their experiences of social interaction as part of their allied healthcare education.

3.2.2 EDUCATION OF NURSING STUDENTS AND DEVELOPING PROFESSIONAL IDENTITY

The development of a professional identity among nursing students has received increased attention in the literature as a popular area of research in recent years. This growth in interest could have been influenced by the relatively recent move to degree status for nursing qualifications at undergraduate level, with increased recognition of the professional status of nurses alongside their peers in other healthcare professions. Research on the development of professional identity tends to be concentrated – as for most studies in professional identity formation among students – around the early and later years of the educational process in nursing.

Browne et al. (2018) describe nursing students' perceptions of the nursing profession as they begin their degree studies. As part of a broader study helping to identify nursing students' understanding of culture and communication in the profession, students were asked to draw what they believed constituted a 'typical nurse' as they were participating in an orientation week open day. They were also asked to write down any significant features they wished to emphasise. The students were then encouraged to brainstorm the qualities, characteristics and duties they may associate with being a nurse. A thematic analysis approach was used to explore the data (which were comprised of drawings, words and phrases). Drawings were also analysed through Rose's (2001) critical visual methodology framework of interpretative engagement, as proposed by Guillemin et al. (2014). Four key themes were identified as part of this process by Browne et al. (2018: 90), including (i) 'To be a nurse I have to look the part'; (ii) 'To be a nurse, I have to perform in a variety of roles'; (iii) 'To be a nurse, I have to connect with others'; (iv) 'To be a nurse, I have to care for myself'. The theme of 'To be a nurse I have to look the part' included references to the female gender stereotype, as well as reference to nursing equipment and expected professional behaviour. The theme of 'To be a nurse, I have to perform in a variety of roles' encapsulated the various roles, including considering the nursing role as both a carer and competent practitioner. The third theme of 'To be a nurse, I have to connect with others' had the associated subthemes of 'collaborative practice', 'communication' and 'cultural understanding'. The fourth theme, 'To be a nurse, I have to care for myself', aimed to encompass the positive and negative connotations of self-care (including resilience, health, being tired and overworked that can often be associated with the profession). Having 'to connect with others' via 'collaboration' and 'communication' speaks to the important role social interaction plays in the achievement of these desired attributes among nascent nursing students.

Teskereci and Boz (2019) also conducted a study with nursing students at the outset of their education, exploring diary entries of first-year nursing students as they reflected on their initial experiences in clinical practice. Analysing the data via thematic analysis (van Manen 2014), four main themes were identified: (i) conflict between feelings and professionalism; (ii) trying to act like a nurse; (iii) growth through challenges; and (iv) care outcomes. The theme of 'conflict between feelings and professionalism' was informed by students' references to their efforts, at times, to hide their feelings so as to appear more professional. References to the students' questioning of themselves and their own decision to become a nurse on entering the clinical environment with the associated responsibility of care also informed the identification of this theme. Within the theme of 'acting like a nurse', some students reflected that once they were carrying out nursing procedures and tasks, including caring behaviours, they felt more like the professional they were to become, thereby helping their identity formation in this context. As for many healthcare professional students, the challenges that accompany clinical practice can have positive effects on personal growth and maturity. Captured within the theme of 'growth through challenges' were student references to the care that their supervisors afforded to them on placement, which went some way to diminish the stress and anxiety felt by some. The hospital environment also posed challenges for some students, making adjustment difficult. Finally, the fourth theme identified as 'care outcomes' comprised references by the student nurses to issues of their value and that value being appreciated by other fellow healthcare professionals. Other student accounts reported satisfaction with being able to deliver care to patients, even at the very early stage of their education. A 'sense of belonging' also gradually emerged for some, contributing to their sense of professional identity.

Most, if not all, of the themes identified among the diary accounts analysed by Teskereci and Boz (2019) referenced (directly or indirectly) contexts of social interaction which brought about change or developments in student learning. Whether it was being satisfied with an interaction with a patient or being valued by another healthcare professional, these critical learning experiences grew from social interaction contexts in their nursing practice which influence identity formation, both personal and professional.

3.2.3 EDUCATION OF PHARMACY STUDENTS AND DEVELOPING PROFESSIONAL IDENTITY

The transition from the pharmacy student to the qualified pharmacist – like many other healthcare disciplines – has its opportunities and challenges, and as such calls into focus professional identity formation in this discipline. In a recent scoping review, Noble, McKauge and Clavarino (2019) report on their analysis of 22 studies (from an initial 137 articles retrieved and published within the last decade) concerned specifically with professional identity formation. The studies reviewed met the following inclusion criteria: (i) explicitly addressed professional identity formation, (ii) involved pharmacy curricula, and (iii) focused on students registered in pharmacy degree courses or their experiences of the curriculum. Most of the studies retrieved for review were Australian in origin (n=10; 45%), with lesser numbers from elsewhere in the world (but including studies from the USA, UK, South Africa, Canada and Lebanon).

Noble et al.'s (2019) main findings describe how many students in the studies reviewed struggled with their professional identity formation, particularly with reconciling their value and belief systems with what they experienced in clinical practice. Although many of the studies reviewed reported some innovative pedagogical practices related to professional identity formation, these practices were not routine or fully integrated into curricula and failed to include other important stakeholders in the design (e.g. practice educators/supervisors, patients and other healthcare providers). As in other areas of healthcare, Noble et al. call for more research in professional identity formation as integrative to pharmacy curricula and clinical training.

What is of particular interest to this volume is those studies reviewed by Noble at al. (2019) that specifically referenced or focused upon social interaction as part of that development of professional identity. Just four of the studies reviewed had social interaction at their core, with two predominant themes emerging: 'identities lacking social recognition' and 'identities remaining unresolved' (Noble et al. 2019: 28). The former theme suggests that pharmacy students' identity formation was dependent upon, and highly relevant to, their social interaction while on placement with the various relevant stakeholders involved in their field of practice (e.g. pharmacy staff, patients and other healthcare workers) (Noble et al. 2015). In terms of 'identities remaining unresolved', a further two studies in Noble et al.'s (2019: 28) review referenced interactions with others as being at the core of this challenge: as students struggled to become their professional self 'as a pharmacist', experiences such as their advice not being accepted or their inputs being met with 'disinterest' or even 'anger' challenged their confidence and identity formation (Noble et al. 2015). A similar finding was reported in McCartney and Boschmans' (2018) study which explored the lived experiences of 33 final-year students in South Africa. Following a 15-week placement, feelings of insecurity and doubt about their role reportedly negatively impacted their developing identity as hospital pharmacists.

Finally, in the context of the education of pharmacists, a study by Bridges (2018) explored first-year students' reflections on their experiences of 'interacting for learning', hence placing social interaction at the core of their study. Along with the expected benefits of amiable interactions, learning about others and increased confidence, Bridges (2018: 290) also found that students 'reflectively considered their own stance in the light of others' experiences and healthcare perspectives; and started to gain a wider world view, potentially informing their future interactions with patients and colleagues'. Hence, social interaction seemed key in the early stages of pharmacy education, not unlike other programmes of allied healthcare education. The centrality of social interaction to identity formation cannot be ignored in these contexts of allied healthcare educational experiences.

3.2.4 EDUCATION OF PHYSIOTHERAPY STUDENTS AND DEVELOPING PROFESSIONAL IDENTITY

Physiotherapists have long considered what it means to be a member of their discipline and what the key aspects of their identity as practitioners may be. In a 1992 study, Miles-Tapping et al. (1992) used an open-ended questionnaire to explore physiotherapists' perceptions of their own identity. Interestingly, a mere 15% of the population surveyed identified themselves as a member of a caring profession with a career that was rewarding, despite many respondents acknowledging that their skills had 'potential benefit for patients' (p. 31). Since the early 1990s, there has been a growth of studies in professional identity formation in the physiotherapy context (e.g. Lindquist et al. 2006; Korpi, Peltokallio and Piirainen 2014; Kyte, Frank and Thomas 2018). Identity, then, for this group of AHPs was – and continues to be – an issue of concern, as it has been for most practitioners outside the core medical teams of nurses and physicians.

Hammond, Cross and Moore (2016) explored professional identity within physiotherapy, employing a qualitative methodology using collective memory work (see Crawford et al. 1992). Their study focused on the analysis of 17 hours of discourse data collected from regular meetings of eight physiotherapists over a six-month period, where ethical dilemmas and issues of identity were discussed. Hammond et al. (2016: 71) concluded that:

> Participants co-constructed the meaning of being a physiotherapist within intra-professional and inter-professional communities of practice. Patients informed this, and it was mediated by workplace and institutional discourses, boundaries and hierarchies, through an unfolding career and the contingencies of a life story.

Of interest here is the acknowledgement of co-construction through interactions, not only with fellow professionals of their own or other disciplines but with patients they work with and as part of their own 'life story'. Hammond et al.'s assertion that identity is 'dynamic' and not a static notion also fits with our own beliefs about identity as discussed in Chapter 2 of this book, as does the understanding that identity is constructed and 'fed by the individual's feelings and how one makes sense of the interplay between personal and professional identities and experiences' (p. 75).

Shifting the focus to the student experience and their developing identity in the pre-registration context, Rappazzo, Seagrave and Gough (2022) conducted a scoping review to investigate how professional identity is considered in physiotherapy curricula. To identify key themes within the review, a meta-synthesis was carried out of qualitative studies sourced (n=21) to gain a more nuanced appreciation of the arguments presented. The following five themes were identified: *self* (e.g. 'finding a voice', 'self-awareness', 'self-reflection), *skills* (e.g. 'confidence', 'knowledge', 'teamwork' etc.), *curriculum* (e.g. 'course progression', 'collaborative practice', 'interprofessional learning'), *programme* (e.g. undergraduate, postgraduate and doctoral studies) and finally, *location* (e.g. 'community engagement', 'university', 'home', etc.). These themes resonate with the discussions to follow in this text, demonstrating how some commonality across allied healthcare educational concerns around identity are core to the teaching and learning student experience. (The reader is referred to this review for a more in-depth consideration of the themes identified.)

3.2.5 EDUCATION OF SPEECH AND LANGUAGE THERAPY STUDENTS AND DEVELOPING PROFESSIONAL IDENTITY

As with the other disciplines discussed thus far, 'identity' issues are equally pertinent and increasingly relevant to the discipline of speech and language therapy, not least because of the common and persistent misunderstandings surrounding what speech and language therapists (SLTs) actually 'do'. Such misunderstandings are helped in no small part by a discipline name that is at best reductive, falling well short of transparency to reflect the diversity of the scope of speech and language therapy in working with a wide group of people who may have voice, communication and/or swallowing disorders as part of their clinical presentation (be that congenital, neurodevelopmental or acquired). Hence, role ambiguity is not uncommon (American Speech and Hearing Association (ASHA) 2019) in speech and language therapy, which only highlights the focus on identity issues by students and practitioners alike. However, for clarity we include a definition of the SLT role here (Irish Association of Speech and Language Therapists (IASLT) 2022) that may help readers appreciate the discussions to come around identity concerns in speech and language therapy:

> SLTs assess, diagnose and provide a broad range of interventions and supports to people across the lifespan, with a variety of disorders and/or concerns regarding communication, voice, feeding, eating, drinking and swallowing (FEDS). SLTs also have a broader societal role in advocating for and developing services for all those with communication and swallowing needs.

Beginning speech and language therapy students – like fellow students in other allied healthcare courses – are not immune from misunderstandings about the role and multidimensional nature of their chosen profession. From our own experience as lecturers on undergraduate programmes, it is not unusual to find that first-year students are genuinely unaware of the diverse scope of the profession of speech and language therapy; they may also be unaware of what personal qualities or aspects of their identity may come to the fore as they learn to interact with others in clinical and non-clinical contexts.

Jagoe and Walsh (2016) explored identity work among first-year students in speech and language therapy. As part of a foundational module which aims to provide the student SLT with some experience in interacting and conversing with people with language and communication difficulties, students were invited through a reflective writing task to write 'letters to self' (i.e. 'Dear me...' letters) both before and after a series of weekly pre-clinical meetings involving people with aphasia (i.e. the language and communication impairment that may follow a stroke). The purpose of these weekly home visits to people with aphasia was for the student and the person to engage in naturalistic, social-conversational interactions. The substance of the written 'before' and 'after' student reflections was then analysed thematically.

Concepts and themes related to the 'before' reflections included the following: 'anticipation', 'hope' and 'feelings', with many of the students' commentaries looking forward to their future identity as an SLT and welcoming the 'face-to-face practical experience' ahead:

> I also look forward to the chance it is giving me of having this face-to-face practical experience to develop my knowledge and skills of [sic] dealing with disorders such as aphasia as I believe it will be a huge learning tool in helping me through the 4 years in college and for when I qualify and begin my career as an SLT (M1). (Jagoe and Walsh 2016: 178)

Similarly, another student's comment was also forward-looking to their future self and the requisite 'valuable communication' skills needed:

> I hope by the end of the process that I will have learned valuable communication skills and better understanding of what it's like living with aphasia, which in turn will help me to develop the skills I need to be a future SLT (Q1). (Jagoe and Walsh 2016: 180)

The follow-up 'Dear me...' letters, which were written after the series of visits to people in the community, also referenced the students' concept of their future selves or developing identities as a healthcare professional. 'Relationships' and 'changed' were two key concepts that were identified in the data, once again reflected in the student comments, such as:

> At the beginning of [the programme] I had the perception that I would form a strong bond of friendship with my conversation partner, and although I have enjoyed his company, I am also glad to say that I have been able to separate myself personally from the programme and have discovered an important boundary capability for my career with clients (P2). (Jagoe and Walsh 2016: 182)

Jagoe and Walsh (2016: 169) conclude that their analysis of these student written reflections revealed students demonstrating 'a broadening view of a more "considered self" and an increasing acknowledgement and consideration of the "other" (i.e. another person)', thereby laying preliminary groundwork for future identity work as a healthcare professional in a caring and altruistic role. The findings of this study clearly show that professional identity work begins early on in the student's learning journey, with social interaction with others being the conduit to kickstart this preliminary work.

In a mixed methods study involving second-year speech and language therapy student volunteers also interacting with people with aphasia as co-workers, Nikkels, Berns and Neijenhuis (2023) note the students' increased confidence and improvement in knowledge and communication skills following a Dutch communication partner training programme (called Training Con-tAct). The students' performance was evaluated through pre- and post-measures via a quantitative video analysis, a self-report questionnaire and student focus group interviews. Of interest here are some of the observations made by the students which reference the social interaction dimension of their experiences, even hinting at identity development through this programme and best reflected in the following comment: 'an SLT talks to a person and not to a disorder. The disorder is just a part of that person' (Student 5; Nikkels et al. 2023: 8).

O'Leary and Cantillon (2020) extended the focus on student awareness of identity by considering it in contrast to recent graduate identities in speech and language therapy (i.e. those therapists qualified for less than two years). Data were collected via in-depth interviews and analysed thematically. Unlike the findings of Jagoe and Walsh summarised above, O'Leary and Cantillon (2020: 781) found that 'undergraduate professional identity was characterised by dependency, self-centredness (as opposed to patient centredness), and a naïve role concept'. This finding was also in direct contrast to their findings on the analysis of the data from recent graduates, whose identity was informed by client-centredness and a sense of self-sufficiency. These authors call for greater involvement by students in patient-centred roles and clinical decision making in consideration of identity-focused work in undergraduate curricula.

3.2.6 EDUCATION OF OCCUPATIONAL THERAPY STUDENTS AND DEVELOPING PROFESSIONAL IDENTITY

Like speech and language therapy, occupational therapy also suffers from misunderstandings of what the discipline entails and what the specific role of an occupational therapist is as part of healthcare teams. Once again, in the interest of clarity we provide a definition by the Association of Occupational Therapists of Ireland (AOTI), who define occupational therapy as:

> a healthcare profession offering support to people with physical, psychological and social problems to enable them to live life to the fullest. Occupational therapists help people to do the everyday activities they want and need to do when faced with illness, injury, disability or challenging life circumstances or events. (www.aoti.ie/what-is-ot)

Like its fellow allied healthcare disciplines, occupational therapy also has focused on professional identity issues. Just over two decades ago, Ikiugu and Rosso (2003) recognised the need to explore identity in occupational therapy students through a consideration of students' enhanced sense of professional identity, following their participation in a graduate course on the theory of occupational therapy (which included aspects such as philosophical, social, economic and political factors impacting the discipline, as well as models of practice and the history of occupational therapy). Edwards and Dirette (2010) also considered professional identity in occupational therapy, and its relationship to burnout within this profession, taking into consideration the often-expected broad reach of occupational therapy practice. Related to the burnout and role ambiguity, Turner and Knight (2015: 664) suggest that issues around identity in occupational therapy stem from a 'lack of deep knowledge of the profession's unique beliefs', with therapists consequently having a sense of being 'undervalued'.

Focusing on the student occupational therapist, Gray et al. (2020) explored the developing professional identity of second-year undergraduate students as part of an assessment task in which they were asked (i) to describe why they had joined an occupational therapy programme of education, (ii) how they envisaged themselves in the role of an occupational therapist, and finally (iii) to consider who their role models might be. The findings suggested a variation in identity profiles within the same year group, with some students showing an advanced sense of their professional identity linked to their choice of role models, while the majority demonstrated a developing sense of identity in the early stages.

Finally, in a recent scoping review, Walder et al. (2022) concluded that identity in occupational therapy was multifaceted in nature and identified four main themes in the analysis of 89 papers on the subject. Themes included 'developing a shared ontology', 'embracing the culture', 'enacting occupational therapy' and 'believing in occupational therapy' (Walder et al. 2022: 175). This latter theme of 'believing in occupational therapy' resonates with Turner and Knight's (2015) consideration of the need for occupational therapists to recognise the discipline's unique beliefs about their profession to aid their sense of a unique professional identity.

3.3. INTERPROFESSIONAL PRACTICE AND PROFESSIONAL IDENTITY

Having briefly reviewed how professional identity has been explored across medicine, nursing and some of the allied healthcare professions (i.e. pharmacy, physiotherapy, speech and language therapy and occupational therapy), it would be remiss not to include in this chapter some consideration of how identity is viewed within interprofessional contexts and in allied healthcare educational contexts. Discussions of interprofessional practice and interprofessional teaching and learning (education) contexts have become increasingly popular in recent years. Recognition of the need for healthcare professionals to work with and alongside other professionals from different disciplines has fuelled this increased focus. It seems that interprofessional contexts of interaction provide the ideal fora for identity issues to become salient, offering an opportunity to view discipline-specific and discipline-generic identities through a multidisciplinary lens, therefore adding to our overall understanding of what professional identity means.

Interprofessional learning is fast becoming a staple part of healthcare education, as the workplace requirement for inter- and multidisciplinary collaboration across healthcare settings is recognised as a key professional competency to be achieved. New graduates are expected to be able to enter the workplace with these interprofessional skills and to 'hit the ground running', so to speak. This interprofessional awareness and readiness is one of the goals of interprofessional teaching and learning activities that are now an ever-increasing growth area in undergraduate education. Interprofessional learning activities are common across many spheres of education, from business studies to healthcare programmes. In healthcare education, interprofessional learning activities can be found across the years of undergraduate programmes in, for example, pharmacy, speech and language therapy, dental science, occupational therapy and physiotherapy, as well as programmes in core medicine.

Interprofessional learning, by its very nature, entails social interaction, which in turn drives this learning. Students from different disciplines come together to discuss, argue, problem solve and share ideas. For many, it may be the first time they get to formally meet other students from different disciplines (outside of the social activities that are leisure related). It can be a daunting experience for some who are nervous or feel threatened when they must share teaching and learning experiences. In fact, the fear of being 'exposed' in terms of 'not knowing' can prevent active participation and involvement among some students, while others are more confident in sharing what they know or how their particular discipline can contribute to the learning task under discussion.

Considering interprofessional practice, McNeil, Mitchell and Parker (2013) discuss the issue of 'threat' to identity in such interprofessional contexts. Despite acknowledging the positive literature base and the potential benefits of this kind of working, McNeil et al. (2013: 291) also consider the negative aspects of interprofessional practice and argue that 'a key cause of failure can be attributed to interprofessional conflicts based on differences associated with, and threats to professional identities'. Of interest is their consideration of 'professional identity faultlines' (p. 291) after the earlier introduction of the concept of 'fault line' in relation to social identity by Lau and Murnighan (1998: 328) and defined as 'hypothetical dividing lines that may be split a group into subgroups based on one or more attributes'. McNeil et al. (2013) consider these faultlines as potentially being revealed, for example, when professional groups are treated differently by organisations or when discrete professional values are perhaps not respected.

The notion of 'professional identity faultlines' is a useful one to consider within the context of interprofessional teaching and learning contexts. The authors' own experiences in this regard have seen the potential in interprofessional learning contexts for those 'faultlines' to be exploited in the differentiation of roles, role responsibilities and even identities in these teaching and learning contexts. Guinan et al. (2018) explored health sciences students' attitudes to interprofessional education. Involving over 400 students from disciplines including medicine, nursing, pharmacy, occupational therapy and speech and language therapy, Guinan et al. evaluated their attitudes to this form of learning over the course of interprofessional workshop experiences (i.e. pre-workshop, the workshop itself and post workshop), also considering the students' online preparation for engagement. The workshops involved interdisciplinary discussion of a hypothetical medical case (e.g. a patient following a stroke), where all disciplines were expected to contribute, having a potential role to play in the case management. Attitudes to the interprofessional learning were found to improve following engagement in the structured workshops that brought these student learners together, further underlining the added value of social interaction in this teaching and learning context. Interprofessional teaching and learning contexts or interprofessional education will be revisited in later stages of this book as students and practitioners reflect on this aspect of their educational experiences.

3.4 SUMMARY

Professional identity and professional identity formation are rapidly growing areas of research among allied healthcare disciplines and educational contexts. Building on the foundations of literature on identity in the general medical fields (most particularly on physician training), the allied healthcare disciplines have also come to consider identity issues as a core concern both at the professional and student level. Professionals who may struggle with role delineation (e.g. occupational therapists and speech and language therapists) may have to work harder to establish their unique attributes and contributions to healthcare while working on their own sense of identity as a professional in their chosen field. Increasingly, this identity work is gaining focus at undergraduate levels, where educators (who are often qualified healthcare professionals themselves) see the value of adopting a critical stance to identity development and formation at an early stage of a programme of study and instilling in their students an appreciation of what it means to be (or become) a professional in their respective discipline. Interprofessional teaching and learning contexts, where some (or many) students from different disciplines come together to learn side by side, have been shown to be beneficial in helping to form a sense of a profession-specific identity while being cognisant of a broader profession-generic identity as healthcare workers. The next chapter, Chapter 4, explores where such identities may be challenged in the social interactions of the workplace, emphasising the need to pay attention to identity work in all its contexts and forms.

4

NEGOTIATING WORKPLACE IDENTITY THROUGH SOCIAL INTERACTION: AN END GOAL OR WORK IN PROGRESS FOR THE STUDENT PROFESSIONAL?

Learn as if you were not reaching your goal and as though you were scared of missing it.
Confucius

4.1 INTRODUCTION

It has been discussed in the previous chapters that identity is something that is constantly in flux and not something that is static. Its dynamic nature is honed by context and, as we argue in this text, by social interaction. Allied healthcare professionals (AHPs), by the very nature of their work and the context of their workplace, interact constantly with other professionals, both within and outside their profession. It is within such interactions that profession-specific – and even profession-generic identities – are honed. Much of the work of healthcare teams is grounded in social interaction as individuals work together as a unit to support and intervene with families and individuals who are seeking care. Their identity is also shaped by those they serve, the service users who attend clinical contexts for support. But how do the workplace and one's workplace colleagues shape and influence identity? Is this something that evolves over time as one grows within or with a service? Is this potential evolution of professional identity something that healthcare students can be prepared for during their education?

This chapter will explore these questions by focusing on a partial set of the findings from a larger study by Ryan (2018) within the context of a Child and Adolescent Mental Health Service (CAMHS). Through in-depth interviews, Ryan (2018) explored how identity is navigated, even challenged, in times of change to service provision. This study is of relevance here for three main reasons. Firstly, it is clear from the findings of this research that identity is something that is valued and 'owned' by professions, and it is only when the unique ownership is challenged or threatened that it becomes even more urgent to protect it. Secondly, the findings also speak to the identity-as-social-interaction idea, where reports of team interactions precipitate reflections on profession-specific identity. Finally, the findings of this study also inform our education focus in this book, where a professional identity is seen as both an evolving process and an end goal for those in education and training. Considering this workplace identity has important implications for how identity work can be shaped in undergraduate education.

4.2 BACKGROUND TO WORKPLACE STUDY

As referred to above, Ryan's (2018) larger study explored the experience of mental health professionals working in CAMHS in Ireland. Mental health services, including CAMHS, have undergone significant development over the past decade in the Irish context. Such development has put professions under the spotlight so to speak as they navigate their work and identity against a tide of shifting service models and provision. The development and changes largely occurred within the context of the publication of the national policy document *A Vision for Change* (Department of Health and Children 2006), which set out a framework for mental health services across the lifespan. Unfortunately, despite its ambitious aims, the updated version of this policy, *Sharing the Vision* (Department of Health 2020), has been met with disappointment among allied healthcare communities due to the lack of recognition and visibility of the diversity of professionals needed to deliver optimum care to this population.

Identity is explored in this chapter by drawing on the experiences of healthcare professionals working in CAMHS contexts. Through a series of in-depth semi-structured interviews with six multidisciplinary professionals from the disciplines of social work, speech and language therapy and clinical psychology, the healthcare professionals discussed aspects of their respective roles both within and outside the CAMHS multidisciplinary setting. Participants described their unexpected journey to establishing a professional identity and being part of a multidisciplinary team. They also spoke about the hierarchical nature of the team and how their experience of the elevated status of psychiatry (the usual lead discipline on such teams) led them to having to compete for their voices to be heard in establishing their identities.

4.2.1 NOTES ON METHODOLOGY

In-depth interviews with three social workers, two psychologists and one speech and language therapist were transcribed and analysed for this study. All professionals had from 5 to 15 years' experience working in the CAMHS context. Participants were advised that the purpose of the study was to hear about their experiences working in CAMHS and their views on the services. Open-ended questions were asked to encourage the participants to express their opinions and talk freely. The initial questions were broad (e.g. 'How did you end up working in CAMHS?') and became more specific as the interview progressed (e.g. 'How would you describe the public's understanding of CAMHS?'). Probes such as 'Can you tell me more?' and 'Do you mean...?'were used for clarification and elaboration as required. Follow-up questions were asked based on the participants' responses to thoroughly listen to what was being said and to understand the wider context of the views expressed (Rubin and Rubin 2005).

As referenced elsewhere in this book (i.e. in Chapters 5 and 6), an interpretative phenomenological analysis (IPA) was the analytic methodology adopted to help make sense of others' experiences as related by the professionals during the interviews. In keeping with IPA, (i) getting at the lived experience requires a 'double hermeneutic' as the researcher is attempting to make sense of the participant making sense of their experience (Smith and Osborn 2003), and (ii) while the researcher attempts to understand the experience of the participant and appreciate the phenomenon from their point of view (i.e. an empathic stance), the researcher also attempts to move away from what the participant said and adopt a more curious and critical style in their interpretation (i.e. a questioning stance). Once all the interviews were completed, they were transcribed verbatim. The data were then analysed according to the step-by-step approach described by Smith, Flowers and Larkin (2009). As these data were analysed prior to Smith et al.'s more recent revision of IPA terminology (i.e. see Smith and Nizza 2021; Smith, Flowers and Larkin 2022), the original terms for the identification of themes will be retained here to honour the original analysis (i.e. emergent theme, superordinate theme, master theme); subsequent analyses in later chapters adopt the updated terms of experiential statement, personal experiential theme (PET) and group experiential theme (GET), respectively.

4.3 NEGOTIATING AN IDENTITY IN THE WORKPLACE

An overall master theme of 'I think everybody's finding it a challenge to be honest' was identified from the data analysis of the larger study, with three associated superordinate themes: (i) negotiating identity in the workplace, (ii) power in CAMHS and (ii) the changing nature of CAMHS. The theme of 'negotiating identity in the workplace' is the focus of discussion in this chapter, although it is not hard to see how the two additional themes could have a bearing on identity formation and ownership, not least because of hierarchical nature of a CAMHS team (led almost exclusively by a consultant psychiatrist) but also because any change to service delivery can precipitate cause to reflect on specific professional identities in flux.

The superordinate theme of 'negotiating identity in the workplace' was best expressed by the quote from one participant: 'I suppose it's been a bit of a rollercoaster'. The three associated emergent themes are listed in Table 4.1 and are as follows: (i) my professional background, (ii) adapting to the context of the workplace and (iii) being part of a multidisciplinary team, will be discussed below. Throughout the discussion of these themes, extracts from the interview data will be used to support the points made. In these extracts, pseudonyms are used for participants and line numbers refer to the initial line of the extract, followed by the abbreviation 'ff' to denote 'and following lines' (e.g. 'Matthew, lines 518ff').

The 'rollercoaster' analogy is one that one participant invoked to describe their journey to establish their identity within a CAMHS team. All professions, through their education and training, establish a profession-specific identity honed and shaped over the years of their undergraduate courses. Once in the workplace, that identity may be further shaped or even challenged. CAMHS settings are no exception in this regard, where the professional must find their 'place' among other professions represented on the multidisciplinary team. Such professions can include a wide array of highly skilled healthcare workers, including psychologists, psychiatrists, psychiatric nurses, occupational therapists, speech and language therapists,

Table 4.1 Superordinate theme of 'negotiating identity in the workplace' and its associated list of emergent themes

Superordinate Theme	Emergent Themes
Negotiating identity in the workplace: *'I suppose it's been a bit of a rollercoaster'*	• My professional background • Adapting to the context of the workplace • Being part of a multidisciplinary team

social workers and, sometimes, play therapists. The day-to-day work of the multidisciplinary team requires social interaction, both in terms of (i) interacting with the children and families attending the service, and (ii) by virtue of the social interaction that is necessary in working as a multidisciplinary team, where case conferences, family meetings and other consultations all require varying levels of interaction.

The participants interviewed reported a marked uncertainty around their role in CAMHS settings. Trying to preserve and reconcile their own specific professional identity against a backdrop of a diversity of professions that they interact with daily proved a real challenge for some as they tried to 'fit in'. As Ryan (2018: 36) states: 'The very nature of working in CAMHS means that the participants are not working in silos; they are part of a group of other professional disciplines'.

4.3.1 MY PROFESSIONAL BACKGROUND

An emergent theme within this superordinate theme, 'my professional background', sees the professionals explicitly talking about this struggle to fit in, both to meet the needs of the CAMHS team but also the families and individuals they serve. A social worker interviewed for the study (under the pseudonym 'Matthew') spoke about his awareness of families looking for a more medical-model type of intervention, as opposed to that which he was trained in:

Extract 4.1

I think that, yeah and this was a struggle for me early on in my CAMHS career, is that sometimes people want that certainty of a professional who's going to assess, diagnose, treat. In the same way a doctor, a medical doctor, would with a medical ailment. And sometimes people seek that, sometimes it satisfies them because it fits with their view of the world and with their view of their difficulties. **(Matthew, lines 518ff)**

Ciara, another social worker, talked of her own identity being linked to the strong ethical dimension of the role, even if it is less defined than other professions. She referred to social work identity as like a 'cuckoo', one that is an eclectic mix of 'borrowing' from other professions yet firmly grounded in the 'social work position':

Extract 4.2

It's kind of, eh I mean social work borrows from all over the place, it's kind of a bit of a, a bit of a cuckoo. Is it a cuckoo going around stealing other birds' eggs? (laughs) ... It's a little bit like that, borrows from all over the place. So, we have a strong social work position but when you're going into therapeutic social work, it's all a bit kind of, well you can kind of pick and choose. **(Ciara, lines 159ff)**

The social work identity, according to Ciara, is not easily defined and can seem vague (or 'woolly') in comparison to other disciplines:

Extract 4.3

(Sighs) This does sound really, it does sound woolly, doesn't it? Eh I suppose we're less wed to formalised assessment than other disciplines, it's less part of what we do in our assessment ... So when you meet a family, you're doing a lot of assessment through conversation and through observation and, rather than going through a tick-box assessment. **(Ciara, lines 253ff)**

Of interest in this quote is the description of a 'woolly' identity emerging as a product of social interaction with families ('when you meet a family'), where 'conversation' and 'observation' is the order of the day, as opposed to what she sees as a 'tick-box' type of interaction. Here, without the fallback of standardised tools or measures ('less wed to formalised assessment'), this social worker described how her role may be perceived as vague and indeterminate, which does not help in portraying a clearly delineated identity.

Like Ciara, Deirdre, also a social worker, described how families attending CAMHS are often confused about her role; she feels the need to explain why she is part of the multidisciplinary team. The connotation for some families of the term 'social worker' suggests an expectation of being part of a social welfare system, including assessment of parents' ability to look after their children ('we don't want you to be kind of coming out to us because our kid isn't going to school'):

Extract 4.4

Eh so everybody has a different idea. I went out on a home visit last week and eh I clarified my role and all that they kept talking about was you know, 'We sort of, we don't want you to be kind of coming out to us because our kid isn't going to school' ... Another eh, most other sessions when I mention when I'm doing an initial assessment eh here, most sessions they eh when you say, 'I'm a social worker and this is the clinical nurse specialist', they gravitate the eye contact towards me and 'Oh'. So, there's always that sense of 'Mmm social worker', you know? And then you you clarify that, you know that your role on the team is different and then you you balance it by clarifying that the clinical nurse specialist doesn't work with, you know this this and they work with their voice ... So, you kind of try and kind of clarify it like that. **(Deirdre, lines 187ff)**

Once again, we see the negotiation of identity being precipitated by the social interactions of the professionals with the families they are working with, while at the same time doing that work alongside other different, and perhaps more easily recognised, healthcare workers (e.g. a nurse in the case described above).

Likewise, a speech and language therapist interviewed for the study, under the pseudonym 'Caroline' spoke of her attempts to explain her role in a CAMHS context (i.e. 'you have to explain yourself') when parents perhaps expressed surprise at her involvement with their child who had been referred for a mental health issue such as 'severe anxiety':

Extract 4.5

And often, I think it confuses people sometimes when they're coming into the department and you know, their child might be, have severe anxiety, exceptionally bright and they're seeing a speech and language therapist? (laughs) They're going, 'What's going on?' And then you have to explain yourself and once you explain it, it's fine. **(Caroline, lines 486ff)**

Interestingly, Mary, another participant who is a clinical psychologist, defined her role within the context of others, as suggested above. In this interview, Mary talked of her work being caught up with families and individuals she termed the 'chronic ones', identifying psychology as the discipline which is seen to have the skills and the experience to do so:

Extract 4.6

Whereas now, well certainly for psychology you'd be getting the chronic ones, you wouldn't getting the easy ones. If there was an easy one, usually the nurse or another discipline would often take those eh... **(Mary, lines 311ff)**

Mary subsequently gave an example of a 'chronic one' as a young person who is engaging in repeated self-harm and an example of an 'easy one' as a child with developmental difficulties. She therefore perceived her role as a psychologist as more specialised than that of her colleagues. Mary further defined her discipline as being separate to others (e.g. occupational therapy and speech and language therapy) in this regard:

Extract 4.7

I mean obviously speech and language are similar, have similarities as does OT, but I suppose for me just coming here there's a whole range of different stuff that I know I could do that would be useful. **(Mary, lines 820ff)**

Therefore, it seems that the identity of the discipline is important here as participants talked of holding on to it, as defined by both its similarities and its perceived differences.

4.3.2 ADAPTING TO THE CONTEXT OF THE WORKPLACE

'Adapting to the context of the workplace' – in this context a CAMHS service – was another emergent theme identified in the data of relevance to identity formation. The workplace and the activities therein can have an influence on the evolving identity of healthcare practitioners.

One participant in the study, Deirdre, reported how she and her social work colleagues initially experienced significant uncertainty and doubt about their role in the context of CAMHS. Consequently, they adopted temporary identities and 'turned into mini-regs [medical registrars] and mini-nurses and mini- whatever until we got some sense of where we might fit' (lines 363ff). Over time, and with the support of a new line manager as well as proactively developing some key documents about social work in CAMHS, they developed a stronger sense of themselves and felt more able to do their own work. In the context of reviewing her role in CAMHS and trying to broaden her skill set and expertise, Deirdre also decided to pursue a qualification in family therapy. Three years later, this decision was causing her some upset, and she wondered why social workers in CAMHS feel a need to pursue further training. In the following extract, there is a sense of social work not being 'good enough' (i.e. 'hasn't got the value') to work in CAMHS and having to address this sense of deficiency by pursuing further 'retraining':

Extract 4.8

Eh so yeah, it saddens me because I just feel like you know that social work should have. Like what is it about social work that hasn't got the value on its own you know? ... Like you know, what is it that? So, like eh you know for example a nurse or a psychiatrist can come in here with their title and you know there's not the same, you know (sighs) level of retraining you know? 'Cause it's, 'cause they do psychiatric nursing but for social work, I think again it's around that general term. But like, that's the value, that's the best thing about social work. And then we try and pare it down, by you know 'cause we don't fit. So then when we don't fit, how are we going to fit? So, we put a psycho-something before our name or after our name, you know? And then, then people might appreciate. **(Deirdre, lines 634ff)**

For Deirdre, additional therapeutic qualifications are seen as being more useful on the multidisciplinary team than the core social work qualification. She lamented that social workers 'don't fit' and posed the question of 'how are we going to fit?'. Furthermore, she wondered if putting a 'psycho-something before our name or after our name' would help, leading to greater appreciation by others. To be appreciated by others speaks to the need for others to respect and perhaps help define their role and help with identity formation and recognition.

As a speech and language therapist in CAMHS, Caroline explained how working and adapting to CAMHS led to her developing another professional identity as 'a mental health worker' (line 384). Although Caroline suggested that that she may become deskilled in some of her core speech and language therapy skills, she has embraced this new identity as a 'mental health worker'. She described it as a natural consequence of her role in CAMHS because 'the working life of a clinician on a CAMHS team isn't, it's not straightforward, it's not sort of compartmentalised. It's not neat, you know' (lines 210ff). However, Caroline also spoke about some difficulties she has experienced in adapting this identity of a 'mental health worker'. She gave an example of applying for funding to attend a short training course on loss and bereavement. Her application was queried by the management team because she is a speech and language therapist, and it was not clear to them why she would be interested or needed to attend a course on the topic of loss and bereavement. It seems that while Caroline sees herself and her colleagues as being 'mental health workers', the management team may not share this understanding. Caroline pointed out that 'it's really hard to kind of explain to somebody who doesn't understand our remit that we're not just speech and language therapists, we're not just psychologists. We have two hats; we are mental health workers' (lines 204ff).

In summary, each of the participants recognised the need to adapt to the context of CAMHS and to its concomitant context of social interactions with families and other professionals outside of their own. While they attempt to remain true to their professional background, they have also developed ways to adjust to working in CAMHS and to negotiate their identity accordingly. It is particularly interesting to note the adoption of a new – or additional – identity for some, talking of belonging to a wider group of 'mental health workers' and referring to themselves by the collective inclusive plural pronoun 'we' ('We have two hats; we are mental health workers', Caroline, lines 204ff)

4.3.3 BEING PART OF A MULTIDISCIPLINARY TEAM

The third and final emergent theme to be discussed within this chapter is that of 'being part of a multidisciplinary team'. Being part of a such a team seems to help inform the identity as a 'mental health worker' referred to above. To function effectively as a multidisciplinary team, a considerable amount of social interaction takes place as professionals from an array of disciplines come together to discuss the children and their families in their care via case conferences, joint therapy sessions or agency meetings.

Many of the participants spoke about being part of a multidisciplinary team in CAMHS and how this also shapes their practice. While it can take a while to get to know their colleagues and to get used to working together, the participants generally spoke about their positive experiences of being part of a multidisciplinary team. Mary explained that her decision to continue working in CAMHS was largely influenced by her experience of working on her team. Joanna, a clinical psychologist, explained that she and her colleagues do not always have the opportunity to do joint work together as they are often working in different locations. However, they committed to supporting and helping each other out when the need arises and in relation to difficult cases. Joanna continued say that she feels a greater loyalty and 'allegiance' (line 1036) to her multidisciplinary team than she does to her colleagues in the department of psychology. She also reflected that she is able to have a better understanding of other disciplines based on her experience of working on the multidisciplinary team.

Meanwhile, Caroline was clear that being part of and interacting with a multidisciplinary team is one of the main reasons why she enjoys working in CAMHS. She had earlier described how her previous role as a speech and language therapist involved working with developmental communication difficulties and visiting schools as part of her typical working day. This led to her working primarily 'out of her car' and in quite an isolated way. In contrast, she is surrounded by colleagues on the multidisciplinary team in CAMHS and spoke highly about this:

Extract 4.9

`But what I really liked about CAMHS was just being part, part of the multidisciplinary team, learning from colleagues, and just the whole new area. And the fact that you know it was... it was quite different to core SLT work. ... Learning from colleagues was something I really enjoyed and continue to enjoy.` **(Caroline, lines 22ff)**

In summary, the participants are individual clinicians working in CAMHS and they are also clinicians working as part of a multidisciplinary team. Working as part of and interacting with a multidisciplinary team appears to bring challenges as well as rewards and is another way in which the participants negotiate their identity in this workplace context.

Overall, then, it seems that the participants' experiences of negotiating identity in the workplace can be understood as a process in which they recognise their professional background and adapt this background to the particular context of their workplace. While there are some similarities in the participants' journeys to negotiating an identity, it is also clear that each participant's journey is unique to them. In addition to their professional background and attempting to 'fit' into CAMHS, the participants also familiarised themselves with their colleagues and learnt how to work as part of a multidisciplinary team. Negotiating identity is therefore 'a bit of a rollercoaster' (Joanna, line 75), but one which lends itself to the adoption of numerous complementary identities, both profession specific and profession generic (i.e. 'mental health workers'). The notion of an evolving identity is useful here to capture that fluidity which characterises one's identity as professional careers progress. Furthermore, it is not hard to gain a sense of identity under threat as professionals forge a pathway for themselves in the changing workplace context and its concurrent adaptation of work duties and activities.

4.3.4 IDENTITY UNDER THREAT

In concluding this chapter, it is interesting to note that the findings of Ryan's (2018) study are supported by a more recent study by Porter and Wilton (2020) which explored the professional identity of healthcare staff within a service that was undergoing restructuring. As noted above, contemporary healthcare is ever-changing and professionals are expected to move with those changes while at the same time maintaining their core professional identity. During periods of organisational restructuring, professional identity can be threatened, and anxieties emerge as professionals cling to what they know and are familiar with.

In this Australian study, Porter and Wilton (2020) surveyed allied healthcare staff, including social workers, physiotherapists, speech and language therapists, occupational therapists, dieticians and allied healthcare managers and assistants. The groups were surveyed using an online scale which helps to rate the individuals' strength of professional identity with their own professional group. The online scale was administered at two time points (before and after service restructuring) and at two years apart to an average of 200 staff. Restructuring involved reconfiguration of teams and reporting relationships, moving away from purely discipline-specific professional teams and reporting lines to more mixed clinical teams, with 'a dual reporting relationship to allied health managers for professional governance and to programme managers (of any health professional background) for operational management' (Porter and Wilton 2020: 1105). Their findings showed that despite professional identity being found to be high before and after restructuring, overall professional identity declined significantly post restructuring, leading to the suggestion that 'as staff work and interact more in interprofessional teams, they identify less with their professions' (Porter and Wilton 2020: 1106). However, Porter and Wilton are careful to point out that a multiplicity of factors may have affected this outcome, not least the differing demographics of the cohort under study, in terms of length of service, for example, and professional education. Of interest here is the observation that more recently qualified staff were more likely to have experienced interprofessional learning as part of their education (e.g. the 'Millennials') as compared to those qualified for longer periods, hence preparing them for a shift in work practices of an interdisciplinary nature.

4.4 SUMMARY

This chapter focused on professional identity issues as played out in the workplace – in this case a CAMHS service – where many disciplines come together to work on a common goal of supporting children, adolescents and their families to navigate mental distress that may manifest itself as emotional and behavioural difficulties. The negotiation of identity in this workplace context seems therefore to be linked to many factors, including what other professionals may be doing and as constructed by the individuals they care for, along with (re)structuring of teams and workplace organisation. The following question is posed, then, is negotiating a professional identity an end goal or work in progress for the student professional? The growth of interprofessional learning in undergraduate education (as discussed in Chapter 3) speaks to this question and interprofessional learning some way addresses this need for identity work as student learners. What is of interest here is how the social interaction opportunities during education prepare professionals for not only the profession-specific identity but also a profession-generic one, as in the example above. In other words, how are students of healthcare prepared for the often 'fluid' identity that the workplace may demand? It seems that the advances in the focus on professional identity formation and interprofessional learning in healthcare education contexts may have something to contribute to this consideration.

5
CLINICAL INTERACTIONS: TOWARDS INHABITING A 'FULFILLED' PROFESSIONAL IDENTITY

We know what we are, but not what we may be.
William Shakespeare

5.1 INTRODUCTION

In this chapter, our focus shifts to the social interactions between clients/patients and healthcare professionals as a fertile site for the exploration of how a professional identity awareness is developed, honed or challenged by interactions with those attending services. Here, we draw on the analysis of a discrete set of data gathered from discussions which took place via focus groups comprising healthcare professionals. The data being considered here were taken from a larger body of collected material for another research project undertaken by the second author, concerned with therapeutic relationships in clinical contexts. As such then, we were keen to consider these data through the lens of social interaction given that such interactions are core to all clinician encounters. The question in focus is how a consideration of social interaction, as taking place between a client/patient and healthcare professional, informs the development or evolution of a professional identity in the allied healthcare context. We want to consider in this chapter what we interpret as a journey or a trajectory to inhabiting what we term the 'fulfilled' identity role and the inherent challenges on the road to that destination.

The data we draw upon come from healthcare professionals who are all speech and language therapists with varying extents of clinical experience. As explained in Chapter 3, speech and language therapists work with a wide variety of clients and families, who may present with speech, language, communication and/or swallowing needs in a therapeutic milieu of support and facilitation. The data were collected via two focus group discussions (comprising four and eight participants, respectively), with the participants reflecting on clients and families they have encountered and interacted professionally with. The focus group context provided a space for reflection for these practitioners as they discussed their experiences in their day-to-day roles as speech and language therapists. Reflecting on experiences as part of clinical practice is not new to healthcare practitioners, as it is viewed as a core part of both undergraduate training and continuing professional development (see the seminal text by Schön (1983), for example). Reflections provide fertile data for analysis, and making sense of such data by honouring the intended meaning and integrity is key to a robust qualitative analytic methodology. (The use of reflection and reflective practice is considered in more detail in Chapter 6, where it is discussed as also relevant to the data analysed in the remainder of this book.)

As for other data sets considered in this text, the choice of analytic methodology was interpretative phenomenological analysis (IPA), with the revised terminology for the description of themes outlined by Smith, Flowers and Larkin (2022) also being employed here. Small numbers of participants within focus groups are justified for an IPA analysis (Smith et al. 2009), as it is the in-depth nature of the analysis that is core to IPA, not the quantity of participants.

5.2 SOME BACKGROUND TO THE STUDY OF CLINICAL INTERACTIONS

Before exploring the data relevant to the trajectory of experiences in identity awareness, it would be useful to briefly review similar considerations in other healthcare professional domains. In the practice of psychotherapy, for example, Urban (2013: 525) speaks of what she has learnt from interactions with her clients, that is, 'the connections of emotional depth that occur out of an impelling connection for relatedness'. Burges Watson et al. (2012) detail how a paramedic's identity is strongly influenced by their interactions with patients, that is, the treatments they employ and the relationships they foster with those they serve. Wong and Trollope-Kumar (2014) describe how just sitting in silence with a patient and that patient's reaction to that quiet company was comforting, and that it helped the practitioner understand 'the importance of his role as a witness to a man's suffering' (Wong and Trollope-Kumar 2014: 494). Such examples highlight how social interactions with patients can impact the professional identity of a healthcare professional.

In more recent years, there have been texts published in the popular press of clinicians working with clients, describing how those interactions have impacted their sense of identity as healthcare professionals in differing ways. Many of these texts – frequently emanating from the field of psychiatry and forensic psychiatry – foreground the social interaction dimension of their involvement with their patients as they describe in varying detail the encounters in their therapy rooms and over time (e.g. Lucey 2014). Deisseroth (2021) discusses case studies, sharing stories of his clients while working in emergency psychiatry. Similarly, Adshead and Horne (2021) share stories of interactions with clients in forensic settings and their impact. Others look to the more general medicine domain of practice (e.g. de Visser 2021). What these texts have in common is the overwhelming sense of being affected by others, patients or clients in practice, as played out in the routine clinical interactions that are ubiquitous to healthcare, whatever the field of speciality. What is core to all these examples is that sense of 'connectedness' brought about by the social interaction that is at the core of healthcare clinical interactions.

5.3 THE DATA: FOCUS GROUP DISCUSSIONS

The data discussed in this chapter were collected from recordings of two focus group discussions, involving a total of 12 participants from within the profession of speech and language therapy and divided into two groups of four and eight participants, respectively. The data were collected with a notetaker present along with the principal researcher (the second author of this book). The focus groups each lasted for approximately one hour. All participants were female speech and language therapists, with differing experiences working in, for example, hospitals, disability settings and child development clinics. Eight of the participants had been directly involved in student clinical education in addition to their clinical work. The eclectic mix of workplace settings represented, and hence the consequential differing client groups being discussed, made for a rich data set in terms of diversity of experience. Furthermore, the focus group context allowed for the sharing of experiences across clinical areas of practice.

Examples of probes for the focus group discussions are outlined in Table 5.1. The probes sought to elicit considerations of professional identity and specifically how professional identity had been impacted by interactions with clients. In keeping with the focus of this book, the data reported here have social interaction as their focus.

The recordings were transcribed soon after the focus groups took place and in consultation with the notetaker for clarification of any issues in the discursive content. The data were analysed via IPA methods and are summarised here, with a focus on the role of social interaction as reflections are explored and referenced according to the identified themes.

5.4 SOCIAL INTERACTION IN CLINICAL CONTEXTS AND ITS IMPACT ON PROFESSIONAL IDENTITY

In the extracts from the data presented here, various clinicians reflected upon their transition from being a student to fully inhabiting their professional role as a qualified speech and language therapist. During this transition phase, there is a sense of realisation of the reality of the clinical working world, as experienced through interaction with the client. Clinicians reflected upon how they might not always be able to

Table 5.1 Examples of probe types used in focus group data collection

Probe Type	Example
Opening	Early in your career, what activity or behaviour did you do that made you think 'I'm a speech and language therapist now!'?
Transition	Have you ever reflected before on the influence of a client/clients/the client upon your professional identity and if so how and why?
Key	Have there been any moments, perhaps preparing for another client or in other clinical interactions, that you have been reminded of this client? In what ways did this reflection help?

'fix' certain situations (or provide a 'cure' in the medical sense of the term) for clients in the speech and language therapy contexts, but rather it is about enabling the client to cope and adapt to the current circumstances (e.g. living with a speech, language or communication disorder). Furthermore, the clinicians discussed how sometimes it is encounters and interactions with more challenging clients/scenarios that prompt them to question themselves and their identities.

The clinicians also reflected upon using the more challenging times that they have encountered to reassure clients that success will come in time. Success for clinicians is defined by collaborative work, communication and problem-solving with the client. The clinicians further conversed about inhabiting both the role of client and clinician and how this may influence their approach to practice (i.e. we have all been 'patients'). Other clinicians discussed their role and social interactions in the context of the multidisciplinary team. It seems that it is the combination of challenging times, experiences, reassurance, reflection and acceptance of the reality of the working world that enables clinicians to fully inhabit their 'fulfilled' professional identity.

The themes for consideration in this chapter are listed here and are informed by extracts from the data set to aid contextualisation and grounding within the data (i.e. the words of the participants). Through IPA, the group experiential theme identified is entitled 'towards inhabiting a fulfilled identity'. This theme seeks to reference how clinicians described reaching this state, through reference to their growth as healthcare professionals being influenced significantly by their interactions with clients, families and other clinicians as they go about their daily clinical work. The personal experiential themes within this group experiential theme of 'towards inhabiting a fulfilled identity' were identified as follows:

- The journey from student to clinician
- Clinician identity being challenged and shaped by clients
- Progress, success and identity
- Identity within the context of the multidisciplinary team
- The dual identity of client and clinician

Each one of these personal experiential themes will be presented below, with supporting extracts from the data for illustrative purposes. The numbers following each extract refer to the participant number and the initial line of the extract, followed by the abbreviation 'ff' to denote 'and following lines' (e.g. Participant 6, lines 270ff).

5.4.1 THE JOURNEY FROM STUDENT TO CLINICIAN

The personal experiential theme of 'the journey from student to clinician' was recalled and referenced by several of the participants in the data set. Emanating from the idea that 'we were all students once', the wisdom that experience brings facilitates informed reflections on that journey to becoming a qualified clinician. One clinician spoke of not having that 'magic wand' to 'fix' a client's problems, and repetition of the idea 'to fix' in the following extract communicates her emphasis on this point:

Extract 5.1 (a)

I think it's that concept as well that when you come out of college, well it's like I can fix things for people. We're not able to fix things and you learn when you work with patients and their families you may never be able to fix something that has happened to them. **(Participant 6, lines 270ff)**

This clinician went on to explain that through interaction with the client and the family, the clinician facilitates the family to make changes and adaptations and indeed to 'harness' their 'resilience':

Extract 5.1 (b)

It's how you help them to adjust and adapt and that resilience that you mentioned earlier and how we harness that for people. But it's never about having that like, they come to us and it's like this magic wand that is perceived that we have. And as much and all that we would love to have it, we don't, and it's about how we can use these other tools that are available in our system to help [get] results. **(Participant 6, lines 270ff)**

That wisdom of the qualified clinician, in recognising what they can and cannot do with families, suggests a sense of self-assuredness within their own professional identity. This idea is illustrated in the following extract right from the start with the phrase 'I always say to students'. This clinician explained how she reassures the fledgling clinician, explaining to them that 'it's ok not to know' about what to do with clients:

Extract 5.2

I always say to students it's okay not to know because you're not going to all of a sudden, just because you've got this degree in your hand, all of a sudden [click of the thumb] have acquired everything. And there's always going to be things that come through the door that you don't know and it's okay to say to somebody if they ask you a question, 'I don't know but I'll find out' and then you have lots of resources to go and find out afterwards. And people are happy with that as long as they know you've listened and that you're going to come back to them. **(Participant 1, lines 94ff)**

The latter part of Extract 5.2 references the key role of 'listening' in any social interaction with clients (i.e. 'as long as they know you've listened') and is sage advice for any nascent clinician. The central function of 'listening' in any part of a clinical interaction was once again brought to the fore in this theme (Extract 5.3a) by another clinician who reflected and almost regretted that she did not listen more to her clients earlier in her career:

Extract 5.3(a)

I think just listening to what people say. Asking, asking questions and listening to the answers. So I think as students and certainly me as a student, you know, I had these fabulous session plans and I was going to go in there and it was like a steam train I'm gonna do this 'bang, bang, bang' and I look back on a lot of what I did and I think 'sure, I don't know how much use any of that was'. I never asked the client or the child's parents did they – were they – worried about the child's speech. Half the time I mightn't have done ANYTHING. **(Participant 8, lines 102ff)**

Looking back as a qualified clinician and seeming more assured of her own professional skill resulted in this clinician suggesting that simply 'asking questions and listening to the answers' – an obvious interpersonal communication skill – is often not done in an authentic and meaningful way. Admitting and stressing that 'half the time I mightn't have done ANYTHING' further underpins this self-assuredness as a now wiser and more informed clinician. In Extract 5.3(b), this healthcare professional further reflected on what she has learnt, and what she would now do differently, stressing this point using the repeated assertion 'I would have' as follows:

Extract 5.3(b)

If I had them [client/family] in front of me today, I would have asked more broader questions at the beginning about [what] they would have wanted and what they were looking for and what their expectations were and em (.) I think I would have wasted a lot less time so asking questions about what people are there for and that why like, 'why are you here' question. The answer isn't, is rarely what you think it will be. **(Participant 8, lines 102ff)**

This clinician's conclusion seems to evidence her learning, that is, asking relevant and meaningful questions while proactively listening to the responses in clinical interactions is crucial. Her final comment is a realisation of sorts that the answers to questions asked in the clinic room are 'rarely what you think', further underpinning her status as an experienced clinician who is open to expectation in interactions with clients.

5.4.2 CLINICIAN IDENTITY BEING CHALLENGED AND SHAPED BY CLIENTS

Reflecting on past interactions with clients, both in terms of what has been learnt from those clients by the qualified clinician (as in the above examples) and what has specifically taken place in clinical consultations, seems to feature in the data, particularly related to the personal experiential theme of 'clinician identity being challenged and shaped by clients'. In the examples to follow we see clinicians, through their personal statements, reflecting on specific experiences and interactions with clients, which prompted them to consider or question their role and perhaps their identity in a myriad of ways.

One participant (Participant 5), questioned her identity as related to her professional title: 'I think if anything, sometimes I kinda wonder "speech therapist", what is, you know, what is that? What am I, what am I doing?' In this clinician's reflection in Extract 5.4, she seems aware that it is via her interactions with clients that her identity, not only as a speech and language therapist but as a healthcare professional who advocates for her patients, is honed:

Extract 5.4

Yeah, I suppose, yeah, everyone is so, everyone that I meet is very, very different and asks very different things of any professional that is involved in their case. And I suppose I learn something new from each of them and the more I learn, the more I don't, the more grey things become as well sometimes. And you realise your role as an advocate, you relate your role as all these non-speech therapy related things. **(Participant 5, lines 152ff)**

Of interest here too in this extract is the learning that takes place from interacting with different clients and families (i.e. 'I learn something new from each of them'), adding to this clinician's realisation of the 'grey' areas in patient involvement, with patient advocacy emerging as a key role in allied healthcare.

It seems from the data that the act of questioning one's own identity as a professional can even spill over to out-of-work hours, as the following examples illustrate. Reflecting on what happened in interactions during the day is something that seems common to responses in the data. Reflecting on interactions that provoked 'conflict' or concern about severity of 'impairment' is illustrated in Extract 5.5:

Extract 5.5

The ones I think about when I get home possibly might be the ones that either a) that there's been a conflict - the parent is not happy, they're not happy with you or they're not happy with the service; b) the second one that would make me reflect would be somebody who has a really, really severe communication impairment and that feeling of am I doing enough, could I do more? **(Participant 2, lines 159ff)**

Here, questioning attempts to help or of 'doing enough' is also echoed in the following extract, where this clinician (Participant 6) reflected on work with a patient and family that may be experiencing a 'life-altering' health event.

Extract 5.6

That concept of, well are we doing enough? Are we supporting the person and their family who are dealing with this life-altering event not just for the person themselves but for those around them? **(Participant 6, lines 175ff)**

Once again, we see a clinician critically evaluating her role, questioning if her work as a professional is sufficient for that client and 'those around them', thereby extending the caring remit to beyond the patient. Of interest also in this extract is the use of the first-person plural pronoun 'we', that is, the inclusive 'we' referring to their discipline-specific profession or their identity as a healthcare professional in general; 'are we doing enough?' suggests a collective responsibility in patient care, part of a collective identity as healthcare professionals. Similarly, another clinician (Participant 7, lines 145ff) reflected on those clinical cases 'that didn't work out' or 'where you didn't feel you could help', emphasising that such experiences have a greater ('bigger') impact on professional identity compared to experiences with clients where 'things went well':

Extract 5.7

It was a wakeup call for me that those are the clients that sort of, have had an impact on my professional identity rather, more, bigger... sorry bigger, much bigger, impact than ones who say we had a good rapport, things went well, they achieved their goals.
(Participant 7, lines 145ff)

Describing this realisation as a 'wakeup call' suggests that the learning gleaned from differing experiences with clients can be related to levels of perceived success in clinical interactions.

Having your identity as a clinician 'shaped' by interactions with clients, then, is a salient issue in the data. This is further evidenced by a clinician who drew on positive experiences of getting to 'meet people every day', explaining how she is continually 'surprised' by them as they challenge her preconceptions:

Extract 5.8

I think that they [people] are surprising and that they are a bit unpredictable and that's a quality I think that has shaped me. I would have gone in with quite rigid expectations of who people were and what they would be like ... I think that's always being prepared to hear something new or thinking 'I think this is how this is going to go' or thinking 'I could be wrong, something else might happen'.
(Participant 7, lines 214ff)

Moreover, the realisation of the need to be 'prepared' for something different and perhaps of being 'wrong' about a person is also acknowledged here, once again referencing an identity that is flexible and open, both of which are key and desirable professional attributes in any healthcare professional. Such influences and impacts on professional identity seem not uncommon in the data and inform the personal experiential theme of 'clinician identity being challenged and shaped by clients'.

5.4.3 PROGRESS, SUCCESS AND IDENTITY

The thematic content in the above extracts also references 'progress' or lack of it, and how those experiences can impact one's professional identity. We now turn briefly to another related personal experiential theme identified in the data, that of 'progress, success and identity'.

The personal experiential theme of 'progress, success and identity' is informed by clinicians' reference to progress (or lack thereof) and success in interventions with their respective clients and how that measurement of progress affects them in their role and in turn their sense of identity. Once again, we see how social interaction is referenced throughout the clinicians' reflections as the clinicians recall meetings or encounters with clients and families to make their point.

In Extract 5.9a, a clinician (Participant 7) reflects on her interactions with clients and families and wonders if it is the clinical 'relationship' or the established rapport that mitigates a lack of progress, recognising this as the 'hard part' of identity considerations:

Extract 5.9(a)

`I think that can be a hard part with your identity if it's a case where maybe impairment wise em (.) it's hard to make progress, ... but you might have had a good relationship with [him/her], so they got maybe that out of it that you were a support to them or a counsellor ...` **(Participant 7, lines 179ff)**

This same clinician elaborated on this realisation of being like a 'counsellor', as follows:

Extract 5.9 (b)

`... that leads me to question my identity, going well what am I then? Like am I just a nice person who was a good support to them and a help to them if we didn't actually effect any change with their communication? Like a lot of people I see would leave my care still with the same severity of communication impairment and nothing has changed. And well maybe not nothing has changed, maybe something has changed in terms of their confidence or their hap- you know, their satisfaction but sometimes I think that can be jarring with your identity of am I [a] counsellor, friendly counsellor?` **(Participant 7, lines 179ff)**

Casting herself as 'just a nice person' or a 'friendly counsellor' in the case of little progress being made due to the severity of a client's communication impairment suggests that this therapist was naming this counselling role as informing her potential identity in such contexts of interaction. However, it seems that this perceived role is one that 'jars' with her, perhaps due to the ambiguity suggested by the term 'friendly counsellor'.

In a similar vein, another clinician reflected on her own experiences of working with clients whose 'prognosis may be poor' and who thus may be slow to make 'progress' in treatment due to the nature of their illness (e.g. chronic neurological conditions such as motor neuron disease (MND)). Here we see the clinician reflecting upon the fact that it is these kinds of clients that have the greatest impact on her identity:

Extract 5.10(a)

... where the prognosis is very poor so it's, you're not, you're not targeting any improvement or like definitely some of the people I've worked with that have had the most impact on me is [those with] progressive neurological, MND and you're doing, what has al- what I've learned as a therapist is what I strive to do is to be collaborative. **(Participant 5, lines 185ff)**

In expanding upon and emphasising the notion of 'collaboration', this same clinician referred to the need for joint problem-solving as part of that collaboration while keeping the patient 'at the forefront' of such interactions and discussions:

Extract 5.10(b)

You know, you are problem-solving with this person to try and impact what is important to them at that time and that might be tiny, and it might leave you feeling a bit 'oh I'm not sure I did all that much there'. But just keeping that person at the forefront, this is a collaborative piece - whether it's a child or whether it's an adult I think it's always collaborative. **(Participant 5, lines 185ff)**

Working and interacting with the client and their family around problem-solving is therefore important for this clinician, who acknowledged that collaboration is something 'she has learned as a therapist'. Interestingly, the comment 'oh I'm not sure I did all that much there' echoes earlier references in the above extracts, which see the clinicians' self-questioning being part of their established identities as professionals who perhaps do not have all the answers but remain open and willing to learn as part of being healthcare professionals.

For others, however, the flip side of a lack of progress is the experience of success when interacting with clients and its impact on their sense of identity. In the next extract (Extract 5.11(a)), we see a clinician reflecting on a 'breakthrough' in therapy, where the client became the storyteller through aided communication, a role not evidenced until that moment in therapy:

Extract 5.11(a)

I had em (.) a client recently who I had been working with for a very long time who had very, very severe communication difficulties. And after a LONG time we got a particular day where we kind of got a breakthrough with em sort of alternative communication and the person was able to spell out a story of how she had met her boyfriend. And the story just was so funny ... but just that we got the story out that day, and it was very like I won't forget that day you know. **(Participant 7, lines 248ff)**

This clinician further reflected upon that shift in roles, and how it served as a reminder of the possibilities and potentials that are part of clinical interactions.

Extract 5.11 (b)

Yeah, and that person being in a story-telling role, which they hadn't been in for a very long time, and it sort of at the time reminded me as well that they could be in that role. Sometimes, we, not forget, but you kind of are doing all the talking for that person for a long time, you know it's kind of a good reminder. **(Participant 7, lines 250ff)**

For another clinician, the notion that 'there is progress happening' over time, despite the acute upset, 'grief' and challenges around accepting a 'diagnosis' is described in detail in Extract 5.12(a) and (b) as follows:

Extract 5.12(a)

You know and obviously the grief is still there you know but not there in the acute 'my life is falling apart crying phase' but actually doing something and there is progress happening. And that's helpful to reflect on that when you are in the moment. **(Participant 8, lines 258ff)**

In the next extract, reference here to 'it's not always going to be like this' sees the clinician expressing her reflections in such moments of stress and upset in clinical interactions. Moreover, this clinician seemed to take comfort in her professional knowledge as a clinician 'that there is potential for change' in such cases and 'huge acceptance'.

Extract 5.12(b)

... and you know at least not that you say it to them but at least I know, that 'look actually it's not always going to be like this'. That's helpful for me to know at least, you know they don't know it at that moment but that, like that there is potential for change and there is potential for huge acceptance. **(Participant 8, lines 258ff)**

Thus, in the personal experiential theme of 'progress, success and identity', we see a range of clinical outcomes influencing how the clinicians view themselves and their identity as healthcare professionals. In explaining how they view themselves, the clinicians continually referred to social interactions with their clients, family members and others to illustrate their points and their reflections on their identity as clinicians.

5.4.4 IDENTITY WITHIN THE CONTEXT OF THE MULTIDISCIPLINARY TEAM

A fourth experiential theme identified in the data is 'identity within the context of the multidisciplinary team'. This theme relates to clinicians' reflections on their identity within their respective multidisciplinary teams (MDTs). We saw in Chapter 4 how being part of an MDT has consequences for how one views oneself as a clinician and the potential impact on an evolving identity within a service and as a healthcare professional.

In Extract 5.13, a clinician spoke of her role as advocate (a role and function already referenced in Extract 5.4 above). In this context, the clinician seemed to be fulfilling a necessary role, in her words, 'in a system where there aren't many advocates for people':

Extract 5.13

`I think advocacy as well, like working in a system where there aren't many advocates for people is what makes you want to keep being an advocate even when you don't feel- feel, like they at least need somebody to speak up for them or to be a voice for them, even if you don't always feel like you are fixing them-making them better. You're at least advocating for people and that there aren't many of us as speech therapists and so I suppose if you drop off and quit then they'll be down one advocate- you know they'll be down one less person like fighting for people with communication needs and for swallow needs, so.` **(Participant 7, lines 280ff)**

For this clinician, the responsibility seemed to weigh heavily upon her (i.e. 'you know they'll be down one less person like fighting for people with communication needs and for swallow needs'). Another role which has an impact on a clinician's identity within the MDT is that of the bearer of bad news (e.g. in the case of a cancer diagnosis):

Extract 5.14

`And when I worked in head and neck cancer, I can't count how many people came to me ... for pre-radiotherapy work and I would say blah blah blah blah blah and 'the cancer...' and they'd say 'what-what cancer? I don't have cancer' ... they just didn't know. And that's not always to say they weren't' told, they might not have been in the headspace to process it but we're definitely mopping up! The speech therapists are definitely mopping up what people haven't heard, haven't been able to be told.` **(Participant 7, lines 306ff)**

The notion of 'mopping up' after having inadvertently disclosed bad news (that was assumed already communicated to the patient) was referred to here as a role that seems reluctantly adopted by the clinician, a role that perhaps ought to have been fulfilled by another MDT member (with the repetition of the phrase 'definitely mopping up' further emphasising the point made). In the next extract (Extract 5.15), another clinician identifies herself as the 'hang on person', reflecting on her need to speak up when other MDT members are perceived to be rushing into a clinical situation:

Extract 5.15

And there needs to be someone who's, like I always think if I can do nothing, I could be the person who's the 'hang on person' who says 'hang on now a second!' So, team are like 'go go go go go go go go go' and I'm always like 'hang on now a second' and that's who I feel my identity is. **(Participant 3, lines 284ff)**

Finally, within this theme, the title of a profession as linked to identity and perceptions of others was called into question by this same clinician who suggested that if there was a name change from 'speech and language therapist' to 'experts in communication', then those professionals might be seen to be adding more 'value in actual normal everyday exchange of information or conversation I think' (Participant 3, line 313), both with the MDT and within the wider healthcare context.

5.4.5 THE DUAL IDENTITY OF CLIENT AND CLINICIAN

The final experiential theme to be discussed in this chapter is that of 'the dual identity of client and clinician'. Here we see clinicians reflecting on interactions that would have taken place for them when they too were in the 'client' role and how this has impacted upon their own sense of identity, including ways of behaving as a clinician. One clinician recalled interactions with professionals, both as part of their own work and being 'on the other side' as a client, as follows:

Extract 5.16

... feedback was given and the wording that was given still sticks with me. And I realise the importance of that on another side for like when I'm delivering feedback to families on say an assessment or something, you know, that actually you will still remember the exact room and the exact language and you hear that. But when you're experiencing that yourself on the other side, it becomes real and you realise how important it is to get it right for the families you work with, you know. **(Participant 4, lines 265ff)**

This clinician – when in the role of the client herself – explained how what was said to her 'still sticks' with her. Moreover, the emphatic reference to the 'exact room and the exact language ... you hear' further explains her experience as a client but also her learning as a clinician in attending to how to communicate in a professional way with families and clients. These points are echoed by another clinician's reflection on giving 'catastrophic feedback on corridors and stuff' and how she would 'never ever,

ever do that' (Participant 8, line 276), while another advised clinicians to be attentive to their communication as 'they [the patients] hang on your every word so be careful what you say because they'll remember those words' (Participant 4, line 267). Finally, on a more positive note, learning professional and appropriate styles of interaction from other clinicians was also evident in the data; as one clinician observed, 'I love the way she [the consultant] approached that [the consultation], I should do more of that' (Participant 2, line 263).

This final experiential theme addresses the notion that even healthcare professionals are clients or patients too at times, and so can learn from their own social interactions in the service user role to inform their professional practice. This learning as relevant to being a good communicator is core to the identity of a caring, considerate and empathetic healthcare professional

5.5 SUMMARY

It seems for the clinicians involved in this focus group study that reflections on their own social interactions with clients, as part of a multidisciplinary team or being a client/patient themselves, prompted consideration of their own identity – or identities – as healthcare professionals. From recognising their own 'journey from student to clinician' to appreciating that their identity can be both challenged and shaped by clients, it seems that past interactions with clients play a pivotal role in increasing an awareness of their own identity and the nuances therein. Their identity can be honed even further, it seems, by experiences of clinical outcomes in terms of progress (or lack of progress) and/or success. Finally, viewing their identities from within their multidisciplinary teams and when in the role of client/patient further informs that sense of an evolving identity as caring and compassionate healthcare professionals.

6

ALLIED HEALTHCARE PROFESSIONAL EDUCATION AND IDENTITY IN THE CONTEXT OF SOCIAL INTERACTION: METHODOLOGICAL CONSIDERATIONS

6.1 INTRODUCTION

In Chapters 4 and 5 of this book, we explored qualified clinicians' reflections on their evolving professional identities and how those identities can be influenced by their social interactions in the workplace setting with colleagues and with the clients they serve. The remaining chapters of this book (Chapters 7–10) see a shift to a focus on the student healthcare professional and how they navigate identity issues as they reflect on social interactions that pervade their education in clinical and academic domains of teaching and learning.

The data collected from both in-depth interviews and focus groups have been discussed in the previous chapters to explore issues of identity and as related to experiences of social interaction in clinical contexts. The aim of the data analysis reported in the following chapters is to explore professional identity as it can be identified through written reflections via responses to an online survey (with questions adapted from Sharpless et al. 2015) on the educational experiences of a subset of allied healthcare professional (AHP) students, specifically speech and language therapists, occupational therapists and physiotherapists (and/or physical therapists). The objective is to consider how the development of profession-specific and profession-generic identities can be mapped across domains of practice and stage(s) of learning, among several international allied healthcare education sites. We are concerned with how social interaction is referenced within these reflections of student teaching and learning experiences and if it – as a process – can be viewed as a key contributor to identity development.

This chapter begins with a brief consideration of other methods used in the study of identity, before giving the reader more background on the notion of reflection and reflective practice as relevant to healthcare. The methods intrinsic to interpretative phenomenological analysis (IPA) (Smith, Flowers and Larkin 2022) (i.e. the methodology already invoked in the data analysis reported in Chapters 4 and 5) are considered in more detail here.

6.2 METHODOLOGICAL CONSIDERATIONS IN STUDIES OF ALLIED HEALTHCARE IDENTITY FORMATION IN EDUCATION

Studies investigating professional identity and professional identity formation among qualified professionals and students have drawn upon a variety of quantitative and qualitative methods, with the latter being the most popular among the studies reviewed here.

Matthews, Bialocerkowski and Molineux (2019) outline the limited quantitative analysis employed in relation to professional identity research in allied healthcare, nursing and medicine. Their research aimed to identify the validity and reliability of professional identity measures as psychometrically tested through a systematic review, in order to provide further understanding of the concept of professional identity. Similarly, the work of Ashby, Adler and Herbert (2016) employed descriptive statistical analysis to explore occupational therapy students' perceptions of professional identity, with the results identifying both professional education and professional socialisation as the biggest determiners of professional identity formation for medical students.

However, qualitative approaches to data analysis seem to be the most popular in this area of study. More specifically, thematic analysis seems to be the method of choice in many studies in both medical education (Browne et al. 2018; Noble, McHauge and Clavarino 2019) and allied health education (Binyamin 2018; Volpe et al. 2019). Other qualitative methods used to explore identity in social interaction in healthcare education include van Manen's (2014) thematic analysis, which was employed to identify how nursing students in Turkey were influenced by their experiences (Teskereci and Boz 2019). In a scoping review of professional identity research conducted by Snell et al. (2020), it was suggested that over 50% of the studies that met the criteria for inclusion in their review were conducted using qualitative methods. Furthermore, Snell et al. (2020) commented upon the continued growth in understanding of the concept and research relating to professional identity formation, calling for more longitudinal studies to be considered to (i) further understanding of the process of professional socialisation as students progress through their programmes of learning and (ii) to help identify similarities and/or differences in the professional socialisation trajectory between different AHP programmes.

The main tenets of IPA, the methodology of choice employed here, will be described in Section 6.5. First, however, we describe the study design (Section 6.3) and the participants who acted as respondents to our survey (Section 6.4).

6.3 THE STUDENT PROFESSIONAL: STUDY DESIGN

The study adopted a descriptive cross-sectional design, and data were collected via a popular survey tool, SurveyMonkey™. The online tool was chosen primarily for its ease of distribution and its potential to capture an international sample in a timely and efficient manner. The online survey mode of data collection was also employed for its flexibility and cost-effectiveness, while remaining aware of the limitations as well as the strengths of this mode of data collection (see Evans and Mathur 2005, 2018).

Not least among its limitations is the sole reliance on what the respondents report on the survey and gaps in data due to skipped questions and incomplete responses. However, in this instance, the advantages outweighed the disadvantages in capturing a sample of responses to open-ended questions from an international group of undergraduate and graduate students, which otherwise would not have been as easily gathered. Full ethics approval from the host research institution was granted prior to distribution of the survey. All data were transcribed from the responses and formatted in preparation for analysis.

6.3.1 STUDENTS AS PARTICIPANTS

Participants were drawn from undergraduate and graduate students from Ireland, the USA, Malta, South Africa and India, with the distribution of respondents represented outlined in Table 6.1.

Given the nature of the area of enquiry, purposive sampling was undertaken. Inclusion criteria specified that the respondents were students in their pre-final or final year of undergraduate education or in pre-final year or final year of graduate programmes in the allied healthcare disciplines of speech and language therapy, occupational therapy and physiotherapy (including physical therapy). Table 6.2 outlines the distribution of student respondents according to stage of educational programme in allied healthcare education. The majority of the student respondents came from the final two years of their undergraduate education.

Table 6.3 outlines the distribution of student respondents according to allied healthcare discipline, with the largest proportion coming from the discipline of

Table 6.1 Distribution of student respondents according to country of origin

Country of Origin	% of Total (n)
Ireland	30.43 (14)
Malta	23.41 (10)
India	21.74 (10)
United States of America	17.39 (8)
South Africa	6.52 (3)
Total	*100% (45)*

Table 6.2 Distribution of student respondents according to stage of education

Stage of Educational Programme	% of Total (n)
Final year (undergraduate programme)	45.45 (20)
Pre-final year (undergraduate programme)	30.43 (14)
Final year (graduate programme)	19.57 (9)
Pre-final year (graduate programme)	4.35 (2)
Total	*100 % (45)*

Table 6.3 Distribution of student respondents according to allied healthcare discipline

Allied Healthcare Discipline	% of Total (n)
Speech and language therapy	40.30 (18)
Physiotherapy/Physical therapy	30.43 (14)
Occupational therapy	28.26 (13)
Total	*100 % (45)*

speech and language therapy, followed by physiotherapy and occupational therapy, respectively.

It is clear from the Tables 6.2 and 6.3 that, overall, the number of respondents may be considered small. Given the small number of responses per international site (i.e. ranging from 3 respondents from South Africa to 14 from Ireland), we do not consider inter-ethnic differences in the chapters to follow. Rather we are concerned with capturing the nuances of the collective experience of AHP education in the larger group of learners, as a whole (n=45). This total figure is not unusual in this kind of study, for example, in Snell at al.'s (2020) scoping review which included 96 similar studies, over half of these studies had fewer than 50 participants.

6.3.2 THE STUDENT PROFESSIONAL SURVEY DESIGN

The survey was designed on a popular online platform (SurveyMonkey™) and completed anonymously. For the purposes of the survey and for clarity, we proposed the following definition of professional identity as an introduction to the survey:

> Professional identity formation can refer to how we see ourselves as emerging professionals through education and training, as we engage in the process of 'becoming' an allied health professional (i.e. an OT, PT or SLT). It can also be defined as our own professional self-concept, based on our experiences, beliefs and values.

The questions used in the development of our own survey were adapted from those used by Sharpless et al. (2015) in their study of medical education. These questions reflected our concern and interest in professional identity formation and could easily be extended and presented to AHP students. Of specific interest also was what seemed to be a tacit reference to social interaction, as Sharpless et al.'s questions referred to, for example, the process of 'pretending', 'formal and informal aspects of the curriculum', 'relationships' and 'interactions'. In addition, the fact that the questions do not explicitly lead students to address social interaction provides the opportunity to explore how students reference social interaction as salient in the absence of specific prompting. Such reference to social interaction becomes powerful evidence for the role of social interaction in identity formation. We also welcomed the open nature of these questions to allow for personal expression of ideas and details. On closer review, we decided to adapt the original questions to broaden the scope for the inclusion of AHP students and to separate out some of the questions for increased clarity. To appreciate the adaptations we made to the original content and format of Sharpless et al.'s questions, we list the original questions in Table 6.4 before showing our adaptations to them in Table 6.5.

In our revisions to the original wording of the questions, we substituted 'allied healthcare education' or 'allied healthcare students' for 'medical education' or 'medical students'; we also substituted 'clinical placement' for 'residency programme' as necessary; 'dieticians and psychologists' was substituted for 'nutritionists' and 'pharmacists'. We also reworded and reordered questions to enhance clarity, cognisant of the fact that we were working with an international cohort of respondents, some of whom would not have English as a first language.

Finally, we added a question on how the participants might communicate their specific role to other students. We therefore increased the overall number of questions to seven. The survey was piloted on a group of students outside of the target group and no changes to wording were deemed necessary. The questions posed to the participants via our online survey are outlined in Table 6.5 (with our adaptations highlighted in bold font).

The written responses to each survey question were downloaded, transcribed and formatted to allow for exploratory notes and in preparation for the implementation of an IPA. Prior to outlining the nature and processes of IPA and given that we analysed data drawn from written reflections prompted by means of an online survey, we consider in the next section what 'reflection' is and its growing use in terms of reflective practice in healthcare education and practice.

Table 6.4 Original questions used to prompt written reflections about professional identity formation in medical education (Sharpless et al. 2015)

1. Several authors have written about a stage of identity formation in which medical students feel like 'imposters'. What role, if any, does 'pretending' currently play in your professional life? If applicable, what have you done or what has allowed you to cross the line between 'pretending' to be a medical professional and fully inhabiting your professional role?
2. What incidents or relationships during your medical education (whether in the context of your study/work or in your life outside of medical education) do you perceive as critical or meaning making for your PIF?
3. What formal or informal aspects, if any, of the curriculum provided at your medical school or in your residency program have you found to be particularly valuable in supporting your PIF and nurturing your personal growth? What, if anything, do you believe teachers or mentors could do differently in medical education to facilitate your process of PIF?
4. If relevant, how have your interactions with other health care professionals (nurses, therapists, nutritionists, pharmacists, etc.) during your training affected your understanding of your own professional identity? How, if at all, do you differentiate and/or reconcile your medical professional identity with an interprofessional identity?

Table 6.5 Questions adapted from Sharpless et al. (2015) and supplemented for use in student online survey

1. What aspects of your university course, or clinical placement, have you found to be particularly valuable in supporting the formation of your professional identity, and in nurturing your personal growth?
2. **Thinking about your study or work in your life outside allied healthcare, can you think of** any experiences or relationships that have influenced the formation of your professional identity
3. Several authors have written about a stage of identity formation in which **allied healthcare students** feel like 'imposters'. What role, if any, does 'pretending' currently play in your professional life **as a student of allied healthcare education?**
4. What, if anything, has helped you to cross the line between 'pretending' to be an allied healthcare professional and fully inhabiting your professional role as a **student of allied healthcare education?**
5. What, if anything, do you believe teachers or mentors could do differently **in allied healthcare education** to facilitate your process of professional identity formation?
6. If relevant, how have your interactions with other healthcare professionals (other therapists, nurses, doctors, **dieticians, psychologists,** etc.) during your training affected your understanding of your own professional identity?
7. **How if at all, do you communicate your specific role (as a SLT, OT or PT student) when meeting or working with other students from other disciplines. Give an example of what you might say.**

6.4 REFLECTION AND REFLECTIVE PRACTICE

6.4.1 DEFINING THE CONCEPTS

Reflection and the use of reflective practice are common to many professions. The importance of self-reflection in education and professional practice has increasingly gained attention in recent decades across, for example, the worlds of business (e.g. Bailey and Rehman 2022), education (e.g. Sellars 2017; Malthouse and Roffey-Barensten 2020) and specifically English language teaching (e.g. Mann and Walsh 2013; Mann and Walsh 2017), healthcare (e.g. Launer 2022) and allied healthcare (e.g. Kinsella, Caty and Jenkins 2012). Attention to the value of reflection and adopting reflective practice is largely due to the foundational work of both Dewey (1933) and, 50 years later, to the work of Schön (1983), as relevant to learning and professional contexts, respectively (Schön's ideas are considered in more detail in Section 6.4.2.).

Reflection is seen as key to learning and professional development, whether during education or in the workplace. In its simplest form, 'to reflect' suggests 'unhurried consideration of something recalled to the mind' (www.merriam-webster.com/dictionary/reflect). The notion of 'unhurried consideration' is key here, in that the process of reflection allows for one to take time to pause, to stand back from the classroom or the busy workplace, in order to think about what has been experienced and what can be learnt from those experiences while at the same time heightening awareness of the impact upon one's personal or professional development. However, to proactively and meaningfully reflect in this 'unhurried' way in the context of education and workplace contexts often needs structured guidance if reflection is to be used in an optimal manner and with maximum effect. Therefore, students and qualified professionals often benefit from instruction in the process of reflective practice (e.g. Cross et al. 2004; Philip 2006), with pedagogical models being developed to maximise its teaching (e.g. Joyce-McCoach and Smith 2016).

Reflective practice – or the practice of reflecting – has been defined in many ways, from simple, basic definitions to those that are more complex and detailed. Koshy et al. (2017: 1) offer one such simple yet pragmatic description of reflective practice, reassuring the reader that 'what you may not have considered is that you have been subconsciously reflecting your whole life: thinking about and learning from past experiences to avoid things that did not work and to repeat things that did'. However, Loughran (1996: 21) introduces the *conscious* nature of the act of reflecting, describing it as 'the purposeful, deliberate act of inquiry into one's thoughts and actions through which a perceived problem is examined in order that a thoughtful, reasoned response might be tested out'. Similarly, Machost and Stains (2023: 1) define the practice as one which considers 'past or present experiences, learning from the outcomes observed, and planning how to better approach similar situations in the future'. However, definitions like these, as Mann and Walsh (2017: 8) point out, while referencing 'experience' fail to fully consider other important aspects of reflective practice such as 'action', 'interaction' or adopting a 'critical' stance to the reflective process:

> While most definitions highlight the importance of experience, they vary in the extent to which they foreground interaction or action. Most included the intellectual and the affective (what you think and how you feel). Two other elements of many definitions are 'action' and 'critical' though again there are huge variations in emphasis.

Incorporating, more explicitly, notions of action and interaction, for example, makes sense when one considers how reflective practice is enacted. Reflective practice allows one to not only reflect on one's own interactions but also to reflect *through* interaction with others. Hence, reflective practice can take many forms, from open discussions in small groups (e.g. see Miller 2005; McDermott 2020) to online peer-led group interactions (e.g. Palacios et al. 2024) and in supervision contexts (e.g. Carroll 2009; Ravalier et al. 2023). The mode of reflection can be spoken (e.g. Farr 2005) or written as part of learning portfolios (e.g. Pais Marden and Herrington 2022) or other written tasks (e.g. Jagoe and Walsh 2016). Mann and Walsh (2013: 292–3) note that reflective practice in professional education is often conducted on an individual basis and 'dominated by written forms of reflection at the expense of potentially more beneficial forms'. They call for consideration of a more 'dialogical/collaborative view of reflection' (p. 303) which written forms may preclude if not shared or discussed (such dialogic forms of reflections were the substance of the focus group transcribed data discussed in the previous chapter (Chapter 5)). Likewise, in their systematic review of reflective practices in medical education, MacAskill et al. (2023) consider other forms of reflection beyond the written mode to further ascertain the use of more creative means of reflective learning. Their review (from 15 studies) identified five alternative modes of reflection or reflective activities: 'viewing' (e.g. artworks, photographs), 'performing' (e.g. theatrical activities), 'imagining' (e.g. role play), 'creating' (e.g. digital storytelling, poetry) and 'mind-body' activities (e.g. relaxation and meditation). Some of these ideas will be revisited in Chapter 10 of this book, as we consider further directions in this area of practice in allied healthcare. However, for the researcher, written forms often lend themselves to more immediate availability for analysis, as is the case in the data collected from our online survey that are discussed in the remainder of this book. In our data to be presented and discussed in the following chapters, respondents (i.e. final-year AHP students) reflect on their personal and clinical 'interactions' while looking forward to 'actions' they may adopt as they prepare to enter the professional workforce.

6.4.2 REFLECTIVE PRACTICE IN HEALTHCARE AND ALLIED HEALTHCARE EDUCATION AND PRACTICE

In Chapter 5 we referred to the work of Schön (1983), specifically his treatise entitled *The Reflective Practitioner*, as seminal to any discussions of reflective practice for professionals. Schön's work provided the touchstone for the serious consideration of the value of reflection in healthcare and allied healthcare practice. One of Schön's foundational ideas is the fact that professionals know a lot more about their practice than that learnt from formal teaching via curricula content, published scientific papers and academic textbooks. Schön (1983: viii) states that 'this knowing-in-practice is largely tacit; thus, competent practitioners know more than they can say'. Getting at this embedded, professional 'tacit' knowledge that develops with experience and practice is central to the principles of reflective practice. Bringing that knowledge and experience to the fore is the concern of reflective practice, in other words, to put those insights to work for further and future learning. Schön's distinction between 'reflection-in-action' and 'reflection-on-action' is particularly helpful. The distinction offers a way for the healthcare professional to consider what is happening in the current moment, the 'here and now' (i.e. 'what am I doing in this clinical interaction, what should I change now?') and at a time removed (e.g. 'what did I do in that clinical interaction, what could I have done differently?'). Of relevance to the data to follow in this book is also the extension of these ideas to 'reflection-for-action' (Killion and Todnem 1991). This idea allows for the reflective act and the reflective practitioner to look forward and adopt action or agency, thereby enabling identification of 'steps or guidelines to follow to succeed in a given task in the future' (Mann and Walsh 2017: 8). Such agency is a consideration for many healthcare practitioners on the cusp of, or as they progress through, their professional careers as allied healthcare clinicians.

Schön's work, and that which has followed, has had such an impact that use of the terms 'reflection' and 'reflective practice' have become ubiquitous in healthcare education and training. Healthcare disciplines such as medicine (e.g. Koshy et al. 2017;

Winkel et al. 2017) and nursing (e.g. Rolfe, Freshwater and Jasper 2001; Wilding 2008; Miraglia and Asselin 2015; Howatson-Jones 2016) have long espoused the principles and implementation of reflective practice. Recognising the value of such practice is not lost in the education and practice of (allied) healthcare professionals (e.g. Artioli et al. 2021) across such disciplines as radiography (e.g. Baird 2008; Abrahams and Brady 2013; Brackenridge 2013), pharmacy education (Mantzourani et al. 2019), physiotherapy/physical therapy (e.g. Clouder 2000; Caeiro, Cruz and Pereira 2014; Ziebart and MacDermid 2019), speech and language therapy (e.g. Caty, Kinsella and Doyle 2015; McCluskey, Gallagher and Murphy 2021; Cook, Messick and McAuliffe 2023), and occupational therapy (e.g. Boniface 2002; Knightbridge 2019; Guy et al. 2020).

6.4.3 PUTTING REFLECTIVE PRACTICE TO WORK

Introducing critical reflection and reflective practice from the outset of training or education in healthcare is crucial. Many disciplines have firmly established a place for the theory and practice of reflection in healthcare curricula; others have explored how reflective practice is assessed. Many of these models and adapted templates have been developed from the work of Kolb's (1984) 'Reflective Model of Experiential Learning', Gibbs' (1988) 'Reflective Cycle' and Rolfe et al.'s (2001) 'Three-Stage Model of Reflective Practice' (What? So what? What next?).

Koshy et al. (2017:1) summarise the main questions posed in reflective practice, considering both 'things that go wrong' and 'things that went well' and as applied to many dimensions of practice (e.g. an interaction with a patient who may be dissatisfied, a diagnosis that may have been missed, an experience at a seminar or a challenging procedure carried out successfully etc.). Put simply, Koshy et al. (2017: 1–2) delineate stages, or probes, for reflective practice, drawn from many accounts of the processes engaged in, and these are listed in Table 6.6.

For the experienced and competent practitioner, these questions are probably well integrated into their patterns of professional thinking and acting. However, for the student and nascent healthcare professional, these questions provide a roadmap – or template – for professional conduct in practice, whether that be as core to supervision with seniors, mentors or peers, or unspoken in personal reflections and considerations.

Table 6.6 Stages or probes in reflective practice, as outlined by and adapted from Koshy et al. (2017: 1–2)

Probes	Focus
What, where and who?	The situation
How did it make you feel?	Your emotional state
Why did it happen?	Making sense of the situation
Could you have done anything differently?	Critical review and development of insight
What will you do differently in the future?	How will this change your practice?
Re-enforcement	What happens when you put this into practice?

For a student or healthcare professional to develop and hone their reflective practice, the issue of assessment has been a sticking point for many educators. However, how does one evaluate a learner's performance in this regard and feed back this evaluation for further growth without affecting the process of reflection? It is obvious that if a student knows they are being assessed on 'reflection', they may write, report or discuss the issues differently. As Mann and Walsh (2017: 19) point out, 'there are clearly tensions in assessing a process which is intended to be formative and enhance professional development'.

Assessment in the form of evaluative tools for reflective practice in healthcare was the focus of a recent scoping review by Préfontaine et al. (2021) and speaks to the complexity within and nuances of the practice of reflection. No less than 34 different evaluation tools were identified (across 45 papers), referencing 11 components of reflection in all. Tools to assess a myriad of spoken and written reflective activities (such as verbal reflections, maintenance of portfolios, journaling, student observation and reflection worksheets) were all included in the review, which highlights the vast array of reflective activities that may be used in healthcare. The review called for more attention to context in the assessment of reflective practice, given the vastly different experiences and formats encountered by both students and their assessors in the reflective domain.

It seems then that reflective practice is core to healthcare education and ongoing professional development, occupying an important place in any practitioner's toolkit. Whether written or verbal, online or in person, small group or peer to peer, it is clear that a lot can be learnt by both instructors and their students in this regard, including assessment and evaluation processes.

We now turn to the format and analytic method adopted for the data collected, which the remaining chapters of this book focus on. It will be shown how considerations of social interactions are particularly referenced in the written reflections which form the content for analysis. These written accounts required a suitable means of analysis beyond surface-level interpretations, given that respondents were relating their own personal experiences as probed by survey questions. It was important to give voice to their accounts to help understand their experiences and to help inform allied healthcare education and practice. IPA was chosen to satisfy the concern of really 'getting at' the students' experiences while in teaching and learning contexts across the disciplines of speech and language therapy, occupational therapy and physio/physical therapy. In the next section we describe the main tenets of this approach and the steps undertaken in the analysis.

6.5 INTERPRETATIVE PHENOMENOLOGICAL ANALYSIS (IPA)

Qualitative research is usually concerned with the intent of an action or experience. IPA is a method that aims to capture an individual's lived experience and how they make sense of this experience in the context of both their personal and social worlds (Smith and Nizza 2021; Smith et al. 2022). IPA is increasingly being employed as a research methodology, favoured by many who wish to somehow make sense of others' experiences. For example, IPA has been used to explore such diverse experiences as (chronic) pain (e.g. Lavie-Ajayi, Almog and Krumer-Nevo 2012; Smith and Osborn 2015), involuntary childlessness (Smith and Fieldsend 2021), experience of Parkinson's disease (Eatough and Shaw 2019) and the lived experiences of children and adolescents with obsessive-compulsive disorder (Sravanti et al. 2022), to name but a few areas in which IPA has been employed.

In the world of the healthcare professional, phenomenological enquiry has also been popular for some time. For example, in relation to nursing, Taylor (1993: 171) asserts:

> Given that nursing occurs in 'the real world of practice', the view is forwarded that a research method chosen to understand nursing practice must be able to generate meaning from the people who are involved in nursing, that is, the nurses and patients in everyday practice settings.

We have seen in Chapters 4 and 5 that attention was paid to the healthcare professionals' voice as they recounted their experiences of working as part of a multidisciplinary team and with clients, respectively. The origin of these reflections was 'the real world of practice', and likewise it is to the 'real world' of the student to which we now turn, and their experiences of education and clinical practice. We aim to explore these experiences through their written reflections in response to the adapted survey (Table 6.5). Through IPA, we aim to 'generate meaning' from the students' accounts of experiences as we make sense of them making sense of their own experiences (in keeping with the main tenet of IPA, i.e. the 'double hermeneutic', Smith et al. 2009). Furthermore, given the complex nature of professional identity in the socio-cultural context of healthcare, IPA was deemed the most suitable analytic methodology to 'get at' these experiences, most often recounted with reference to student social interactions with educators, supervising clinicians, peers, clients and families. The main concepts and principles underlying IPA are explained in Table 6.7 and further discussed in Section 6.5.3.

Table 6.7 Principles and explanations of key IPA terms (Smith et al. 2009; Smith et al. 2022)

Phenomenology	The phenomenological principle of IPA refers to the study of the human experience. This typically involves the use of first-person accounts that encapsulate an individual's life experiences as well as how people perceive events to make meaning of their lives.
Hermeneutics	Hermeneutics refers to the theory of interpretation. IPA employs a double hermeneutic in which the researcher aims to make sense of the participant making sense of their own life experiences, leading to a greater understanding of the person and their social realities,
Ideography	Ideography refers to a focus on the narrative and lived experience of a particular individual in particular circumstances.

Section 6.5.3 will consider IPA and the notion of phenomenology, further extending and justifying our use of this methodology to analyse the student data – the focus of the remaining chapters of this book (Chapter 7–10).

6.5.1 DATA ANALYSIS

Following the data collection phase, data were transcribed from the responses and formatted in preparation for analysis. Data were formatted under each respective question to provide the most appropriate means of exploring professional identity in AHP students.

It should be noted that, in recent times, modifications to some terminology within IPA have been introduced. There has been a change to some of the terminology used in the analytical process, as noted in Chapter 4. Of note, emergent themes are now called 'experiential statements'. Furthermore, a group of related experiential statements now make up a 'personal experiential theme' (PET), previously termed superordinate themes. We use the new terminology throughout the data analysis discussions to come. Moreover, it should be noted that there has been no change to the process of analysis per se with this new terminology; rather, the change only applies to the terms used to describe the themes identified to more clearly reflect what is being done in the analysis, that is, to honour the personal nature and experiences of the participants' data (Smith et al. 2022).

6.5.2 STEPS TAKEN IN IPA ANALYSIS

Step 1 – Multiple readings and exploratory notes

The authors undertook multiple readings of the data for the purpose of familiarisation. Analysis of similarities and differences in the segments of text, words and sentences of participants attempted to understand what the experience may mean for each individual participant. The notes produced were intended to be comprehensive, including descriptive, linguistic and conceptual comments, as described in Table 6.8.

Table 6.8 Types of exploratory notes in IPA analysis (Smith et al. 2009; Smith et al. 2022)

Descriptive Comments The researcher provides a summary of what the participant has explicitly said. Descriptive notes aim to identify the structure of participants' experiences and thoughts at a basic and face-value level.
Linguistic Comments These types of comments focus on exploring the specific ways a participant uses language to make a point within the data. Linguistic comments aim to provide an insight into both the cognitive and affective state of the individual.
Conceptual Comments These types of comments tend to explore the data at a more conceptual and interrogative level, exploring the potential meanings and detailing deeper interpretation of a participant's response.

Step 2 – Formulating experiential statements

The exploratory notes in Table 6.8 provided the basis from which experiential statements could be formulated. Experiential statements aim to provide a concise summary of the meaning of the experience for the participant, as well as the researcher's understanding of the participant's experience.

Step 3 – Finding connections and clustering experiential statements

Once experiential statements had been identified, the authors aimed to review and refine these experiential statements to more accurately define the key features of the experience of the participants. By continuing to refine and group experiential statements together, cluster groups of experiential statements began to emerge.

Step 4 – Compiling the table of personal experiential themes

Following the clustering of the experiential statements, each cluster could then be named as a personal experiential theme (PET). Each PET identifies the experiential statements within each theme.

6.5.3 PHENOMENOLOGY: SOME FURTHER CONSIDERATIONS

Our discussion above has considered IPA from the points of view offered by Smith and Nizza (2021) and Smith et al. (2022), building on the original work of these authors over a decade earlier (Smith et al. 2009). Before we show how we employed their methodology in the analysis in our student data chapters (Chapters 7–10), it is worth reiterating and considering exactly what we are aiming to do in this text and what we mean by the 'phenomenon' of what we are exploring.

We are concerned with the 'phenomenon' of an evolving identity of the allied healthcare education student, as viewed through the lens of social interaction activities which are an integral part of education in clinical education programmes. We are drawing on reports of the student experience as a starting point; however, we also move beyond these accounts of *what* our participants say in their responses, and *how* they are saying it, to consider *what* it means for the phenomenon of the AHP student identity. In other words, we consider the experiential accounts, interpret them from a phenomenological perspective and engage in a process of abstraction and deliberation in our presentation of the findings.

However, it is necessary at this juncture to consider the notion of 'phenomenology' in research, as it is a term that may be used differently according to research contexts and researchers' relative understanding of the concept. In this regard, van Manen (2017) provides an insightful editorial entitled 'But is it phenomenology?' where he interrogates the notion of phenomenology as used and misused by researchers. His thoughts prior to the more recent research of Smith and colleagues (Smith and Nizza 2021; Smith et al. 2022) force us to consider exactly what we are doing when we engage in phenomenological research. Referring to his interpretations, we are examining 'how a particular group of individuals in a certain place or institutional context have certain experiences' (van Manen 2017: 775), and we are moving beyond (or even with) those experiential accounts to consider the phenomenon of professional identity. Van Manen (2017: 775) references the prominent phenomenologist Jean Luc Marion (2002) in this discussion, who emphasises that 'phenomenology is the study of how things show or give themselves'. Applying this idea and terminology to what we are doing in this book, we are concerned with how the 'thing' of the student identity formation experience, occurring through social interaction, 'shows itself' and 'gives' of itself to inform the phenomenon of identity under study. This is in keeping with van Manen's (2017) warning of drifting into analysis that may render 'psychological themes and not eidetic phenomenological themes' (p. 778), the latter revealing what is the *eidos* (unique meaning) of what shows itself or gives itself in living experience' (p. 776).

If we fast forward, so to speak, to the intended outcomes of our research as presented in this text, we believe we are striving to provide, as van Manen (2017: 776) asserts, that which is 'the topmost coveted prize of phenomenological human science research ... the promise of depthful understanding and meaningful insight'. Van Manen (2017:777) explains further what the outcome of a careful phenomenological study may look like, in his words:

> a full-fledged reflective text[s] that induce[s] the reader into a wondering engagement with certain questions that may be explored through the identification, critical examination, and eloquent elaboration of themes that help the reader recognise the meaningfulness of certain human experiences and events.

6.6 SUMMARY

This chapter has outlined the main procedures undertaken to collect and analyse the data of relevance to the research discussed in this book. The survey design and general demographic information about the student respondents were summarised. Phenomenology is a popular qualitative analytic methodology in the field of professional identity research, and specifically IPA (Smith et al. 2022) was briefly outlined as the approach used to analyse the data collected for this study. We have also considered here exactly what we are striving to do and our understanding of 'phenomenological' research as adopted in this book.

The following chapters (Chapters 7–10) will describe the findings, with extracts from the data to support the points being made. For ease of reference, the extracts will be denoted as follows: profession name/country of origin/respondent number. For example, 'OT-Ire36' refers to an occupational therapy student from Ireland respondent number 36; 'SLT-SA45' denotes a speech and language therapy student from South Africa respondent number 45, and so on for students from physiotherapy (PT) and the other represented countries of origin United States (US), Malta (Mal) and India (In).

7

'WE FAKE IT 'TIL WE MAKE IT': THE ROLE OF PRETENDING (OR NOT) IN SOCIAL INTERACTIONS AS ALLIED HEALTHCARE PROFESSIONAL STUDENTS

The greatest way to live with honour in this world is to be what we pretend to be.
Socrates

7.1 INTRODUCTION

'Pretending' or 'imposter syndrome' is not a new concept to the experience of healthcare education and student learning. Many studies have referenced this phenomenon as reported by students and even new graduates or novice clinicians. When it is used it seems that pretending is manifest and played out in the social interactions that make up the activities of clinical practice, including interactions with clients/patients and their families, and even extending to interactions with supervising clinicians. This chapter will focus on how and why students employ pretending in their clinical interactions. We will show that students use 'pretending' with the right intentions – to impress and behave professionally towards supervisors and patients when feeling challenged or out of their depth – it is not something that is undertaken to do harm or to deceive in the negative sense of the term. Put simply, *to pretend* is defined as: '*to give a false appearance of being, possessing, or performing*' (www.merriam-webster.com/dictionary/pretend).

Students were asked to address questions in our survey around their experience of 'pretending' during their education. The following questions (see Table 6.5; Q3 and Q4) from our survey were posed:

- Several authors have written about a stage of identity formation in which allied healthcare students feel like 'imposters'. What role, if any, does 'pretending' currently play in your professional life as a student of allied healthcare education?
- What, if anything, has helped you to cross the line between 'pretending' to be an allied healthcare professional and fully inhabiting your professional role as a student of allied healthcare education?

It is the analysis of the responses to these question that are the focus of this chapter. The identified experiential statements which inform the personal experiential themes described in this chapter will show that for students of allied healthcare education, 'being' a professional, 'possessing' knowledge and clinical acumen, along with 'performing' requisite clinical skills, are important attributes of a student clinician, so much so that pretending is necessary to give that impression in some instances.

In the data, a nuanced interpretation of 'pretending' is identified, that is, there is a variety of views expressed in terms of whether such behaviour is beneficial for or useful to the learning experience as a healthcare student.

Two personal experiential themes were identified in the data related to the notion of 'pretending' and will be discussed along with the associated experiential statements in Sections 7.2 and 7.3 in this chapter, respectively. Table 7.1 lists these associated experiential statements.

Table 7.1 Personal experiential themes related to 'pretending' and associated experiential statements

Personal Experiential Themes (PETS)	Associated Experiential Statements
Role of pretending in professional life as a student of allied healthcare education	• Pretending as a coping mechanism • Pretending as a barometer of progress and experience • Pretending (or not pretending) as a natural process of growth and development • Pretending and knowledge • Pretending and confidence • Multiple opportunities for pretending
Crossing the line between 'pretending' and becoming a student of allied healthcare education	• Verbal communication-focused strategies • Non-verbal communication-focused strategies

7.2 ROLE OF PRETENDING IN PROFESSIONAL LIFE AS A STUDENT OF ALLIED HEALTHCARE EDUCATION

7.2.1 PRETENDING AS A COPING MECHANISM

The experiential statement of 'pretending as a coping mechanism' is illustrated in several ways in the responses analysed. The act of pretending is closely linked to confidence for some students. The data suggest an inevitability about pretending on the part of the students, in that it was a normal part of the behaviour of students on clinical placement:

Extract 7.1

`I think that sometimes we're doing things on placement without even realising and we sometimes feel like we know a lot less than we actually do because we feel like 'just students'.` **(OT-Ire36)**

Appearing to others as confident in social interactions is regarded as a routine practice or 'daily occurrence' while learning:

Extract 7.2

Pretending to have confidence when on clinical placements is a daily occurrence. I feel like I have to 'sell myself' as a student to my Practice Educator (the occupational therapist who supervises me while on placement) as it is them who will determine whether I pass or fail placement - feel like I have to know the answer to everything & appear confident so as not to look bad. It can be hard in this sense to discuss professional limitations & areas for development. Also feel for clients you have to pretend to be knowledgeable & confident even if you are doubting yourself so that they can trust you as a therapist. Often given very difficult assignments - have to pretend in a sense that I have completely grasped & understood the topic at hand to obtain a high grade even if I may not have fully achieved this. **(OT-Ire41)**

Of note in the above quote is the pervasive extent of pretending across contexts of social interaction and engagement. The student referred to having to pretend to be confident to the practice educator (clinical supervisor), the client/patient and also to academic staff in the submission of assignments. However, pretending here is also linked to wanting to be awarded a high grade in clinical practice and academic work, while engaging confidently with the client is related to building trust. Faking confidence with the client was noted by another student as playing a 'key role' in helping the client 'feel more at ease and comfortable with your abilities' [as a student] (SLT-Ire1).

Being concerned that a practice educator also has confidence in a student's abilities was also noted by another student. This interpretation of confidence was linked to perceived expectations of a supervisor as a student progresses through a programme:

Extract 7.3

I feel that at the start of each placement I have experienced this [pretending] as, in each new work environment there are so many new things that I have not experienced yet. In third and final year I think this might be experienced more as expectations of the student are higher. For many, third or final-year placement is likely to be in an area that they have not had experience in before (e.g. mental health or paediatrics) but yet the student has quite a large base of knowledge at this stage so an element of 'pretending' is almost necessary in order for the practice educator/supervisor to have confident [sic] in the students' abilities. **(OT-Ire40)**

There is an apparent desire here from the student that the practice educator becomes confident in the student's abilities. Behaving like a professional is also an act of pretence for some, as they reported not knowing what was expected of them. Pretending, therefore, allowed them to function in the clinical context to 'remain professional' and 'act as a professional':

Extract 7.4

It [pretending] helps me to remain professional. **(SLT-SA45)**

Extract 7.5

Sometimes clients trust you with their personal experiences and difficulties, and since you are still a student and you're still growing in knowledge and professionalism [it] makes you feel that you are not the ideal person to carry out intervention for them. Still, you need to act as a professional and trustworthy therapist. **(OT-Mal32)**

The data suggest that the students were not always sure what the correct behaviour is – or should be – because of tacit expectations that are not expressed (e.g. 'this is how to act as a professional'). Pretending, therefore, it seems is used by healthcare students as a coping mechanism in social interactions to overcome self-doubt and appear confident to others, patients and supervisors included.

7.2.2 PRETENDING AS A BAROMETER OF PROGRESS AND EXPERIENCE

The experiential statement of 'pretending as a barometer of progress and experience' was also identified in the analysis of the data. For some students, pretending served as a tool to measure their own progress and confidence. Some suggested that the more exposure they, as students, have, the more the act of pretending would reduce their interactions with others. For example, pretending somehow enabled this student to find 'more confidence' in their skills, as follows:

Extract 7.6

'Imposter syndrome' hit me hard when I first started my graduate programme. I hadn't had any clinical experience, and I felt like a fraud. But once I began my clinical experiences, I found I was able to 'fake it till I make it' and eventually found more confidence in my skills. At times, I still 'fake it' but it happens less often now as I gain more varied experience. However, whenever I have a new experience, I always go back to that 'imposter feeling' for a least a short while. **(SLT-US27)**

Of interest here is the use of 'pretending' when necessary ('at times I still "fake it"'). In other words, for this student, the act of pretending is something to fall back on when exposed to new experiences. The data analysis also suggests that despite initially feeling the need to fake it for a large part of the programme of study (SLT-US24), for some students a reduction in pretending seems more likely as confidence grows and in the latter years of student training (e.g. SLT-Ire34; OT-Mal31). The following quotes (Extracts 7.7–7.9) from the data illustrate this point:

Extract 7.7

'Fake it til you make it' seriously applies here. Students might feel incapable and doubt themselves often. I personally felt like I didn't belong, or someone made a mistake letting me into the programme, for a good portion of my time in the programme. As I build my professional confidence, I find myself 'pretending' less and less. **(SLT-US24)**

Extract 7.8

I feel that 'pretending' is an inevitable part of being a student clinician. Pretending has largely faded by the end of fourth year, but it played a larger role for me in previous years; I feel it was particularly apparent on my second-year placement. I still saw my role as primarily a student in second year, and certainly felt somewhat of an imposter in a busy acute hospital. **(SLT-Ire34)**

Extract 7.9

Sometimes it is hard to think on the spot and you need time to refer back to notes or research in order to formulate your professional opinion about something. All years before final year, I felt like an imposter during placement! **(OT-Mal31)**

It seems that up to the latter stages of a programme, feeling like 'an imposter' is evident, but for some students that feeling gradually fades with the knowledge and experience accumulated by 'final year' (OT-Mal31). It seems, then, in other words, that a measure of less pretending means for some students that 'I am making progress'.

7.2.3 PRETENDING (OR NOT PRETENDING) AS A NATURAL PROCESS OF GROWTH AND DEVELOPMENT

Analysis of the data also identified the experiential statement of 'pretending (or not pretending) as a natural process of growth and development'. This experiential statement suggests that for some students, 'pretending' was perceived as a part of their natural growth and development as an AHP student, while others did not feel the need to pretend.

Pretending as just being a part of all AHP development and 'the only way to do it' was referenced by one student as follows:

Extract 7.10

We fake it till we make it - in all professions, inclusive of our allies. We simply just try to keep pushing on till we feel comfortable and have the knowledge. It's the only way to do it. **(SLT-SA44)**

However, of interest here is the notion that it may be a transitional phase until the student feels 'comfortable' and has 'the knowledge'. Also of interest is the reference to a collective identity of allied healthcare professional (AHP) students (i.e. 'allies'). For another speech and language therapy (SLT) student (SLT-Mal16), getting some 'idea of the workplace' suggests some acceptance of the imposter syndrome being part of the process to becoming an AHP:

Extract 7.11

It [pretending] gives me an idea of what the actual workplace will be and feel like but also give [sic] me an inside perspective into the hierarchical structures of a job. **(SLT-Mal16)**

Availing of opportunities provided by a supervising clinician was also referenced by some students when reflecting on the role of pretending. The following SLT student (SLT-Ire2) made a comparison to 'playing "House"' as a contrived situation, with interactive role plays as the means to practise skills provided by the supervising clinician:

Extract 7.12

When a professional educator provides role plays or situations rather than opportunities to demonstrate skills, it can feel like one is playing 'House' as the situation is contrived and controlled, unlike a clinical situation. **(SLT-Ire2)**

Moreover, this same SLT student (SLT-Ire2) explained that often pretence seems to be reinforced by others, such as when the client or service user 'belittles' you as a student or bypasses you to talk to the clinician, as follows:

Extract 7.13

At times, it can also feel like 'pretending' when service user parents or the service user (if elderly) belittle you by referring to you as a child or give feedback on your performance rather than listening to your clinical judgement! Or if the parent/service user listens to you, doesn't acknowledge what you said but instead turns to the qualified clinician seeking answers. **(SLT-Ire2)**

This quote suggests then that – for this student – an identity of 'imposter' is almost reinforced and co-constructed by others, in this case the client's parents or service user. The pretence was perceived as being maintained through the social interaction occurring with others. For others, if the supervisor provides opportunities to deal with 'actual clients', this seemed to lessen the need to 'pretend':

Extract 7.14

I think it also depends on the supervisor that you are assigned to. If you are given opportunity to practise with actual clients, I don't believe that as a student you are pretending, but rather you acknowledge the fact that you are learning and make that known to the client. Hence, they know that they can trust you to be able to contribute well to their well-being. **(OT-Mal30)**

For this occupational therapy (OT) student, acknowledging that they are learning and making that 'known to the client' engendered 'trust.'

However, 'pretending' had no role to play for some other students according to the data analysis (e.g. 'no role', PT-In28); 'no pretending', PT-In21), while others referenced the lack of a need to pretend, explaining their own rationale as follows:

Extract 7.15

I feel like I do not have to pretend to be anyone else, as I like interacting with people. **(SLT-Mal13)**

Extract 7.16

None [no role for pretending]. I am proud to be a student of physiotherapy and make it clear that I am as such. I acknowledge that this is a transitional phase towards becoming an AHP and am proud of this. People around me value my opinions on matters and do seek my advice but are cognisant of my limitations. Nevertheless, I am honoured to be identified in my community and social circles as being someone who is aspiring to be an AHP and actively studying towards this goal. **(PT-Mal29)**

A SLT student (SLT-Mal13) referenced the fact that they liked 'interacting with people' and therefore did not see a need to pretend. Moreover, a physiotherapy (PT) student referenced the fact that they are 'proud' and 'honoured' to be an AHP student (PT-Mal29), with no need for pretence. Here, both students seemed to also hint at their personal identities by referencing lives outside of their professional training ones (e.g. 'I like interacting with people', SLT-Mal13, and reference to 'social circles', PT-Mal29). Furthermore, both profession-specific (i.e. PT) and profession-generic (i.e. 'aspiring to be an AHP') identities were also referenced by PT-Mal29. Of note here too is the reference to how experiences of social interaction outside of workplace experiences seemed to influence or aid the interactions as a healthcare student.

7.2.4 PRETENDING AND KNOWLEDGE

Thus far, the discussion has focused on 'pretending' and its role in the activities of a clinical placement, with requisite clinical skills when interacting with patients and supervisors and links to confidence. We now turn our attention to the reference by some students to 'knowledge'. The experiential statement of 'pretending and knowledge' is identified here. Being more specific about the role of pretence in knowledge, with reference to self-doubt, is interesting as the following quotes illustrate:

Extract 7.17

Sometimes I don't feel like I know as much as I do so I feel like I'm pretending. **(SLT-US26)**

Extract 7.18

I do feel like I am currently suffering from imposter syndrome ... I feel I have acquired my OT degree but not worthy of it. I feel somewhat of a fraud with my patients; however, it gives me heart that they benefit from my services even if I still have that imposter feeling. **(OT-Ire42)**

For others, there is no place for pretending as far as knowledge is concerned:

Extract 7.19

Many times in my clinical internships, I feel that I am pretending to be more confident than I am in my abilities. However, I avoid pretending to have knowledge that I do not have because this is a poor habit for healthcare providers to develop. **(PT-US9)**

The quote that 'I avoid pretending that I have knowledge' is of interest here. As stated at the outset of this chapter, it seems that from the students' descriptions, there is not an intent to purposely deceive but more to appear confident in interactions and in control in dealings with others while learning. This pretending for some did not extend to having knowledge as this was suggestive of being unethical: pretending in this context, therefore, is a 'poor habit for healthcare providers to develop'. Of note here is the reference also to the values that the AHP must hold, a reference to the profession-generic identity and the need to uphold its values.

Other AHP students seemed to reflect on the fact that the feeling like an imposter during placement was confined to 'all years before final year':

Extract 7.20

Sometimes it is hard to think on the spot and you need time to refer back to notes or research in order to formulate your professional opinion about something. All years before final year, I felt like an imposter during placement! **(OT-Mal31)**

Even having graduated with the academic and clinical knowledge to be awarded their degree, another student (first referenced in Extract 7.18 above) talked of still having 'that imposter feeling' despite knowing her patients are gaining from her input:

Extract 7.21

I do feel like I am currently suffering from imposter syndrome ... I feel I have acquired my OT degree but not worthy of it. I feel somewhat of a fraud with my patients; however, it gives me heart that they benefit from my services even if I still have that imposter feeling. **(OT-Ire42)**

It seems then that many students and new graduates seem to harbour those feelings of pretence, despite having the experience and knowledge to do the job. Of note, however, is the awareness of those 'imposter' feelings and being able to acknowledge and express them.

7.2.5 PRETENDING AND CONFIDENCE

The experiential statement of 'pretending and confidence' illustrates how many of the students linked confidence to the act of pretence in their responses. Their responses suggest that feigning confidence seemed important when interacting with others while learning on their chosen programme. For SLT-SA45, the feigned confidence in socially interacting with clients helps to overcome doubts about her own abilities:

Extract 7.22

Pretending to be sure and confident in your abilities when talking with a client even when you unsure of yourself or [your] capabilities. **(SLT-SA45)**

Likewise, for this SLT student (SLT-US25) (Extract 7.23), pretending to have 'greater confidence' helps her when working directly with clients and building 'credibility':

Extract 7.23

I 'pretend' to have greater confidence in my skills and knowledge than I do. This helps me establish credibility with clients and gain their cooperation during treatment. **(SLT-US25)**

Feeling that she 'didn't belong' and that 'someone made a mistake' in offering her a place on the programme directly affected another student's confidence in studying SLT (see also Extract 7.7 above):

Extract 7.24

I personally felt like I didn't belong, or someone made a mistake letting me into the programme, for a good portion of my time in the programme. As I build my professional confidence, I find myself 'pretending' less and less. **(SLT-US24)**

However, building 'professional confidence' seemed to allow this student to be less reliant on the need to pretend as she finds herself pretending 'less and less'.

7.2.6 MULTIPLE OPPORTUNITIES FOR PRETENDING

'Multiple opportunities for pretending' as an experiential statement captures the fact that pretending extends beyond the need to pretend to have knowledge or skill in interactions in the workplace. For some, pretending seemed to permeate many of the contexts of social interaction required while learning to become a healthcare practitioner:

Extract 7.25

I am more interested in working with adult clients but to be professional in paediatric contexts I 'pretend' I am just as interested. Not showing any bad mood in a session requires 'pretending'. 'Pretending' to be more confident than you actually are in front of clients. **(SLT-Mal7)**

Pretending to be interested in other areas of healthcare practice (e.g. paediatrics), to 'be professional', was expressed by this student. That pretending was linked to appearing being professional is of interest, suggesting that it is important to give a good impression to those the student interacts with in the clinical context. Moreover, this student reported extending the need to pretend to her 'mood', that is, 'not showing any bad mood in a session requires pretending', an idea that is perhaps also linked to the need to appear 'professional'.

The quote from this OT student (OT-Ire41) also speaks to the multidimensional, or all-pervasive, nature of 'pretending' for her as part of the social interactions that take while on placement. For this student, pretending is a 'daily occurrence' and linked directly to appearing 'confident':

Extract 7.26

Pretending to have confidence when on clinical placements is a daily occurrence. I feel like I have to 'sell myself' as a student to my Practice Educator (the occupational therapist who supervises me while on placement) as it is them who will determine whether I pass or fail placement - feel like I've to know the answer to everything & [sic] appear confident so as not to look bad. It can be hard in this sense to discuss professional limitations & areas for development. Also feel for clients you have to pretend to be knowledgeable &[sic] confident even if you are doubting yourself so that they can trust you as a therapist. Often given very difficult assignments - have to pretend in a sense that I have completely grasped & understood the topic at hand to obtain a high grade even if I may not have fully achieved this. **(OT-Ire41)**

Pretending to be confident is also linked to achievement for this student (i.e. passing a clinical placement or doing well on an assignment); appearing confident seemed important 'so as not to look bad'. However, this OT student was also aware that pretending often prevents opportunities 'to discuss professional limitations &[sic]

areas for development'. Finally, 'trust' was also referenced in this illustrative quote in the context of patient trust, and pretending to be confident has a role in building that trust.

7.3 CROSSING THE LINE BETWEEN 'PRETENDING' AND BECOMING A STUDENT OF ALLIED HEALTHCARE EDUCATION

The follow-up question posed in our survey (in Table 6.5) to further probe the concept and experiences of 'pretence' in allied healthcare education was 'What, if anything, has helped you to cross the line between 'pretending' to be an AHP and fully inhabiting your professional role as a student of allied healthcare education?' Here we were interested in what helped or supported students to begin to leave the need to 'pretend' behind and move to more confidently be that AHP student of. The students reported numerous and diverse ways of what helped them in making this transition. They reported several strategies that were communication focused and had social interaction at their core, including verbal and non-verbal strategies. Tables 7.2 and 7.3 summarise these strategies, which inform the experiential statements of 'verbal communication-focused strategies' and 'non-verbal communication-focused strategies'.

Table 7.2 Verbal communication-focused strategies in helping to lessen pretence and inhabit a professional role as an AHP student

Nature of Verbal Strategy	Examples
Interpersonal communication	Skills of student and supervisor; naturalness of conversation with patient/client (SLT-Ire30)
Questioning	Being able to answer questions from clients (SLT-Mal7)
	Learning by asking/questioning (PT-US9)
Engagement	Talking with qualified professionals (OT-Ire38)
	Engaging and debriefing with fellow students; debriefing with supervisors (SLT-SA45)
	Discussions with supervisors providing reassurance (OT-Ire42)
	Reinforcement from practice educator (OT-Ire37)
	Explicit praise from professionals and college mentors (SLT-Ire2)
Reflection	Daily reflections (OT-Ire38)
	Positive self-talk/belief increasing self-concept (ST-Mal16; SLT-Ire34; OT-Ire36)
	Being honest with practice educator (OT-Ire36)
	Realisation that it is not all about theory (SLT-Ire3)
	Self-questioning 'do I know the theory?' (SLT-US27)

Table 7.3 Non-verbal communication-focused strategies in helping to lessen pretence and inhabit a professional role as an AHP student

Nature of Non-verbal Strategy	Examples
Observation	Opportunity to observe supervisors (OT-Ire41)
Practice	Gaining experience (SLT-Ire2) Repeated experiences with clinical populations (SLT-Ire2).
Facilitating independence	Allowed to be independent (OT-Ire40; OT-Ire35)

7.3.1 VERBAL COMMUNICATION-FOCUSED STRATEGIES

The student respondents reported a variety of verbal communication-focused strategies that they perceived as helping them to decrease their need to pretend and take on their professional role more authentically. These strategies are summarised in Table 7.2.

Of the verbal communication strategies used to help 'cross the line' from pretending to 'being' an AHP student, it seems that the power of interpersonal communication, the ability to respond to and pose questions, actively engage with one's own community of practice, and using self-reflection have key roles to play in this transition.

The power of your own interpersonal communication as informing and supporting a sense of professionalism was highlighted by one of the students:

Extract 7.27

`Realising it's not all about the books and the theory. Your interaction skills and personality are just as important and you have to try not to lose them while you try to remember all the information you have learned in lectures. When you enter a situation/session and you are able to talk to the person like you would if you met them anywhere else, while still adhering to professionalism - that's when you begin to cross the line.` **(SLT-Ire3)**

Valuing her own 'interaction skills' and her personality seemed to help this student become one who acts in a professional way, leaving the need to 'pretend' behind. Being able to ask others (e.g. colleagues; PT-US9) and answer clients' questions was empowering for others in this regard (e.g. 'knowing how to answer a parent's question when asked'; SLT-Mal7).

Proactively engaging and interacting with those in the community of practice (e.g. qualified practitioners) is important for others as they try to progress from those 'imposter' feelings. One of the OT students (OT-Ire42) openly admitted that she has not yet 'crossed the line' but is taking action about that and using supervision to address those feelings; she explained:

Extract 7.28

`I have not yet crossed the line! I have arranged to meet with a senior OT tomorrow as I have already enlightened her how I feel` like an imposter and we will discuss it more tomorrow. I think it will take some time and more work experience before I settle into my role and feel like I am an OT and not just an imposter OT!!! **(OT-Ire42)**

Others referred to 'debriefing', with (SLT-SA45) and gaining 'reinforcement' from supervisors as a 'big deal' (OT-Ire37) in helping to progress beyond the 'pretending' tendency; another (SLT-Ire2) included 'explicit praise from professionals and mentors at times' as a positive strategy in this regard.

Finally, reflecting on one's own progress and practice was important for others (e.g. 'daily reflections'; OT-Ire38). 'Being honest' in interactions with their practice educator was key for one student which, together with focusing on both her strengths and weaknesses, helped her to 'realise that I do have something beneficial to bring to the MDT even as a student'. The reference to 'even as a student' here is testament to her acknowledgement of her own identity as a learner in this context but with the awareness that she is still offering value to the service and clients she is interacting with. The social interaction that clinical placement brings was seen as a 'stepping stone' to 'inhabiting' the AHP role for another student (SLT-Mal16), who concluded that:

Extract 7.29

Once I stopped looking at it as a class and started believing I could really do this as my job, I felt that I really inhabited my role. **(SLT-Mal16)**

7.3.2 NON-VERBAL COMMUNICATION-FOCUSED STRATEGIES

There were several non-verbal communication strategies that helped the students over that line of 'pretending' to feeling like and accepting being an AHP in education. These strategies are summarised in Table 7.3.

Some of the non-verbal strategies that seemed to aid this process included observation, practice and being given some independence. Practice both within the clinical world and outside of it was key for some (e.g. SLT-Ire2; SLT-US27), as in:

Extract 7.30

Repeated experience in a similar clinical setting with a similar clinical population! ... My experience outside clinical practice (part-time job and volunteer work) has allowed me to utilise clinical skills in a non-clinical setting to gain more confidence in these skills. **(SLT-Ire2)**

Being given some sense of independence was also key to some students, well reflected by this comment from an OT student:

Extract 7.31

`I think definitely being trusted to work on my own projects and seeing the benefit that they have had on clients has helped me to cross that line.` **(OT-Ire40)**

Another OT student explained that 'once the supervisor stopped overstepping me in sessions', they became more confident and able to inhabit the role of AHP student (OT-Ire35). How a supervisor interacts with a student seems to be of importance here in building or inhibiting confidence to develop while learning. In fact, supportive supervisors were reported by many students to be a key ingredient that helped them to move on and leave the need to 'pretend' behind. Some of the key characteristics of such supportive supervisors as shared by students are provided in Table 7.4.

'Good' relationships with a supervisor allowed positive interactions to take place which where conducive to moving on and becoming that AHP student, as one student pointed out:

Extract 7.32

`[Having a] good relationship with my clinical supervisor and not feeling inferior or scared of doing something wrong. When my clinical supervisor treated me as a healthcare professional and was approachable for any concerns or questions that I might have. That is where you feel responsible and capable of doing things.` **(OT-Mal31)**

Interacting with a student in an approachable, supportive and sympathetic way was important to students, helping them to move on in a positive, more confident way, and thereby reducing the need to 'fake it' on clinical practice placements.

Finally, along with supportive supervisors, other students also found confidence in themselves as they recognised how their personal and professional experiences could be mutually beneficial. For some, there was less need 'to fake it' when they realised that they could transfer that which has been learnt or experienced through interactions with the outside world and apply that learning to the clinical world. In other words, the personal and professional lives of the students were overlapping

Table 7.4 Supportive characteristics of supervisors deemed important by students

	Examples
Characteristics of supportive supervisors/mentors	'Approachable' (OT-Mal31)
	'Sympathetic' (OT-Mal32)
	'Allow mistakes to be made as part of learning process' (SLT-SA45)
	'Giving good advice' (OT-Mal31)
	'Offering (explicit) praise' (OT-Mal30; SLT-Ire2)

in positive ways in terms of confidence building. This acknowledgement that they themselves are not 'blank slates' and can transfer learning was a positive observation by many of the participants. For example, the confident statements from this SLT student (SLT-Mal13) (partially referenced earlier in Extract 7.15) is a case in point:

Extract 7.33

I feel like I do not have to pretend to be anyone else, as I like interacting with people. I think working as a playworker in an after-school club gave me adequate skills of preparation for placements in my formation to become a capable allied health professional. **(SLT-Mal13)**

Moreover, socially interacting with their colleagues and getting to know them on a more personal level was helpful for others in gaining that confidence as a student. Being aware of the need to 'push on' together as 'allies' allowed this student (SLT-SA44) (partially referenced earlier in Extract 7.10) to feel more comfortable 'personally' and 'professionally':

Extract 7.34

We fake it till we make it - in all professions, inclusive of our allies. We simply just try to keep pushing on till we feel comfortable and have the knowledge. It's the only way to do it. Getting to know allies on a personal level is greatly beneficial. It has helped me feel more personally comfortable, as well as professionally comfortable - knowing that not everyone knows everything, and that we are there to assist one another and grow one another's knowledge. **(SLT-SA44)**

Being 'there to assist one another and grow one another's knowledge' speaks to the acceptance of close working relationships with fellow students and colleagues.

7.4 SUMMARY

This chapter considered the students' responses to questions on our survey which probed the concept of 'pretending' as part of the behaviour of AHP students in teaching and learning contexts. The personal experiential themes capture the students' reported tendency to use pretending as necessary. They seemed to use pretending not just within the clinic but in the classroom, and not just with their supervisors but with their clients also, in a concerted effort to appear to be professional and knowing. Rather than viewing this 'pretending' in a negative light, it seems that in many cases pretending allowed the students to think themselves into the professional role, or 'fake it until they make it' as a couple of students commented. Pretending, then, in social interactions with supervisors, clients and others in teaching and learning contexts (including college-based contexts) seems to be an important part of the student experience, a tool in their toolbox to facilitate 'acting' and 'doing as' a professional; a certain amount of pretending seemed to also allow the students to grow in confidence. The data also show that verbal and non-verbal communication-focused strategies, along with supportive supervisors, all seemed to help the students mitigate their dependency on pretending and take on their professional role in a more authentic and confident manner.

8

SOCIAL INTERACTION IN FORMAL AND INFORMAL CONTEXTS OF TEACHING AND LEARNING IN ALLIED HEALTHCARE EDUCATION

Don't wait for the right opportunity: Create it.
George Bernard Shaw

8.1 INTRODUCTION

This chapter focuses on the contexts that students reported they found helpful in supporting their professional identity formation while engaging in programmes within allied healthcare education. In their responses to the survey, they reported that a mixture of formal and informal contexts of social interaction aided both their professional and personal development.

Before exploring the conceptual content of the students' responses, in terms of their experiential statements, it would be helpful to briefly outline the teaching and learning contexts that students may be exposed to in allied healthcare education (see also Chapter 2). Given the nature of most professions which are public and outward facing, teaching and learning activities that have social interaction at the core are characteristic of most programmes. Following a general overview of such contexts, consideration is given to models of pedagogy, particularly problem-based learning (PBL) which is popular in the disciplines that are the focus of this book: speech and language therapy; physiotherapy and occupational therapy. This chapter also focuses on the role social interaction plays in the said contexts of teaching and learning, given that social interaction is core to many aspects of healthcare education.

In the second part of this chapter, the focus will shift towards informal contexts of learning and life outside of the formal educational contexts of pedagogy. Life outside the bespoke educational contexts of allied healthcare programmes offers further opportunities for learning and growth, yet is often not acknowledged as part of the learning journey to becoming a healthcare professional. The student respondents to our survey recognised this learning, and their insights and observations will be reported upon in the latter part of this chapter.

8.2 TEACHING AND LEARNING IN HEALTHCARE EDUCATION CONTEXTS

8.2.1 CONTEXTS OF INTERACTION

Students of allied healthcare experience a wide and varied range of contexts for teaching and learning. From the classroom to the clinic room, from individual study to group work, all contexts contribute to the developing professional's acquisition of skills and competency development. In most of these contexts, social interaction is required as students navigate new learning in the classroom and on clinical placement. Clinical placements are usually organised in 'blocks' of time, such as when a student attends the clinic for one day a week, a block of six weeks or over more extended time periods (e.g. a number of months). On their learning journey, they interact with fellow students, supervisors, lecturers and clients or patients. As well as observing qualified professionals at work, students also 'learn by doing' not only in the clinical environment but also in the classroom, often employing simulated scenarios through role play of client interaction during skills workshops. Increasingly, students are also getting the opportunity to interact with 'real' clients or patients in the classroom as the drive towards 'public patient involvement' (PPI) in health education grows (e.g. see Dijk, Duijzer and Wienold 2020). PPI has also been incorporated into interprofessional learning contexts (Cooper and Spencer-Dawe 2006; Towle and Godolphin 2013). In PPI teaching and learning contexts, students get to interact with clients or patients in the 'safe' environment of the classroom, supported by peers and their mentors.

8.2.2 SOCIAL INTERACTION IN THE TEACHING AND LEARNING ENVIRONMENT

More than other programmes of study at undergraduate or postgraduate levels which may be single subject (e.g. English literature, history, chemistry, etc.), allied healthcare studies have at their core a significant requirement for explicit social interaction to take place throughout the course of study. Given that the allied healthcare graduate will directly interact with people, be they patients or other healthcare professionals, being able to socially interact with others is key to a successful professional career and delivery of healthcare. Although being able to successfully interact with others in professional contexts is a desired outcome of such programmes, many students must learn or hone these social interaction skills as they develop personally and professionally through their course of study. Moreover, many allied healthcare programmes introduce teaching and learning activities right from the start to induct students into group or paired learning where social interaction is both part of the learning process and the desired product of a specific learning activity. For example, in some speech and language therapy programmes, students in their first year are introduced to the 'Connect' programme first devised by The Communication Disability Network in the UK and widely written about and evaluated both in the UK and elsewhere (Simmons-Mackie 1998, 2000, 2001; Byng and Felson Duchan 2005;

Turner and Whitworth 2006; Jagoe and Roseingrave 2011). As part of a conversational partner scheme, students are introduced, in pairs, to a person with aphasia (a communication disability which frequently follows a stroke), who they then visit weekly in their own home across the academic year. The purpose of these visits is to provide the person with aphasia with opportunities for successful conversation (i.e. this is not formal therapeutic interaction), and to provide the students with the opportunity to learn about the lived experience of communication disability. These programmes have been found to be successful on several levels (e.g. Cameron et al. 2015; Cameron et al. 2017; Finch et al. 2017), not least in confidence building of the nascent student learner (Jagoe and Walsh 2016) (see also Chapter 3).

Healthcare education programmes may also foreground small group learning, as in many cases where problem-based learning (PBL) or enquiry-based learning (EBL) is adopted. PBL was developed initially in the 1960s at McMaster University in Canada as an innovative approach to medical education (Barrows and Tamblyn 1980). The dynamics of PBL are complex, but self-directed learning and teamwork are central to the teaching and learning philosophy (see Hmelo-Silver 2004; Clouston et al. 2010). In short, students work collaboratively in groups on a given problem, researching what they need to know to address the problem presented to them. PBL was initially adopted by medical curricula ahead of being extended to other areas of healthcare, including dentistry (e.g. see Bassir et al. 2014), nursing (Glen and Wilkie 2000) and other allied healthcare professions, for example, speech and language therapy (Whitehill, Bridges and Chan 2014; Erickson and Serry 2016), physiotherapy (Solomon 2005; Gunn, Hunter and Haas 2012) and occupational therapy (Scaffa and Wooster 2004; Bar et al. 2018).

Curricula delivered via PBL have been found to be highly effective across healthcare disciplines, whether a hybrid (i.e. mixed lecture-based input and PBL) or a more exclusive model (i.e. PBL-only) is implemented (Fincham and Schuler 2001). A recent review by Hallinger (2021) confirms PBL's ever-growing place in educational contexts, suggesting that the bibliometric review undertaken 'identified the accumulation of a substantial interdisciplinary corpus of research on PBL that is significantly larger than the literature on other approaches to active learning', with a marked growth evident within the last decade (2010–19). Dring (2019) calls for the early introduction of PBL in medical training, having experienced it first-hand. Graduates in speech and language therapy programmes have favoured PBL over traditional forms of pedagogy, and especially in the development of clinical skills (Erickson and Serry 2016, 2020). That group interaction can be described as the 'crucible' of social identity formation (Thomas, McGarty and Mavor 2016) is relevant here, and can extend beyond to PBL contexts – small group meetings, tutorials and a wide range of formal and informal contexts of teaching and learning – where students come together in the educational context.

8.2.3 CONTEXTS OF LEARNING: FORMAL AND INFORMAL

The previous sections have referred to many contexts and means of teaching and learning for the allied healthcare professional (AHP) student. The lines between 'formal' and 'informal' contexts of learning can be blurred given the amount and diversity of the student experience. However, 'formal' contexts of learning in general may refer to lectures, tutorials and guided workshops, for example, where teaching is systematic, organised and structured. Informal contexts of learning might include one-to-one tutorials, small group meetings, or student-led or initiated activities, for example.

The acquisition of tacit knowledge is important here – where and how do students learn outside of these contexts, and what do they learn? Hayes et al. (2018: 84) discuss the concept of tacit knowledge in the context of healthcare assistants, defining this knowledge as:

> the intuitive knowledge that is not easy to articulate through dialogue or rational justification in the context of healthcare provision. It depends on a level of sensory awareness or feeling that transcends the need for formalised knowledge in terms of its potential impact on practice ... Tacit knowledge cannot be readily articulated, but its implementation in practice lies at the heart of every human interaction.

However, students' learning is not restricted to the confines of the college, clinic or university campus. Students continue to learn and personally develop outside of these contexts as they socialise with friends, undertake part-time work and care for family, for example. How this learning in other contexts influences their professional development is not lost on students, as the discussion in this chapter will show.

The concept of 'borderlands' may be useful to invoke here as that space between the so-called formal context of learning – that is, the university-led and clinic-focused contexts of teaching and learning – and that which happens at the 'edges' of these worlds at home and in other socio-personal contexts of interaction. What happens in the borderlands brings its own influence to bear on the student professional. Kovarsky and Walsh (2018), and others, have used this term to apply to the client or patient experience navigating the two worlds of life experiences and institutional (or clinic) experiences. Additionally, Mishler (1984) in his highly influential work published as *The Discourse of Medicine: Dialectics of Medical Interviews* uses the term 'lifeworld' in his discussions of medical discourse between doctors and patients. He specifically uses the notion of the 'the voice of medicine' as an institutional voice that often dominates or controls such interactions, and discusses how the 'voice of the lifeworld' of the patient may be inadvertently silenced or at least backgrounded in the pursuit of medical goals. The idea of the 'lifeworld' is also useful here to help conceptualise the world(s) that the student AHP inhabits. Naming these lifeworlds for the purposes of this chapter, as the 'education lifeworld' (i.e. university and clinic-based student learning experiences) and their 'socio-personal lifeworld' (e.g. family/ social/ personal learning experiences), helps in the discussion to follow. Borderlands, then, can be envisaged as the learning and overlapping psychological spaces of those lifeworlds where integration of learning experiences happens and impacts the AHP student's worlds of social interactions. In Figure 8.1, each set of circles may represent a sphere of learning experience, be that within the 'education-lifeworld' or in the 'socio-personal lifeworld', with these worlds constantly overlapping and intermingling against the backdrop of the borderlands between these worlds.

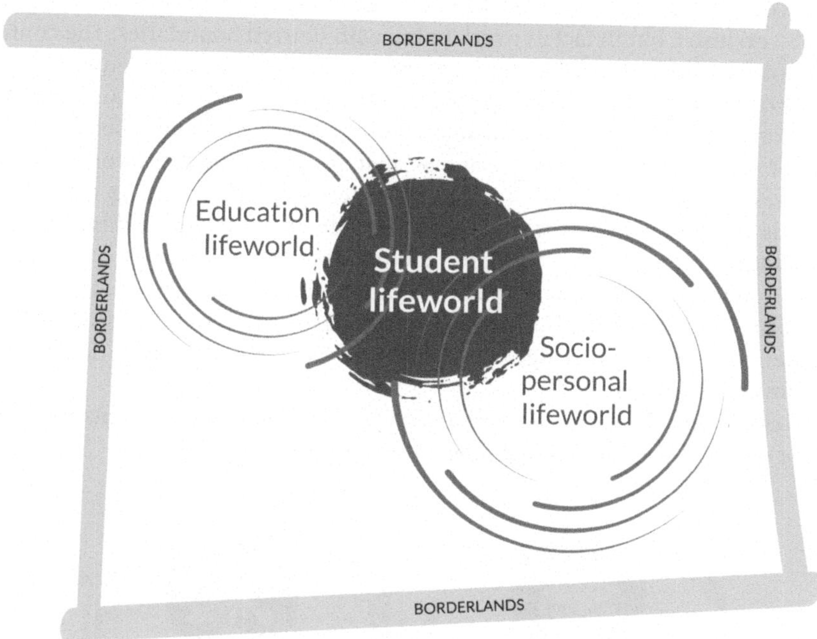

Figure 8.1 The borderlands and spheres of overlapping learning experiences within the student lifeworld and the socio-personal lifeworld of the AHP student

8.3 CONTEXTS OF TEACHING AND LEARNING: WHAT THE DATA TELL US

It is not hard to see, therefore, how contextual factors may affect, influence and shape one's professional identity (Clarke, Hyde and Drennan 2013) that affect, influence and shape one's professional identity. The contextual factors are of interest here as we explore the conceptual content of responses to the following questions (Table 6.5; Q1 and Q2):

- What aspects of your university course, or clinical placement, have you found to be particularly valuable in supporting the formation of your professional identity, and in nurturing your personal growth?
- Thinking about your study or work in your life outside allied healthcare, can you think of any experiences or relationships that have influenced the formation of your professional identity?

The responses to these survey questions suggest that students found an array of experiences valuable in supporting their professional identity and in nurturing their personal growth. The student responses reference both formal and informal contexts of social interaction in teaching and learning. These contexts are not seen as mutually exclusive but in fact as overlapping with blurred boundaries. The contexts are discussed below as 'formal' and 'informal', loosely tied to the environmental contexts of social interaction taking place in the university, the clinic and outside of it (e.g. home life). However, discussing them in this way should not belie the interaction of the lifeworlds discussed above, that is, the 'student lifeworld' and the 'socio-personal lifeworld'. Rather, contexts of learning are occurring within these lifeworlds and are defined by them, a point we will return to later in this chapter via informal learning contexts. Wortham (2006) and others have explored a 'learning identity' among students where there is a mutual interdependence between social identification and academic learning; such fusions belie the complexity of the learning experience yet acknowledge the richness of the student's navigation between and across their worlds

The remainder of this chapter will discuss the experiential statements that informed the two personal experiential themes outlined in Figure 8.2.

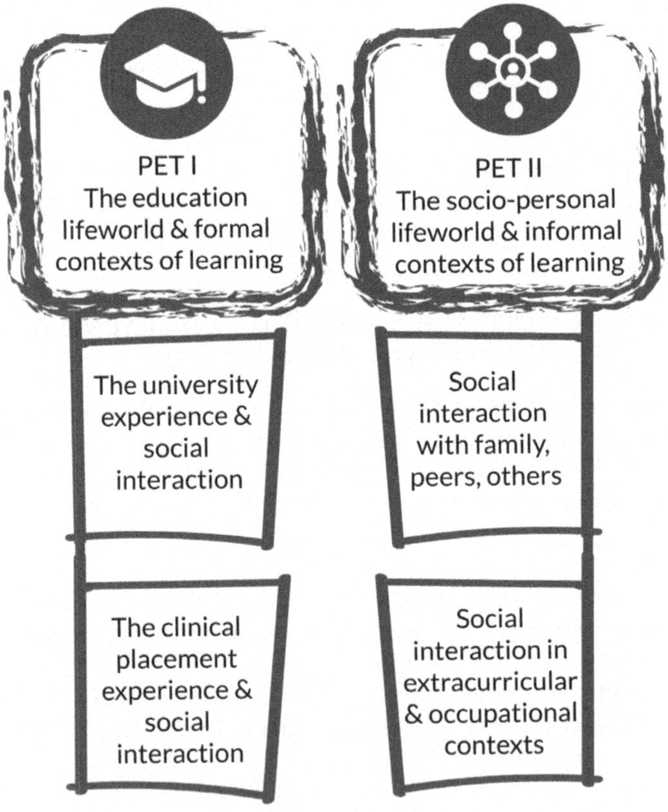

Figure 8.2 The personal experiential themes and summary of associated experiential statements

The experiential statements associated with the personal experiential themes, in the order which they are presented in this chapter, are presented in Table 8.1.

Table 8.1 Personal experiential themes related to social interaction in formal and informal contexts of teaching and learning and associated experiential statements

Personal Experiential Themes	Associated Experiential Statements
The education lifeworld and formal contexts of learning	The university experience and social interaction The clinical placement experience and social interaction • Social interaction with clients • Clinical exposure as a learning experience in the clinical context • Supervision, mentoring and the feedback process
The socio-personal lifeworld and informal contexts of learning	Social interaction with family, peers, others Social interaction in extra-curricular and occupational contexts

8.3.1 THE EDUCATION LIFEWORLD AND FORMAL CONTEXTS OF LEARNING

An experiential statement which informs this first personal experiential theme is 'the university experience and social interaction'. It comes as no surprise that the university experience is an enlightening one for many students in both their personal and professional development, influencing their identity in significant ways. For many students, the university context opens up a whole new world of experiences of teaching and learning. Below are some interpretations of responses to the survey that have been identified as experiential statements to inform the overall personal experiential theme of the 'education lifeworld' and how they inform a developing sense of professional identity and personal growth.

The experiential statements suggest that the formal contexts of learning within the students' lifeworlds were naturally considered critical to their identity development. The physical environment or 'infrastructure' of the university seemed key for some, along with 'the library' (PT-In22). The formal experience of completing a master's thesis (SLT-US25) and the opportunity to engage in research (PT-In22) were referred to by a speech and language therapy (SLT) and physiotherapy (PT) student, respectively, in helping to develop their professional identity. 'All of the coursework' (PT-US10) was a factor mentioned by another PT student along with clinical practicum:

Extract 8.1

All of the coursework and clinical placements have helped me develop professional identity and professional growth. Clinical placements and courses about healthcare issues and PT management has helped me contextualise my professional identity in the larger healthcare system. **(PT-US10)**

For this student, the fusion of both the academic and clinical experience was important, as it is for others in this discipline (PT-US14). Of interest also in the above response is the reference to that identity being framed within 'the larger healthcare system' and not tied to their specific discipline, in this case physiotherapy (PT-US10). Others, for example, an SLT student (SLT-Ire34), mentioned the gains made by maintaining a professional development log (PDL). Maintaining a PDL requires students to systematically reflect on their learning and its impact on their personal and professional development (reflective practice will be further discussed below).

Being exposed to many other viewpoints while learning was significant for some (e.g. SLT-Mal6), along with 'the opportunity for a broadening experience' as noted by others (PT-US14). Part of this wider experience was the experience of interprofessional learning, which in the form of classes and seminars was seen as important for several of the respondents (e.g. PT-US9, OT-Ire35 and OT-Ire37), not least in understanding their own emerging identities while being afforded the opportunity to consider that identity against a backdrop of other student professionals. As discussed in Chapter 3, interprofessional learning offers a unique opportunity for students to socially interact and mix with other student professionals while they are learning. For some, these formal contexts of interprofessional learning may be the first time they meet other AHP students in the learning and teaching environment.

Explicitly addressing issues of professionalism helped other students during their programme of study. For example, an occupational therapy (OT) student referred to the explicit and formal focus in the final year on 'professional issues' and the 'emerging roles' of their profession: 'Final year units about professional issues, leadership & [sic]management and also a unit about emerging roles in occupational therapy' (OT-Mal31). The extent to which this student's 'unit' covered professional identity development specifically though is not known. Trede, Macklin and Bridges (2012) conducted a systematic review to ascertain the focus of professional identity development in higher education contexts, and although theories and pedagogical approaches were discussed in the 20 articles that met the review criteria, there was a lack of a clear link to professional identity formation in the studies identified.

Finally, within this consideration of the formal context of learning as an influence on developing identity, the direct influence of students' lecturers, supervisors or professors seemed key for many (PT-In22; SLT-US26; SLT-US27; SLT-SA45). Significant is one SLT student's reflection on how the impact of 'one caring professor' was important (SLT-US26) to her. Another student's (SLT-US27) response from the same profession further explicates this point:

Extract 8.2

I formed close relationships with many of my professors and employers who have treated me with respect and valued me as an equal. When my opinion is asked for and is received with respect, I feel more like a professional in my field and less like a student. **(SLT-US27)**

It is interesting to note here the repetition of, and hence emphasis on, 'respect' and how being treated with respect helped this student to feel 'more like a professional'. Such reflections underscore the importance of the behaviour of those in the position of teaching roles. Appropriate role modelling and leading by example by those responsible for teaching and learning in allied healthcare education is consequential. Paice, Heard and Moss (2002: 707) define role models as 'people we can identify with, who have qualities we would like to have, and are in positions we would like to reach'. Both SLT student responses above (SLT-US26; SLT-US27) suggest that experiencing both care and respect is critical in students' own identity formation, particularly as related to the kind of professional they may aspire to be themselves. There seems to be a growing body of literature on this topic, particularly in medicine (e.g. Bazrafkan et al. 2019; Mohammadi et al. 2020). Mohammadi et al. (2020) conducted a narrative literature review in the area to ascertain what might make a good role model, as it is not a 'given' that those involved in education fulfil that role (see, for example, a case report on the impact of poor role modelling in medical education, as reported by Mileder, Schmidt and Dimai 2014). Their review included papers which mostly focused on the education of medical students and medical residents, with fewer studies focusing on nursing and clinical teachers or faculty members. The core ingredients of a desirable role model seemed to fall into the following categories: teaching skills, clinical skills and personal/interpersonal qualities. The authors of this review suggest ways that clinical tutors may improve their role modelling, ideas which can easily be applied to other healthcare professions. Key to this improvement is the enhancement of the tutor's awareness of how their role may be having an impact on the professional identity formation of their students.

'The clinical placement experience and social interaction' is another experiential theme which informs the personal experiential statement of 'the education lifeworld and formal contexts of learning'. The students who responded to the survey were fulsome in their reference to the influence of their clinical placements on their personal and professional identity. The 'clinical space' seems to be both the physical and psychological space where development is perceived to accelerate according to the students' reported experiences. 'Clinical exposure' was reported by many students across the allied healthcare disciplines as helping them to form their professional identity (PT-In28; SLT-In12; PT-In21; PT-In22). As discussed elsewhere in this text, clinical exposure by its very nature involves a high degree of social interaction with clients, supervisors and multidisciplinary team members.

Within the theme of 'social interaction with clients' (Table 8.1), the students reported that interacting with clients was significant to them as they progressed through their course of study in allied healthcare education (e.g. SLT-Mal8; SLT-Mal13; PT-In23). One SLT student (SLT-Ire3) commented that:

Extract 8.3

`Meeting clients and hearing their experiences and any positive feedback they have for you on your interactions with them helps you` `grow in confidence and understand why being a health professional is important and what it can really mean for people.` **(SLT-Ire3)**

This student seemed to suggest that the response of clients ('any positive feedback') is important in developing a sense of professional identity. Such client feedback for this student seemed to help her understand the importance of being a healthcare professional and how one may be viewed by the healthcare recipient. Others referenced how meeting a range of clients with different presentations helped them in professional identity formation. An OT student reflected that direct contact with clients who 'all have a different experience of their injury/condition' contributed to identity formation (OT-Mal30). Being exposed to a wide range of age groups was also seen as key to this development:

Extract 8.4

`We are exposed to a range of disorders across multiple ages from *NICU to geriatrics. This allows one to determine where they are happiest working/with what population etc. etc.` **(SLT-SA44)** **neonatal intensive care unit*

Of interest here is the student's realisation that such wide-ranging exposure helps students to decide what clinical population they may be 'happiest working with'. Such realisations may indirectly inform their identity formation as that of a clinician who works primarily with children or one who works with adults, for example. Given that 'exposure' was a concept that many students referenced, it is useful to look more closely at the importance of this for the student professional in clinical contexts.

Within the subtheme of 'clinical exposure as a learning experience in the clinical context', several students specifically referenced 'exposure' as a factor which helped them in their professional identity formation. Exposure within the university, and even more so in the clinical context, seems important for the student learner. For example, one student reported that being made aware of 'different views to therapy' helped him/her (SLT-FU-Ma6), while others cited that specifically 'clinical exposure' (SLT-In12; PT-In21; PT-In22) was a key factor in their professional development. From a simple statement of referencing that such exposure is 'good' (i.e. 'clinical exposure is good' (SLT-In12)) to the more considered response of explaining how such exposure bridges the gap between the more formal contexts of learning (e.g. 'classroom' or 'practicals') and the clinical world, it seems that being 'exposed' to real clients in the real world is significant for many student learners. A PT student summarised this point well in their response: 'The clinical exposure that we receive is invaluable as our learning is not restricted to classroom or the practicals' (PT-In28). Many others referenced the usefulness of clinical placements and practical sessions in general and as linked to professional identity formation. For example, a physiotherapy student (PT-US10) explained how their clinical placements helped in the contextualisation of their identity against the backdrop of the healthcare system as a whole (see Extract 8.1 above).

Other students, such as SLT-US24, referenced the exposure 'outside' of the university setting as being beneficial. This SLT student was perhaps alluding to the experience of the 'college clinic' (i.e. when the clinic is conducted on site at the university), as compared to those clinical placements that may be experienced within the community, in schools or medical centres, for example. Likewise, being exposed to a wide variety of placements was valued by others (e.g. SLT-SA44), especially over the course of study 'to explore interests' and when given the 'opportunity':

Extract 8.5

`Being provided with ample opportunity to develop skills in specific areas and being given the opportunity to explore your interests by being placed in a number of clinical placement settings over the course of the degree.` **(SLT-SA43)**

Others mentioned specific areas of practice where they felt important identity work was happening for them (e.g. in 'paediatrics'; PT-In15). 'Responsibility' and 'ownership' were important for an OT student in their professional identity formation (OT-Mal31), as part of their clinical exposure in the final years of training. 'Ownership' was a salient issue for many students according to the responses and hence will be revisited in more detail in Chapter 9.

Finally, exposure to, and social interaction with, other professionals was a key theme identified in the data from the respondents on the question of what aided their professional identity formation and personal growth. As already discussed, there was learning to be experienced from others in the clinical setting, be they clients or supervisors. However, the respondents (e.g. PT-In23) also specifically referenced other professionals on the multidisciplinary team (MDT) and being able to 'work as a team'. In fact, MDT working was seen as a positive experience for many and valuable to their development. From liaising with different professionals (OT-Mal32; OT-Mal33) to recognising the similarities and differences of roles, MDT exposure seemed to aid the students to develop a sense of their own identity:

Extract 8.6

`Clinical placements where there have been MDTs and there is a good understanding of each other's roles even if there are overlaps at times.` **(OT-Ire42)**

Being able to critically recognise and respect areas of overlap, while respecting discipline-specific expertise, was pertinent for some. (The reader is referred to Chapter 4 in this book for further consideration of critical reflection on role and identity in MDT settings.)

Within the experiential statement of 'supervision, mentoring and the feedback process' (Table 8.1), the students talked of the key role that their supervisors played in their clinical experiences and how feedback and the mentoring process were key to their learning. Snowdon et al. (2020) explored AHPs' perceptions of clinical supervision and what contributes to and facilitates the efficacy of the supervisory process. In-depth interviews across hospital-based allied healthcare professions, including, speech and language therapy, occupational therapy, physiotherapy, dietetics, podiatry, social work and psychology, were conducted. A qualitative analysis of the data from 38 interviews identified three main themes that were key to effective supervision: (i) that the focus of the supervision was on professional development; (ii) that the supervisor was skilled in supervision, possessing the attributes necessary for a relationship that was constructive; and (iii) that the organisation supported the supervisory relationship by providing the right environment for the support of professional development. Although Snowdon et al.'s (2020) study focused on the perceptions of qualified professionals in the workplace, the above themes were echoed to some extent in the AHP student responses in our own study, where the importance of supervisor feedback and mentoring was referenced (e.g. PT-Mal29; SLT-SA45).

Firstly, providing the right supervisory environment seemed to be important for some of the students in our survey. This supervisory experience not only applied to the clinical environment but also the institutional environment of the programme of study, as described by this PT student:

Extract 8.7

Our programme encourages its students to step out of their comfort zone and take on experiences that they might not have taken on before. By doing this, we are able to grow as students and professionals. It challenges us to learn more about our profession and become advocates for our profession so that we can be active participants in the growth of the profession. **(PT-US11)**

Being encouraged to 'step out of' their 'comfort zone' for this student was pivotal to them becoming a professional and an advocate for the profession. Another aspect of the environment that seemed to matter to students was being given the chance to work independently (OT-Ire39; SLT-Mal5) with follow-up feedback from a student's supervisor (SLT-Mal5) to help evaluate that independently led clinical session. Being afforded some degree of 'independence', then, was viewed as central for these student learners.

Secondly, the idea of 'constructive' feedback was critical to supervision for others, as part of the learning journey and contributing to professional identity formation. One SLT student (SLT-Ire4) referenced 'specific and constructive feedback' as being key to this development, and as part of the process of personal and professional growth. This student explained in their response that 'the gradual transition from the role of clinical observer to clinical implementer, followed by specific and constructive criticism from practice educators' (SLT-Ire4) was helpful. Perhaps part of this constructive feedback for others was being allowed to be themselves and to develop their own professional identity (e.g. reflected in the following comment by an OT student: 'The allowance from supervisors to create my own professional identity by modelling from their behaviours' (OT-Ire38)). For another, 'close supervision' was key (OT-Ire40), which enabled identification of the student's learning needs in practising their 'skill of identifying ... own strengths and weaknesses'.

Of relevance here is Quigley's (2021) discussion of the notion of 'feedback literacy', which enables consideration of how learners 'take' the feedback provided to them, that is, 'feedback literacy' enables the receiver's perception of feedback to come to the fore, be examined more closely and optimised to support enhanced student performance and competency development (Quigley 2021: 1121). Supporting AHP students to develop their 'feedback literacy', in other words to make the most of the feedback received, and to use it in a positive constructive way is, according to Quigley, a worthwhile 'investment' to support the student's learning and ongoing development of reflective practice. This need to reflect on experiences and learning was acknowledged by some respondents as beneficial to their development. The maintenance of a professional development log (PDL) was referred to by some students as helpful (as referred to earlier in this chapter). For another OT student, 'daily reflections' (OT-Ire38) were important, while another recognised the need to reflect on many different aspects of their learning activities and at different points on the learning journey:

Extract 8.8

`Reflection post a clinical activity, e.g. client session, MDT [multidisciplinary team] meeting, CPD [continuing professional identity] activity; and at the end of a clinical block placement.` **(SLT-Ire2)**

We have discussed the importance and significance of reflective practice in Chapter 6 (Section 6.4) in both healthcare education and practice, and we will revisit this practice in Chapter 10. As we discussed previously, many have written on the subject, including Kinsella et al. (2012) who provide an excellent overview of the concept, including case studies of AHPs – the fact that the authors themselves come from a multidisciplinary group (i.e. a speech and language therapist, an occupational therapist, an audiologist and a registered nurse) lends further credence to their discussion.

To summarise thus far, and as stated at the outset of this chapter, social interaction is a common characteristic of the formal and informal teaching and learning contexts in almost all allied healthcare programmes, given the nature of the public-facing professions at the core of such programmes. Students reported that they value opportunities to engage in college-based simulated interactions and clinic-based real-world interactions with supervisors, clients and families and other healthcare professionals. Many students acknowledged the learning that takes place in these contexts and the potential impact on their developing identity, from a personal and professional perspective. Others recognised that the impact on their professional development and identity is time-sensitive and is salient at earlier or later stages of their educational journey. Finally, reflecting on feedback and guidance across teaching and learning contexts is a developing skill that students found constructive in their development as a professional.

8.3.2 THE SOCIO-PERSONAL LIFEWORLD AND INFORMAL CONTEXTS OF LEARNING

Below are some interpretations of responses to the survey that have been identified as experiential statements which inform the overall personal experiential theme of 'the socio-personal lifeworld'. Educators in allied healthcare and other contexts have long recognised that all learning does not happen solely in the institutional environments of university and placement sites. Learning is part of life, and life outside formal teaching and learning contexts offers many opportunities to maximise an individual's personal and professional development and growth, influencing their identity formation in interesting ways. Students who responded to the survey, and specifically to the following question (Q2, Table 6.5), recognised this point, as we will show.

- Thinking about your study or work in your life outside allied healthcare, can you think of any experiences or relationships that have influenced the formation of your professional identity?

As detailed in Table 8.1, the personal experiential theme of 'the socio-personal lifeworld and informal contexts of learning' includes the following experiential statements:

1. Social interaction with family, peers, others
2. Social interaction in extra-curricular and occupational contexts

High on the list of experiences or relationships having an influence on students' developing identities seemed to be, perhaps unsurprisingly, the influence and support of family and significant others, captured within the experiential statement of 'social interaction with family, peers, others'. Interacting with family members across the generations seemed key for many. Parents figured high in this context, with other family members also being cited as being constructive in the student's life and identity formation. These 'pre-existing relationships' were recognised by SLT-Ire4 as being significant:

Extract 8.9

Pre-existing relationships with people of significance (across the lifespan), for example, younger siblings, grandparents, friends and so on, provided a foundation on which to base a professional identity. **(SLT-Ire4)**

The analogy of family providing 'a foundation' for that identity to be built upon was echoed by another student who mentioned her father as being pivotal to their development (PT-In22: 'my dad has been the biggest influence of what I am today'). Other respondents recognised the influence of older family members in how they view older clients in their clinical practice. For example, one SLT student (ST-Mal16) cited that 'experiences with elderly members of my family have definitely shaped the way I uphold adult clients'. Likewise, students (e.g. SLT-Mal7) also referenced how their identity as a future AHP may have been influenced by having experience of family members who may have been affected by neurological conditions such as dementia and stroke, or having to access healthcare services through family members (e.g. 'I believe that what mostly influenced me was the ability to observe closely the results of occupational therapy treatment from a young age where a family member was receiving occupational therapy services' (OT-Mal30)). Growing up 'in a family of healthcare professionals' (SLT-SA45) and the influence of a particular 'professor in school' explaining '... whatever I am today I owe it to him …' (PT-In22) were other influences that students cited.

Related to this close social network of family referenced by students was the consideration of the influence of friends and peers. For one SLT student (SLT-Ire3), college friends have been significant in their professional identity formation:

Extract 8.10

My friends from college have been one of the main influencing factors in the development of my professional identity. Through our discussions about our experiences and challenges over the past four years we have shared a variety of perspectives on what it means to be an SLT. **(SLT-Ire3)**

This student explained that it was through social interaction with her friends, via discussions and sharing of 'a variety of perspectives', that allowed her to realise 'what it means to be an SLT'. Explicit discussion of their experiences, including the 'challenges', seemed to help this student realise an identity as a future speech and language therapist. Another student (i.e. SLT-SA44), also referenced peers, both in college, via a mentorship programme, and later 'friends in allied professions':

Extract 8.11

When I was in first year, I had a third-year buddy who absolutely shaped me as a therapist. I was also lucky enough to have friends in allied professions - who helped me link things more coherently and develop interests in alternate areas. **(SLT-SA44)**

Of interest in this response is the use of the phrase 'absolutely shaped me', adding significance and emphasis to the experience of how interacting with a 'buddy' helped in identity formation. Moreover, still valuing the influence of others, this respondent also explained that they were 'lucky enough' to have friends in allied healthcare fields, adding further weight to their social experiences outside of college and their impact. Likewise, for another SLT student (SLT-Ire34), interacting with other professionals in their daily life was seen as beneficial, prompted by reflecting on aspects of the social interactions with them in daily life:

Extract 8.12

I feel that interactions with other healthcare professionals (outside of the college context) have influenced my professional identity. I feel that on a subconscious level, I reflected on the interactions I had when attending other healthcare professionals, e.g. attending a doctor's appointment or a session with a physiotherapist. I feel that I reflected upon the positive aspects of the interaction and tried to reflect on what specifically made the interactions positive. I then tried to bring this forward to my own professional work as a student clinician. **(SLT-Ire34)**

The student had the realisation that such reflection may be 'subconscious' and part of their learning outside of college contexts. At the same time, being able to apply that learning to their 'own professional work as a student clinician' is indicative of a reflective process at work, which perhaps would not be articulated if a prompt (such as a survey question in this case) was not given. It seems then that explicitly naming people and experiences that have influenced identity is part of identity formation, and that recognising and acknowledging that other experiences outside of college have an impact is in and of itself part of the identity formation process.

Within the experiential statement of 'social interaction in extra-curricular and occupational contexts' (Table 8.1), the student responses showed how interacting with others outside of the college or clinic context was significant in terms of their developing identity and personal development. Two specific contexts of interaction where it seems such influences on identity formation were evident for the students are their employment or work activities (i.e. the part-time job sector) and/or the volunteering sphere.

Firstly, within the part-time job context, the reported experiences which are salient to the students' developing sense of identity fall into two contexts: (i) part-time work within healthcare environments while still a student and (ii) working with the public in other sectors. In terms of working in healthcare, for a couple of SLT students, working as 'playworkers' in after-school clubs was reportedly helpful (SLT-Mal5; ST-Mal13), while for an OT student, 'working in similar healthcare area as a part-time job' seemed to support identity development (OT-Ire39). Another OT student (OT-Ire36) explained how her work outside the college context as a care assistant was a 'key aspect' of her developing professional identity:

Extract 8.13

I work part time as a care assistant and this has helped me to gain experience and form collaborative relationships with my clients, all of which are skills I hope to use as an occupational therapist. The key component is to remain client centred at all times and through this job I believe I have developed that skill and it's a key aspect of my professional identity as an OT student. **(OT-Ire36)**

Once again, the naming of the social interaction experiences and the explicit recognition of transferable skills (as in this case) seemed – at least for some students – to aid their professional development in interesting ways (e.g. remaining 'client centred').

Outside of healthcare environments, students referenced their work with the public in service contexts as also being important for them. For example, for a SLT student, 'working as a sales assistant' (SLT-Mal5) was beneficial, while an OT student (OT-Ire41) explained that working in 'customer service – constantly interacting with people and working as part of a team helped me to develop professionally'. Recognising being able to engage in teamwork as a transferable skill was also acknowledged by this respondent. Still other respondents recognised how their part-time work in contexts unrelated to healthcare benefited their sense of identity. An OT student (OT-Ire42) working in 'facilities management and the environment' recognised how their experiences were part of their identity, prompting an application to undertake a course in occupational therapy:

Extract 8.14

I have previous work experience in facilities management and the environment and how it could be adapted to suit the employees who worked there who had a variety of needs (e.g. lactating mothers needed a nursing room, Muslim employees needed a prayer room during the workday, physically disabled employees needed accommodations made to enable them universal access, etc.). This experience helped to develop my interest in OT and why I applied for the course and it is part of my identity. **(OT-Ire42)**

Responding to employees' 'variety of needs' was important for this respondent and helped inform an interest in OT. Moreover, this student recognised that she was bringing an 'identity' to her education within her chosen discipline (i.e. 'it is part of my identity').

In addition to the referencing of part-time job contexts, which seemed to influence the students' developing professional identity and personal growth, volunteering also seemed to have had its own effects. Students from across the disciplines cited their voluntary work (PT-In23; PT-Mal29) and 'volunteering opportunities' (OT-Ire35) as being helpful, including 'relationships with supervisors on and off campus' (ST-US24) being beneficial to them. Being proactive in 'organising or carrying out volunteering and different college committee work' (PT-In23) allowed a PT student to interact with others in different and constructive ways outside of the formal educational or part-time job contexts. Moreover, an OT student noted that 'applying my occupational therapy knowledge to my volunteer work and actually being able to contribute to voluntary organisations makes people value my professional identity' (OT-Mal31), acknowledging the dynamic, two-way nature of identity work, with one context of learning and experience informing the other

Finally, the respondents also cited and acknowledged personal experiences as helping to contribute to their developing professional identities and growth. Experiences of travel helped one of the SLT students 'to see the world in a more diverse light' (SLT-Mal16), while a sense of one's own level of maturity (PT-In20) was cited by a PT student to be beneficial. Other students referenced their previous tertiary-level educational experiences (PT-US10; SLT-US25) as having a constructive influence on their developing identities. Relationships and social interaction within extra-curricular activities such as sports (PT-US9) and 'being a girl guide leader' (OT-Mal31) supported others in physio- and occupational therapy, respectively. Hence, the dynamic nature of identity formation seems relevant here, where different life experiences impact personal growth and development. This idea was aptly summarised by one OT student (OT-Ire38) in the comment 'the relationship that I have with many people with disabilities in my daily life allows me to use these interactions within my practice'.

It seems important, therefore, that students coming into college get the opportunity to explicitly cite, share and discuss their lives and activities outside of college to help them acknowledge and recognise the identities they are bringing to the educational and professional context. This dynamic nature of identity was discussed in Chapter 2 (Section 2.3.3) and is clearly exemplified in this chapter in the students' responses.

8.4 SUMMARY

This chapter focused on the formal and informal contexts of teaching and learning that students, across the allied healthcare disciplines concerned, reported as contributing to their developing AHP identity and their ongoing personal growth. Formal and informal contexts were understood as not only referring to the physical environments (e.g. college, clinic or workplace) where social interaction takes place but to the nature of those social interactions in a diverse range of milieus (e.g. in interactions with supervisors, professors, managers, family and peers). The respondents acknowledged this diversity of environments and experiences, recognising the learning and development as a cumulative or collective attainment in the burgeoning growth of their professional identity. The notion of 'borderlands' was invoked to name those contexts or psychological 'spaces' where overlapping experiential contexts occur and seem to have a constructive influence on identity formation and personal growth.

Such recognition and acknowledgement of this development by respondents suggests that explicit reference to the influences on prior and current identity development should find their way into curricular activities. Explicit reference to this tacit development may help students to further reflect, critically evaluate and 'own' their developing identity and personal growth. The next chapter focuses on this 'owning' as a phenomenon in professional identity formation.

9
OWNING PROFESSIONAL IDENTITY IN ALLIED HEALTHCARE EDUCATION

Be yourself; Everybody else is taken.
Oscar Wilde

9.1 INTRODUCTION

In Chapter 8, we discussed how varying contexts of social interaction can influence and help shape the allied healthcare professional (AHP) student's professional identity. Specifically, we discussed how both formal and informal contexts of social interaction have a bearing on professional identity formation. We also considered how activities and relationships outside of the teaching and learning environments contributed to the developing identities of students. In this chapter, we shift our attention to the concept of 'owning' an identity in allied healthcare education, and how students begin to talk about, explain and demonstrate a sense of ownership of their profession to others while still being a student.

'Owning' an identity is not just an important consideration for the developing healthcare student. Owning our identity as adults in our private and public lives is key to who we are and who we have become (or are still becoming), that is, regardless of our personal or chosen professional life. For example, O'Hare (2021: 25) has written about the concept of 'owning' one's identity in the world of academia. She argues for a culture 'that allows academics to be their whole selves on and off campus'. We have seen in the previous chapter how the physical and emotional lives of students 'on and off campus' have a bearing on their developing identity, recognising and explicitly marking the need to consider their 'whole selves' in any discussion of developing identities in this context. Brown and Everson (2019) also consider the notion of gradually 'owning' one's identity in becoming a professional in education. They focused on interviews with student teachers during their education course, following them into their first year as a professional in employment. They found that the interrelationship between self-esteem and a developing identity was 'complex, shifting and overlapping', impacting feelings of belonging and the student teachers' own 'sense of self as a teacher' (Brown and Everson 2019: 231).

Unlike becoming a professional in a readily recognisable profession (e.g. teacher, doctor, nurse), being a student of allied healthcare can bring with it many enquiries from family, peers, fellow college students and others as to what the exact nature of the student's chosen profession is in terms of roles and responsibilities – or put more simply – what the 'job might look like'. The nature of allied healthcare professions such as occupational therapy (OT), speech and language therapy (SLT) and, to a lesser extent, physiotherapy (PT) is often unclear to the public and others, not least because of opaque – or at times misleading – profession titles that do not help fully explicate to the regular public what their practice involves. It is often not just the public who struggle to understand the 'jobs' of healthcare professionals; even fellow professionals from other disciplines may struggle to fully appreciate the scope of practice of colleagues in a hospital or school setting, for example. Moreover, explaining the nature of one's profession as a student is not often as easy as it may first seem, as they themselves are still in the process of learning about the role and associated responsibilities. Students, as part of their course programmes, are continually learning about the client groups served, how their profession is positioned alongside others in healthcare settings (e.g. acute hospitals, primary care facilities, schools and other settings) and how the work of their profession complements or is differentiated from other healthcare clinicians' work.

Informing others, then, of the nature of the student's chosen profession can be challenging but also empowering as the student through their social interactions explains their role, building on their own clinical practicum experiences and as discussed in college-based lectures, tutorials and workshops. Witnessing, observing and ultimately 'doing' the work of their chosen profession has an impact on the student's developing identity. Moreover, explaining that role to others is in and of itself an act of enacting that identity.

This chapter focuses on how students increasingly come to 'own' their professional identity as they are required to explain to others what being a professional in their area of healthcare entails. The way students approach this telling is of interest in this chapter, that is, *what* they communicate within their social interactions and *how* they communicate what it is they are becoming. Additionally, this chapter also explores the factors that influence that communication, including barriers to getting their message across to others. Finally, this chapter will also consider students' perceptions of how their identity may be honed by the very process that is the heart of this book – social interaction – and in this case social interaction with other healthcare professionals.

The questions posed to elicit this detail from the student respondents were as follows (see Table 6.5; Q6 and Q7):

- If relevant, how have your interactions with other healthcare professionals (other therapists, nurses, doctors, dieticians, psychologists, etc.) during your training affected your understanding of your own professional identity?
- How, if at all, do you communicate your specific role (as a SLT, OT or PT student) when meeting or working with other students from other disciplines? Give an example of what you might say.

The remainder of this chapter will present the findings of the analysis of the responses to these questions. Table 9.1 lists the two personal experiential themes and their associated experiential statements identified within that analysis.

9.2 DEVELOPING OWNERSHIP OF AN IDENTITY THROUGH COMMUNICATION ABOUT THAT IDENTITY

Four main experiential statements were identified as informing this personal experiential theme of 'developing ownership of an identity through communication about that identity' from the analysis of the student professionals' responses to this question and are listed in Table 9.1. The student responses that inform these experiential statements will be discussed below, as they reveal interesting insights into how the AHP students perceived their developing professional identity as they explained and talked about their chosen profession.

9.2.1 *WHAT* THE AHP STUDENT COMMUNICATES

In the responses to the question posed above, putting the person at the centre of their profession was important for many students as they described what they would communicate to others about their profession, captured within 'person-centred care and the holistic and functional nature of the profession' (Table 9.1). Adopting a holistic

Table 9.1 Personal experiential themes and associated experiential statements which inform 'owning' professional identity in allied healthcare education

Personal Experiential Themes	Associated Experiential Statements
Developing ownership of an identity through communication about that identity	• What the AHP student communicates – Person-centred care and the holistic and functional nature of the profession – Highlighting the scope and practice of the profession • How the AHP student communicates about their profession • Factors influencing that communication • Barriers in facilitating that communication
Social interaction with other professionals: Influence on professional identity formation during education	• Other healthcare professionals provide the student with perspective • Other healthcare professionals enhance the student's concept of the multidisciplinary team • Other healthcare professionals provide the student with further understanding of their own and others' professional role • Other healthcare professionals provide the student with insight into others' understanding of one's profession • Other healthcare professionals provide example of how to conduct oneself in the professional healthcare setting • Other healthcare professionals being an inspiration (or not) to healthcare students

stance, focusing on the functional nature of the work of the professions featured in many of the responses. For PT students, explaining what they 'do' with patients seemed to be a good starting point for some, as this direct quote of what a student might say illustrates in Extract 9.1:

Extract 9.1

`Hi, I'm a PT, we rehabilitate people from kids to old people to athletes after their injuries or operations or certain diseases. We also prehabilitate people for a healthier daily life so they can avoid certain posture, occupation-related pain or other such conditions.` **(PT-In23)**

Another PT student explained that 'I tell them we are the ones help you get back towards normalcy maybe after a surgery or an injury' (PT-In28). Of interest here is the use of the inclusive first-person plural pronoun 'we', thereby suggesting a sense of belonging to a profession along with others, not uncommon to the accounts, as discussed further below (see Table 9.2). Referencing belonging to a wider healthcare team of service providers who specialise in the 'body's systems' was the explanation put forward by a PT student (PT-US9), who also referenced the centrality of the patient and the importance of personal goal achievement:

Extract 9.2

`Physical therapists are healthcare providers who specialise in how the body's systems affect movement and pain processing. We work with patients using a variety of techniques to allow them to reach their personal goals for functional mobility and improve their quality of life.` **(PT-US9)**

Similarly, for OT students, keeping the person (and their goals) at the core of their role was key for many:

Extract 9.3

`OTs are there to help the patient/client reach their fullest potential in what they want or need to do. Main focus is to improve the person's independence and quality of life through meaningful, functional activities.` **(OT-Mal31)**

Likewise, the person being part of an environment that influences them and their progress was referenced by another OT student who also referenced her role as a facilitator:

Extract 9.4

`Occupational therapy incorporates the environment around the person and how that is effective, what is important to them to be able to do. OT looks at what the person needs and wants to do and facilitates` the person to be independent in all areas of their life despite and without necessarily changing their own limitations. **(OT-Ire40)**

Continuing with the person-centred focus in many descriptions of what students might say when explaining their profession to others during social interaction, the repeated use of the inclusive 'we' is notable, denoting a belonging to a collective identity of that profession and could be construed as a marker of developing professional identity formation. Examples from OT student responses to illustrate this point are listed in Table 9.2 (with use of 'we' highlighted in bold for ease of reference).

Finally, among these experiential statements was a principled statement from a PT student who simply stated that her profession could be described as one characterised by: 'Treating without medicines. Adding life to years' (PT-In21).

Further informing the personal experiential theme of '*What* the AHP student communicates' about their profession were references to the specific scope and practice of their chosen profession, captured within 'highlighting the scope and practice of the profession' (Table 9.1). From a simple explanation from an SLT student (such as 'Help in communication and swallowing', SLT-Mal8) to a more detailed, almost textbook-like explanation in the following extract (SLT-Mal7), outlining the scope of the work was core to explanation of the role for many:

Extract 9.5

Work with those children/people who have a problem with communication and language. Be it a child who has difficulty acquiring language, or pronouncing sounds, or an adult who has lost ability to speak or communicate due to a disease/accident. SLPs are also the professionals who deal with any problems with feeding and swallowing. **(SLT-Mal7)**

Table 9.2 The use of the inclusive 'we' as a marker of professional identity formation

Student Reference	Response
OT-Mal32	**We** as occupational therapists look at clients from a holistic perspective and address difficulties related with selfcare, work and leisure. **We** also aim to motivate and empower clients in engaging and participating in their daily routine
OT-Ire35	**We** work on everyday activities - these are personal to every individual - it may vary from something as small as tying a shoelace to driving a car or returning to work
OT-Ire38	A lot of other healthcare students already know what **we** do, but I explain to them that we are very much focused on the individual's goals and occupations
OT-Ire41	Often say 'Occupational therapists look at all of the things that people want, need or have to do and how **we** can enable people to achieve these things'

Similar explanations by other SLT students also referenced the full or 'entire' age span of the clinical population ('from kids to old people', PT-In23). This student (SLT-SA44) described her professional remit as follows:

Extract 9.6

I'm in speech therapy and audiology. Basically, we work with anything to do with hearing, speech, language, communication or swallowing. And we work with the entire population age-wise - from premature infants with poor suckling/sucking reflexes (so they can't swallow or feed) all the way to elderly persons with dementia or stroke-related difficulties. **(SLT-SA44)**

Also of interest in this extract is the further explanation provided in parentheses for what 'suckling/sucking reflexes' might mean for infants, that is, 'so they can't swallow or feed'. The need to explain the terminology of a profession, to further explicate the nature of the profession's scope, is another feature that emerged quite strongly in the responses given and will be discussed under the personal experiential theme of 'how the AHP student communicates about their profession' below.

What is communicated in social interactions outside of clinical contexts (i.e. 'in social circles') was referenced by this PT student (PT-Mal29):

Extract 9.7

In social circles and interactions, I always seek to get to know more about other professions. I always emphasise physiotherapy's value in healthcare and seek to educate other future professionals about its contribution to healthcare and how physiotherapy can work hand in hand with their respective professions to ultimately deliver quality care to the patient. **(PT-Mal29)**

In her description here of what she might say to others, this student also referenced the collaborative nature of her profession's work, that is, working 'hand in hand' with others to best serve the patient in their care. Referencing the social interaction with other professionals, another student explained that giving 'practical examples' to others helps to explain how your role may be 'highly dependent on the setting you work in' (OT-Ire43).

For others, explaining the role is often difficult ('As an OT student this is something I find difficult', OT-Ire36), while another OT student stressed the lack of social interaction among student professional groups as a problem in helping to define the scope of practice for others:

Extract 9.8

It is very rarely that there is an interaction between us as OTs and other disciplines. This was clearly evident in lectures where different disciplines used to sit as separate groups. **(OT-Mal33)**

We have discussed the role of interprofessional learning elsewhere in this volume (Chapter 3). However, it is interesting to note in this quote that a lack of social interaction (even in situations where different student cohorts are physically in the same space) is seen by this student as perhaps unhelpful in her professional identity formation as a student, where 'different disciplines' seemed to 'sit as separate groups'. As a contrast to this observation of a lack of social interaction in helping to define or explain roles, the following extract is a counter-example to this. In the following extract, we see a student reporting being proactive in social interactions with others and in pursuance of her own explanation of her role, while also seeking information on other disciplines' roles:

Extract 9.9

When introducing myself as a student SLT, I always state my name, and that I am a student SLT. When meeting with other students regarding a particular client, I usually say something along the line of 'so as you know we work with communication/speech/swallowing', to imply that I understand they are aware of my role already. I then enquire into what that student's goals/assessment results etc. are, and then delve more specifically into the SLT goals/assessments etc. I feel that OT students, in my own experience, have been extremely familiar with the work of an SLT/student SLT. In my experience, physiotherapy students have been less familiar with the role of a student. **(SLT-Ire34)**

Furthermore, in referencing her own experience, this SLT student commented on how familiar or unfamiliar other professions are with her own discipline of SLT. Finally, having to explicitly explain 'with who' one works to help define their role is referenced in the following quote, with this student demonstrating awareness of possible prior misperceptions:

Extract 9.10

I usually have to explain what our role is, and with who. As most people might think that our job is strictly on articulation and voice, and with children and teachers, respectively. **(SLT-Mal13)**

Delimiting the scope of one's profession, therefore, is core to these descriptions in terms of who the professional interacts with in both clinical and non-clinical domains of practice.

9.2.2 *HOW* THE AHP STUDENT COMMUNICATES ABOUT THEIR PROFESSION

The preceding sections of this chapter have dealt with the 'what' or content of explanations that student professionals may give to explain their role and responsibilities. It is now time to turn to their comments on *how* they communicate that information.

AHP students are aware of the need to at times explicitly explain their role to both clients and other clinicians.

Giving 'practical examples' (OT-Ire43) of client groups served by their profession is common among the respondents (see also, for example, an earlier reference by an OT of supporting with tasks ranging 'from tying a shoelace to driving a car', OT-Ire35). One OT student explained that she gives 'Verbal explanations with many examples' (OT-Ire39) to describe her role. Referencing both the clients and what they can do for them is core to other descriptions, as seen in a previous extract (Extract 9.1). Describing her professional discipline of SLT as 'kind of like physiotherapy for talking' is an amusing comparison but one which shows the attempt to communicate the roles and responsibilities in an analogous and jargon-free way to others:

Extract 9.11

I'm doing speech and language therapy, it's kind of like physiotherapy but for talking and understanding. You know maybe if someone has had a stroke and can't talk or had Parkinson's disease, or if a child had a lisp or a stutter, or if someone had cancer and got their voice box removed. **(SLT-Ire3)**

The use of less technical language, (e.g. 'voice box' for larynx and laryngectomy and 'can't talk' for 'aphasia', for instance) is further testimony to ensuring the message is understood easily by others. Comparing one's profession to others to explain that profession more clearly is also evident in the following extract from a PT student (PT-US11) which references the analogy of 'dance' to explain the differences between OT and her own profession, while also referencing teamwork:

Extract 9.12

In terms of the differences between PT and OT, I like to say that an OT will teach you how to get your dancing shoes on and a PT will teach you how to dance. PT tends to focus more on gross movements and body mechanics, while OT tends to focus more on fine motor movements. Each therapist's goal is to help the patient regain specific movements that will help them reach their functional goals. **(PT-US11)**

It is clear from some of the above examples that using simpler, jargon-free language in social interaction with others seems important for the student professionals as they grapple with trying to explain the roles and responsibilities of their respective professions. This SLT student (SLT-Ire4) explained her role as follows, referencing the fact that she intentionally uses 'simple, lay terms' to explain to others:

Extract 9.13

The role of the SLT has to be delineated into three separate functions: speech, language and swallowing. I give a brief explanation of each, using simple, lay terms e.g. 'understanding what other people are saying and being able to put your words together' for language. **(SLT-Ire4)**

Likewise, an OT student (OT-Ire41) echoed this response in her own explanation of using 'accessible language':

Extract 9.14

Often say 'Occupational therapists look at all of the things that people want, need or have to do and how we can enable people to achieve these things'. There's obviously much more to OT than that but I strive to use accessible language that is easily understood. **(OT-Ire41)**

Similarly, another OT student (OT-Ire42) explained her role as follows:

Extract 9.15

As an OT who is currently working in a rehab setting, I would say that our role is to assist people in the area of FUNCTION ... how to do everyday things that patients need to do, like walking, dressing, cooking, participating in social events ... I would emphasise that our work is heavily involved in DOING things ... so that people can achieve optimal independence and function. **(OT-Ire42)**

Of interest here is the student's own marking of emphasis in capitals on the words 'FUNCTION' and 'DOING' in her response, thereby attempting to maximise comprehensibility in her explanation.

It seems, then, that students have a wide range of ways to communicate and explain their respective roles to patients and supervisors alike.

9.3 FACTORS INFLUENCING COMMUNICATION ABOUT IDENTITY: BARRIERS AND FACILITATORS

Some students in their responses considered a range of factors that influenced 'how', 'what' and to 'whom' they communicated about their profession. One SLT student reported how preconceptions of what others thought the role entailed had a bearing on their understanding (i.e. 'I usually have to explain what our role is, and with who. As most people might think that our job is strictly on articulation and voice, and with children and teachers, respectively', SLT-Mal13). Others (e.g. SLT-Ire34) reported how, when socially interacting with other professions during their daily work, they grasped the opportunity to educate others about their role, but in an indirect way, almost 'implying' that others already knew (first referenced in Extract 9.9 above):

Extract 9.16

When introducing myself as a student SLT, I always state my name, and that I am a student SLT. When meeting with other students regarding a particular client, I usually say something along the line of 'so as you know we work with communication/speech/swallowing', to imply that I understand they are aware of my role already. I then enquire into `what that student's goals/assessment results etc. are, and then delve more specifically into the SLT goals/assessments etc. I feel that OT students, in my own experience, have been extremely familiar with the work of an SLT/student SLT. In my experience, physiotherapy students have been less familiar with the role of a student SLT.` **(SLT-Ire34)**

This influence of what is perceived as pre-existing knowledge also extends to models of care of the professional audience, as the above student indicated when she 'enquires' during her interactions what other goals/assessments are being used from other disciplines. It is also this student's experience that she believes occupational therapists are more informed of the SLT discipline than her colleagues in PT, for example. This perception is the result of speech and language therapists having more opportunities to interact with the former than the latter healthcare professionals in many contexts.

Other students, however, reported barriers to communicating their role, and these barriers include a lack of opportunity to socially interact with other healthcare professionals, not just in the workplace but also during their education. For example, an SLT student (SLT-Mal16) explained that despite the idea of working with and alongside other professionals on a 'transdisciplinary team', there are 'unfortunately' not 'enough opportunities to communicate' about the role. For others, this lack of opportunity to interact with others and communicate about roles extends to the educational context, as this quote from an OT student (OT-Mal33) demonstrates:

Extract 9.17

`It is very rarely that there is an interaction between us as OTs and other disciplines. This was clearly evident in lectures where different disciplines used to sit as separate groups.` **(OT-Mal33)**

Hence, social interaction is salient to any discussion of communicating the nature and extent of roles in healthcare. A presence or an absence of opportunities to socially interact with other healthcare professionals outside of one's own discipline has consequences for the communication of roles and responsibilities of specific disciplines and how that is achieved. The remainder of this chapter deals with this consideration, that is, how social interaction with other healthcare professionals (other therapists, nurses, doctors, dieticians, psychologists, etc.) during a student's education affects the understanding of their own developing professional identity.

9.4 SOCIAL INTERACTION WITH OTHER PROFESSIONALS: INFLUENCE ON PROFESSIONAL IDENTITY FORMATION DURING EDUCATION

Six experiential statements were identified in the data to inform the second personal experiential theme of 'social interaction with other professionals: influence on professional identity formation during education', as listed in Table 9.1. These experiential statements were identified following analysis of the responses to the following question (Table 6.5; Q6):

- If relevant, how have your interactions with other healthcare professionals (other therapists, nurses, doctors, dieticians, psychologists, etc.) during your training affected your understanding of your own professional identity?

9.4.1 OTHER HEALTHCARE PROFESSIONALS PROVIDE THE STUDENT WITH PERSPECTIVE

The experiential statement of 'other healthcare professionals provide the student with perspective' encapsulates the notion that the students were receptive to learning how their profession related to others in a broader sense, and to healthcare in general. This in turn had an influence on identity formation, as will be seen from the students' own words below.

The data illustrate that interactions with other healthcare professionals seemed to provide the students with an insight into how their role relates to the wider community of healthcare practice. For example, a PT student commented:

Extract 9.18

They [other professionals] have strengthened my identity, but in terms of how it relates to the larger picture in a patient's healthcare team, I feel like I am able to be more confident in referring patients to other providers because I have a better idea of my scope of practice. **(PT-US9)**

This student recognised how social interaction with other professionals allowed her to develop an enhanced knowledge of her own 'scope of practice'. Similarly, an OT student referred to how the social interaction with a multidisciplinary team in meetings provided a forum 'to voice your purpose and fully understand where it [your profession] fits within other healthcare professions' (OT-Ire39). Likening OT to a 'piece of the puzzle' was expressed by another OT student (OT-Mal31), who explained that:

Extract 9.19

Seeing where our work fits in with the work the other professionals are doing makes me see occupational therapy as a piece of the puzzle and look at the wider picture. **(OT-Mal31)**

9.4.2 OTHER HEALTHCARE PROFESSIONALS ENHANCE THE STUDENT'S CONCEPT OF THE MULTIDISCIPLINARY TEAM

The notion of interacting with the multidisciplinary team (MDT) was referenced again by students and included in the identification of the experiential statement of 'other healthcare professionals enhance the student's concept of the multidisciplinary team' (Table 9.1). The data show that interactions with other healthcare professionals provided the students with an understanding of the role of the MDT and the role of teamwork in healthcare practice. Improving understanding of the MDT (SLT-Mal8) was also 'interdisciplinary' (PT-US14), while valuing every member's role on the MDT (OT-Ire38) was referred to by students across the disciplines of SLT, PT, and OT, respectively. Moreover, recognising that their own discipline was only 'a small part of a very big picture' led to an SLT student's realisation that 'there's no point not working as a team' (SLT-Ire3). These responses underline the idea that your own profession is helpfully defined by interacting with others, as your unique role is recognised while being part of a bigger context of care.

Care for the patient at the centre of healthcare was also recognised by other students in the context of their own developing identity as they interacted with other disciplines, and how at times 'compromise' and some adjustment of opinion is needed to deliver the best treatment in an efficacious manner. A PT student explained this idea as follows, where interacting with an MDT:

Extract 9.20

gave me an overview of how I need to compromise and adjust to opinions of other healthcare professionals; patience and coordination, along with communication with other healthcare professionals, improves the efficiency of treatment provided ... and improves patients' health-related quality of life. **(PT-In22)**

In a similar vein, an SLT student (SLT-SA45) reflected on the need 'to respect one another' within the important context of patient care (i.e. 'the patient comes first', SLT-SA45).

9.4.3 OTHER HEALTHCARE PROFESSIONALS PROVIDE THE STUDENT WITH FURTHER UNDERSTANDING OF THEIR OWN AND OTHERS' PROFESSIONAL ROLE

'Role' is the focus of the third experiential statement in Table 9.1, that is, 'other healthcare professionals provide the student with further understanding of their own and others' professional role'. Here we see that interactions with other healthcare professionals, including as part of a MDT, were the context for the development of this further understanding. Of note is the use of vocabulary and phrases such as 'realise', 'recognise', 'allowed me to see', 'awareness' and 'aided me' among the student responses. That different professions have different bodies of knowledge that they bring to patient care was referred to by some students, from both PT and SLT, as follows:

Extract 9.21

Interacting with other disciplines has helped me identify the unique body of knowledge that PTs have and how that knowledge helps within an interdisciplinary setting. **(PT-US10)**

Extract 9.22

Recognising that physicians and nurses did not share expertise in my field and that my skills/knowledge would enhance their ability to provide effective patient care. **(SLT-US25)**

Other OT students recognised that interactions with other AHPs not only helped them to 'value' their role in general healthcare (OT-Ire38) but also 'to come to terms with the OT role in each particular setting' (OT-Ire36).

Understanding their role enough to feel confident in explaining it to others was also referred to by other students. Being 'sure of your own [discipline-specific] education' (PT-In23) and the 'true meaning' of your profession (OT-Mal32) when interacting with others allowed for easier explanations to other professions of what one's role is. Establishing differences across disciplines also aided this understanding of the discipline's role, especially while on placement, where those social interactions with other professionals were happening in the real world of clinical settings:

Extract 9.23

Clinical placements have aided me greatly in establishing the differences in the roles of OTs/PTs & SLTs as this was something which I was unclear of at times when I was in first year. **(OT-Ire41)**

Extract 9.24

While on placement we had a number of interdisciplinary tutorials with other healthcare students and qualified staff members, which really helped me in communicating and clarifying my role while also gaining an insight into the role of other healthcare professionals on the team. **(OT-Ire43)**

Similarly, simply interacting with the MDT allowed an SLT student 'to realise the vast extent of our [her] scope of practice' (SLT-Ire1). It seems then that the very act of socially interacting with other professionals helps the developing professional to better understand their own role.

However, the benefits of interacting with other professionals are not restricted to better understanding of the students' own discipline-specific role. What was evident in the data, via the identified theme above, was also the added benefit of understanding more about the other professional roles through social interaction. An OT student explained this learning well as central to her identity formation as follows:

Extract 9.25

I feel that part of your professional identity entails understanding the role of other professionals so that you can work effectively as part of a team so increasing my knowledge of each HCP's role has contributed positively to my professional identity. If clients ask me something which is not within my professional remit, I feel confident telling them who will be better equipped to deal with their query. **(OT-Ire41)**

Similarly, an SLT student echoed this account of learning through social interaction, and how that interaction 'helped me to refer cases to other departments' (SLT-In12). Students from other disciplines also acknowledged the benefits of interacting with other professions as an aid to really understanding what that profession can also bring to the content and process of patient care, in other words 'to better identify what skills each member of the team could bring to help the patient' (PT-US11). The opportunity to engage in 'joint sessions' was highlighted by one OT student, who claimed it helped with the often 'grey areas' that may be evident depending on the work context:

Extract 9.26

I have a far greater idea of how the therapists complement each other's approach - there are always grey areas and it may depend on place to place what your role is - joint sessions are definitely useful - one in particular that I learned a lot from was a feeding assessment which was done in conjunction with a SLT. **(OT-Ire35)**

A good summary of how interacting with other professionals serves a dual purpose of not only learning about one's own role but also that of others is illustrated by the following response:

Extract 9.27

Understanding how these other professionals interact with clients and other professionals helped me find out more [about] how I should interact and carry myself in my professional life. **(SLT-Mal13)**

The notion of learning from others of how 'to carry oneself' in 'professional life' shows just how potent the influence of socially interacting with other professionals is to the student professional.

9.4.4 OTHER HEALTHCARE PROFESSIONALS PROVIDE THE STUDENT WITH INSIGHT INTO OTHERS' UNDERSTANDING OF ONE'S PROFESSION

Interactions with other healthcare professionals have provided the students with insights into how others may view their professional role and the potential need for further education of others' understanding of their profession. The responses that have informed this experiential statement seem to stem from a lack of perceived awareness (in general) of the nature and function of some AHPs, such as OT and SLT.

Students of OT referred to the need for better understanding of their professional roles. However, some pointed out that awareness and knowledge is often dependent on the setting or context in which one works (OT-Mal33). Moreover, not unlike SLT, OT seems subject to misunderstandings (i.e. 'OT is only about arts and crafts' and such misinterpretations can be 'downgrading', OT-Mal33). The ignorance of other professionals about OT, for example, was referred to by one student as leading to feelings of the role being 'less important' (OT-Mal32), while others acknowledged that the role was 'respected' (OT-Ire40), even in cases where the full OT role was not understood.

Facing ignorance or misunderstandings of their role led one student (OT-Ire40) to seek out opportunities to 'validate' her profession 'in comparison to others such as PT' (OT-Ire40), for example. This need to validate the discipline is linked to professional identity for others, and linked to 'believing in' the profession they are training for:

Extract 9.28

`In my experience, OT has been usually respected but often other professions have not understood the role of OT so that element of developing my professional identity has involved believing a lot in the profession that I am training in.` **(OT-Ire40)**

Likewise for OT-Ire37, the very act of socially interacting with other professionals outside of their own discipline 'and how they reacted to the OT label impacted my own understanding and identification with the role' (OT-Ire37) influenced the development of a professional identity.

The SLT students' responses were not unlike their OT counterparts in echoing the lack of awareness among other AHPs of roles outside their own, summed up as follows: 'Most are not aware of the SLP's roles unless they have worked with one' (SLT-Mal7). What is common to the responses is how the lack of awareness of each other's roles often only becomes apparent through social interaction with others, which in turn offers opportunities for education about other disciplines through those same interactions.

9.4.5 OTHER HEALTHCARE PROFESSIONALS PROVIDE EXAMPLES OF HOW TO CONDUCT ONESELF IN THE PROFESSIONAL HEALTHCARE SETTING

Social interaction remains at the core for student clinicians, not just to learn more about their own profession but also about other professional disciplines. Moreover, the student responses also indicated that interactions with other healthcare professionals seemed to provide inspiration to some students for how they wished to behave as professionals during client interactions (SLT-Mal16), with some aiming to 'be like them' (SLT-SA45). Others referred to such interactions as providing insight into how to 'carry' and conduct oneself in healthcare settings (SLT-Mal13), referring to the importance of mirroring 'good professional behaviour and care with clients' (SLT-SA45). These students, then, valued learning more about the professional behaviour of their chosen discipline through others while at the same time learning to respect the distinct roles of colleagues and thereby becoming 'less judgemental' (SLT-Mal6).

Some other students linked the value of interacting with other disciplines directly to the development and enhancement of their own sense of professional identity, as illustrated in the following two extracts from SLT respondents:

Extract 9.29

Other professionals have strengthened my professional identity through treating me as an equal in a professional manner, asking me for opinions on clinical scenarios and listening to my recommendations for management. They have also provided opportunities to gain knowledge on their experience of transitioning and developing professional identities by relating to their own personal journey. Some professionals have also asked thought-provoking questions to me about the profession which allowed me to reflect on my professional identity, e.g. the role of an SLT in palliative care. **(SLT-Ire2)**

Extract 9.30

I feel this has influenced my understanding of my own professional identity. In interactions with other healthcare professionals (outside of the college context) I feel I reflect on the interaction afterwards. In particular, I feel the degree of 'comfort' you feel with an HCP is something really valuable in the interaction. I have reflected on what specifically made me feel 'comfortable' in an interaction and have brought this forward to my own work as a student clinician. **(SLT-Ire34)**

Being asked 'thought-provoking questions' (SLT-IRE 2) about their work and reflecting on why they felt 'comfortable' with other AHPs seemed to help inform these students' developing professional identity as novice clinicians. It is clearly demonstrated in the data that students value this social interaction with other AHPs and see it as pivotal in their own learning and professional development, summed up by one student emphatically: 'they have helped me grow immensely!' (SLT-SA44).

However, such positive influences are not the experience of some other respondents in the data, with one respondent talking of quite the opposite effect on their developing sense of professional identity. That is, some students reported that interactions with other healthcare professionals reduced their sense of credibility and professional identity. For one student, once they explained that they were still in training in 'school', they felt that they had lost 'credibility', commenting that:

Extract 9.31

It can be frustrating to speak to people who talk to you as if you are a freshman in college studying business, when instead you are nine months from your masters in speech pathology. **(SLT-US27)**

For another OT student (OT-Mal30), interactions with other healthcare professionals were described as 'minimal' due to the nature of the placement (i.e. just one day per week, as opposed to a block of continuous time) and therefore they were only 'seeing a few clients here and there rather than the holistic experience' of patient care as part of a team.

9.4.6 OTHER HEALTHCARE PROFESSIONALS BEING AN INSPIRATION (OR NOT) TO HEALTHCARE STUDENTS

In the final experiential statement, discussed within the personal experiential theme of 'social interaction with other professionals: influence on professional identity formation during education' (Table 9.1), students reflected on how other healthcare professionals may (or may not) aid their sense of a developing professional identity. In some instances, interactions with other healthcare professionals provided the students with insight and inspiration into how to conduct themselves in the healthcare setting. One SLT student commented that 'other SLTs have been an inspiration as to what I aspire to be like during my interaction with clients' (SLT-Mal16), while another remarked that:

Extract 9.32

Seeing others' professional behaviour makes you want to be like them. It is so important to mirror good professional behaviour and care with clients. **(SLT-SA45)**

Alternatively, in other instances interactions with healthcare professionals reduced the students' sense of credibility and professional identity during social interactions (i.e. 'As soon as you say you're in school [college]...'):

Extract 9.33

Speaking with other health professionals has, for the most part, reduced my feeling of professional identity. As soon as you say you're in school [college], you immediately lose any credibility. It can be frustrating to speak to people who talk to you as if you are a freshman in college studying business, when instead you are nine months from your Master's [degree] in speech pathology. **(SLT-US27)**

It seems from such responses that the way in which students view healthcare professionals' behaviour and how they are communicated with as students can influence their often-fragile sense of a developing identity, in positive or negative ways.

9.5 SUMMARY

This chapter discussed the concept of students coming to 'own' their identity as AHP students. Unlike O'Leary and Cantillon's (2020: 781) findings that within the discipline of SLT 'undergraduate identity was characterised by dependency, self-centredness (as opposed to patient centredness) and a naïve role concept', the respondents in our survey across the healthcare professions of OT, PT and SLT seemed to be more ready 'to step up to the mark' so to speak, to 'own' their identity and accept where they are at in their professional education. This acceptance from students to embrace the unknown of the trajectory of professional identity formation is perhaps part and parcel of an allied healthcare education, where that identity is acknowledged to be continually reinforced and shaped with both time and experience through social interaction.

10

FUTURE CONSIDERATIONS FOR IDENTITY WORK THROUGH SOCIAL INTERACTION IN ALLIED HEALTHCARE EDUCATION

Let us do something, while we have the chance! It is not every day that we are needed. Not indeed that we personally are needed. Others would meet the case equally well, if not better ... Let us make the most of it, before it is too late!
Samuel Beckett, *Waiting for Godot (Act II)*

10.1 INTRODUCTION

As we come to the closing chapter, it is time to summarise what has gone before in this book. We then consider how we may look to the future to support 'identity work' in allied healthcare education, with social interaction as a focus and as a means to contextualise the educational experience. The next section of this chapter (Section 10.2) will summarise our main arguments thus far in garnering support for the place of social interaction in allied healthcare education and practice. We then (in Section 10.3) once again look to the respondents to our survey to guide us on the way forward, attending to the student voice to gain insights into how we as educators can join the learners in their ongoing trajectory of professional identity formation. In Sections 10.3 to Section 10.5, we suggest – based on the students' ideas and concerns – some ways forward in the enhancement of student learning and identity in allied healthcare education and practice.

We as educators have a professional responsibility to our students, and although as 'others would meet the case equally well, if not better' (Beckett), the primary onus is on us, in conjunction with our students, to provide opportunities and contexts for professional identity formation work with social interaction as a conduit.

10.2 A SUMMARY TO THIS POINT: FROM PRETENDING TO OWNERSHIP – IDENTITY THROUGH THE LENS OF SOCIAL INTERACTION

Starting out as we did in this book, outlining our own beliefs on what we understand by identity (Chapter 2), led us to explore how it has been considered across the allied healthcare professions that have social interaction necessarily at their core (Chapter 3). Identity has been foregrounded to greater or lesser extents in studies of the educational experience. However, identity issues are gaining traction as educators, students and prospective employers alike recognise the need to reflect on developing and honing professional identity – both generic as part of the larger body of healthcare professionals and specific as specialists in their chosen discipline. The generic versus specific identity consideration is one that was reflected in our discussion of workplace identity (Chapter 4), prior to considering it as a student goal or experience. Chapter 4 showed that despite well-established career pathways and experiences of individual professionals, challenges to identity are common in the workplace and identity work continues throughout professionals' working lives. Coping with threats to that identity was particularly highlighted within the context of service-level changes, a feature not uncommon in institutional contexts. Chapter 5, which discussed the notion of 'towards inhabiting a fulfilled identity', dealt with clinicians' reflections of interactions they had with clients, families and their multidisciplinary team and how those social interactions prompted them to reflect on issues of identity in interesting and nuanced ways. The power of reflections was seen here in this chapter, only to be reinforced in later chapters where social interaction was again in focus.

Chapter 6 dealt with methodology issues. We included here a discussion of reflection and reflective practice, along with a consideration of IPA. Here, we not only considered how IPA was put to work in analysing the core survey data discussed in this book but also dealt with a broader consideration of IPA's uses, as applied to data discussed in Chapters 4 and 5, which focused on workplace considerations and client interactions, respectively. We conclude that IPA has a lot to offer when considering identity through social interaction, as demonstrated through the data sets presented in this book. We believe that IPA gets at the core of the experiences described by the participants. We appreciate the collaborative nature of this qualitative methodology 'because it explores experiential meanings through the interpretative work between the researcher and the participant rather than being a theory-driven examination' (Smith and Fieldsend 2021: 147). We, like others, also welcome the new terminology used to foreground the highly personal and experiential nature of the substance of the data (i.e. personal statements, personal experiential themes and group experiential themes; Smith and Nizza 2021; Smith, Flowers and Larkin 2022). Van Manen (2017: 779) eloquently defines phenomenology thus:

> Phenomenology, if practiced well, enthrals us with insights into the enigma of life as we experience it—the world as it gives and reveals itself to the wondering gaze—thus asking us to be forever attentive to the fascinating varieties and subtleties of primal lived experience and consciousness in all its remarkable complexities, fathomless depths, rich details, startling disturbances, and luring charms. Genuine phenomenological inquiry is challenging and satisfying precisely because its meaningful revelations must be originary and existentially compelling to the soul.

We do not for one moment believe we have exhausted the analysis of the data presented in this book. However, we do believe we have duly considered the 'phenomenon' of an evolving identity of the allied healthcare education student as viewed through the lens of social interaction activities. In other words, we have exposed 'phenomena' relevant to healthcare professional identity and social interaction as lived by those involved in practice and education, considering healthcare professional students' and practitioners' lived experience in at least some of 'its remarkable complexities' (van Manen 2017: 779).

Chapters 7 to 9 built on the earlier introductory chapters which set the scene for the findings of our survey (administered pre-pandemic) as we strove to explore the dynamic interaction of social interaction and developing professional identity. Not uncommon to qualified professionals and akin to the 'imposter syndrome' experienced by many, the student experience of 'faking it until you make it', discussed in Chapter 7, seems to be a necessary part of the student experience – a common practice to allow one to grow, learn, make mistakes and 'do better'. Perhaps 'faking' it in clinical and teaching and learning interactions is just the practice ground for that identity work, until it becomes more routine and engrained as part of a professional identity. 'Faking it' may be considered as 'doing identity work' as the student assumes the identity of the healthcare professional they are aspiring to be. Chapter 8 explored how social interaction is at the core of many formal and informal contexts of teaching and learning in healthcare education. Formal contexts of learning are often those that get the spotlight or the focused consideration, in other words where 'real work' gets done. However, our data show that students seem to appreciate the incidental learning that occurs within informal interactions and outside the confines of the structured classroom setting or the strictly planned clinic session.

Getting to a state of 'owning' one's own profession and forging and assuming an identity within that profession was the focus of Chapter 9. For many of the students, 'owning' their profession was part of 'becoming' that professional and assuming the identity that they had aspired to in their educational experiences. Many students came to 'own' their profession with pride, further strengthening their sense of identity of who and what they had become or were becoming. This chapter (Chapter 10) takes the notion of developing that professional identity further, that is, exploring what the students themselves thought educators should or could do to enhance that developing identity.

10.3 DOING THINGS DIFFERENTLY: THE FACILITATION OF PROFESSIONAL IDENTITY FORMATION THROUGH SOCIAL INTERACTION

We look to the survey responses to guide us on the way forward, attending to the student voice. The responses to the following question (Table 6.5; Q5) of the survey provide the data for analysis and reflection in this chapter:

- What, if anything, do you believe lecturers or supervisors/practice educators could do differently in allied healthcare education to facilitate the formation of your professional identity?

As in the other chapters, the data were analysed thematically through the lens of IPA to get at the core message being voiced by the student learners. Their voice seeks to tell us what is important to them as experts of their own learning experiences. A total of four personal experiential themes were identified in this section of the data, and these themes are posed as aims here to further underline the action the students are requesting. These four personal experiential themes are listed in Table 10.1, before being discussed and 'unpacked' via students' experiential statements in this chapter.

10.3.1 EMPHASIS ON PRACTICAL COMPONENTS IN HEALTHCARE COURSES

It is not unsurprising that students in their responses called for 'more' in terms of (i) opportunities to engage in more practical/skill-based learning and intervention during their time at university, and (ii) to have more opportunity to engage in reflective practice while on placement.

Requesting 'more' in contexts of both university and clinic-led learning speaks to the referenced desired connection between theory and practice across a number of speech and language therapy (SLT) students' responses in particular (SLT-Ire4,

Table 10.1 Personal experiential themes identified in relation to actions to be taken by educators and as suggested by students through their experiential statements

Personal Experiential Themes	Description
To increase emphasis on practical components in healthcare courses, with emphasis on application of theory to practice	• Students reflected upon seeking increased opportunities to engage in more practical/skill-based learning and intervention during their time in university, and in the application of theory to practice. More guidance regarding reflective practice on placement and the opportunity of discussing more functional aspects of placements during lectures was also highlighted.
To increase collaboration with other allied healthcare students and professionals.	• Students reflected upon seeking opportunities to engage with other AHP students and other professionals
To personalise the student experience	• Students reflected upon the possibility of lectures/ supervisors/practice educators taking a strength-based/ human-based approach to assessment and engagement with students.
To provide more support (including reassurance and encouragement) in becoming an autonomous learner	• Students reflected upon the possibility of supervisors/ lecturers providing more support to students through supervision and personalised feedback. Some students reflected upon the support they have received from their lectures and supervisors throughout their time in university. Students reflected upon the possibility of supervisor providing more reassurance and encouragement to students while on placement and in supporting their autonomy as learners under supervision.

SLT-Mal5, SLT-Mal6, SLT-Mal7, SLT-Mal16). The students envisaged how these links can be made stronger for them and for their learning (e.g. 'Incorporating more functional aspects into lectures – adding the "how" to the "what" and the "why", SLT-Ire4). This point was made clearly by one occupational therapy (OT) respondent, who asserted:

Extract 10.1

Lecturers should allow for more questions from students regarding actual OT practice as this is something which the student has discussed very seldomly while in college- we focused mainly on theory & [sic] while it is obviously incredibly important to our professional underpinnings there are often many discrepancies between theory &[sic] practice, so it is vital to discuss the realities of practice with individuals who have practiced as OTs in the student's opinion. **(OT-Ire41)**

That 'lecturers should allow for more questions from students', coupled with the latter part of this quote (i.e. 'discussing the realities of practice with individuals who have practiced as OTs') speaks to the need for learning through interaction with a qualified person in the university setting. Moreover, providing opportunities 'for more clinical experience' (SLT-Mal16) and to get this experience through more 'interaction about cases' was further outlined by a physiotherapy (PT) student (PT-In23):

Extract 10.2

More practical and skills-based learning/interaction about cases and how to go about them/give an independent patient case so we understand and get used to the responsibility and rules were supposed to follow. **(PT-In23)**

Similarly, another PT student made a similar call for significantly increasing the hands-on dimensions of the work (i.e. 'should include evidence-based teaching/ clinical based training, incorporating more workshops and demo sessions/practical hours should be included/ curriculum modifications/ exams should be objective and application based', PT-In22). At the core, then, is both engagement in and preparation for social interaction in university and clinical contexts as both a means and an end to the development of their professionalism and skill as a healthcare professional. Some respondents recognised the need for this increased exposure and engaged interaction as linked to their stage of education across their programme, with some looking for earlier placement (or placement-like experiences) from the outset:

Extract 10.3

I think increasing the number of hands-on experiences that students have in first and second year would increase the students' confidence when more responsibility is placed on them in third and fourth year. I know that some colleges in the UK expose their first and second years to far more clinical placement in these earlier years. **(OT-Ire40)**

Other students looked to their professional associations as a means of increasing this exposure, especially in the final years, that is, 'encouraging attendance of CPDs, workshops tailored to final year students and inclusion of students in professional organisations' (OT-Mal30). Of interest here is the reference to their future selves as members of their professional association, thinking themselves into this identity, the role and its responsibilities, including as fellow researchers (PT-In21).

The second dimension of this personal experiential theme refers to the students' desire for more 'self-reflection' opportunities in the clinical environment to allow for them to build a greater awareness of their interactions with clients and others. The form of this reflection was also specified by one SLT respondent, who called for a less structured means of reflection:

Extract 10.4

Less structured reflection sheets should be provided- perhaps one main question and a dear diary format would be more beneficial as students can acknowledge all of their feelings in a safe environment and later identify areas to improve on. **(SLT-Ire2)**

10.3.2 COLLABORATION WITH OTHER ALLIED HEALTHCARE STUDENTS AND PROFESSIONALS

A more explicit plea for social interaction with other allied healthcare professional (AHP) students and professionals informs this personal experiential theme. Students seem to want, and desire increased opportunities to socially interact with other professionals, as a means of enhancing their development and learning. Interprofessional learning (discussed in Chapter 3 of this book) features in the students' responses as a positive way forward in their own professional development, as illustrated by the following quotes (Extracts 10.5–10.7) from across the AHP student responses:

Extract 10.5

Have us work with other professionals and discuss our roles in a patient case. **(PT-US9)**

Extract 10.6

I think that modules should be done together with other disciplines- such as generic communication modules etc. which appy to all or group facilitation. **(OT-Ire35)**

Extract 10.7

Inter-professional communication and meetings from the beginning of the courses. Definitely. **(SLT-SA44)**

How interprofessional learning work lends itself to identity work and role identification was also referenced by other students, in this case students of OT. Organising 'talks to other healthcare professional students so they increase the awareness of the role of the OT profession' (OT-Mal33) was further elaborated upon by another OT student (OT-Ire42) as follows:

Extract 10.8

As a profession I think we need to communicate clearly what is within the remit of our roles. I see much confusion, I see even senior OTs who blur their role with others such as PT ... if OTs are confused, then other members of MDT will be too, and clients/patients. **(OT-Ire42)**

Once again, we see students recognising that social interaction is key for their future development as healthcare professionals, both discipline specific and discipline generic.

10.3.3 PERSONALISING THE STUDENT EXPERIENCE

Within this personal experiential theme of 'to personalise the student experience' (Table 10.1), the students reflected upon the possibility of lecturers/supervisors/practice educators taking a strengths-based/human-based approach to assessment and engagement with students. Here then, we see a focus on what students referred to as the desire for positive social interactions with their educators.

The students' call for a recognition of strengths is particularly salient in the data, not only as part of the feedback by a supervisor but also as recognised by the students themselves, and as individual to them. SLT students (i.e. SLT-US24, SLT-Ire2) referenced this aspect of feedback in the statement 'Make comments about strengths and weaknesses more personal to the individual student' (SLT-US24) and as below:

Extract 10.9

Supervisors should explicitly ask the student what they are strong at ... The student knows their own strengths, and this should be discussed more frequently. **(SLT-Ire2)**

Issues of identity were also referenced by students in this context of strengths and of personalising the student experience. One student referred to the desire to be affirmed in her provision of a 'quality service even if we are "only students"' (OT-Ire36). Of interest here is the reference to being 'only students', with this term of reference perhaps being used by clinical supervisors or other educators. Furthermore, issues of identity were also referenced within the context of interactions while on placement, even during the non-clinical time spent in each other's company, for example:

Extract 10.10

Eating lunch with your practice educator is important in my opinion in the formation of your professional identity. It forces you to act like you would act if you were working and interacting socially yet professionally rather than experiencing a kind of teacher/student complex like in secondary school. **(SLT-Ire3)**

A related notion relevant to identity formation was raised by yet another student, and this referred to her belief that some lecturers have a tendency to 'place their identities on students' at the cost of stifling a student's own identity formation:

Extract 10.11

Lecturers especially need to allow the formation of the student's professional identity. I feel that a lot of lecturers try and place their identities on students without allowing the student to form their own opinions on situations. **(OT-Ire38)**

The formation of identity for this student was linked to being allowed 'to form their own opinions on situations' and to get an opportunity to express those opinions. Finally, a call from the students to have their life outside of the educational context recognised by practice educators/clinical supervisors (i.e. 'understand that we are human and that we have worked a life outside of our educational formation', SLT-Mal13) speaks to a point made earlier in Chapter 8, where social interactions outside of the student's allied healthcare educational world (i.e. their informal personal worlds) require recognition and respect by educators as contributing to identity formation.

10.3.4 PROVISION OF SUPPORT IN BECOMING AN AUTONOMOUS LEARNER

This personal experiential theme is multidimensional, as it not only suggests the practical 'support' a student desires but also the personal support they desire in the form of reassurance and encouragement.

The students reflected upon the possibility of supervisors/lecturers providing more support to them through supervision and personalised feedback. Some students reflected upon the support they have received from their lecturers and supervisors throughout their time at university. There seems to be a trajectory or continuum along which levels of support are referenced according to the students. Some students have felt well supported by their educators (SLT-Ire34, OT-Ire35), while others did not report feeling that support in a constructive way (SLT-US27). Those that felt supported linked that feeling to their developing identity as a healthcare professional ('I really felt the college did a great job of reinforcing my professional identity', OT-Ire37; 'I feel that lecturers and practice educators have always been extremely supportive in enabling the formation of my professional identity', SLT-Ire34). Other comments suggest that the lack of support was also linked to a threatened or uncertain development of identity when practice educators were reportedly 'unkind', as in:

Extract 10.12

I do feel that a lot of practice educators can be quite unkind, which then makes students think that the identity is mixed and can have difficulty identifying with it as we did not want to identify with the person who was making us uncomfortable, making the experience unpleasant. **(OT-Ire37)**

Support was also considered by the students in the context of practical direction given and levels of autonomy afforded to them. Some called for a balanced approach (SLT-US27) in this regard:

Extract 10.13

I think there needs to be a more standard balance of autonomy/direction. Sometimes, my supervisor would tell me exactly what to do and become irate if that was not what I did. Other times, I was thrown to the wolves and made to do things on my own. It was very frustrating to go back and forth always. **(SLT-US27)**

However, exactly what that autonomy might look like is open to interpretation here as 'being thrown to the wolves' is quite a stark description in this student's account of her experiences. In a similar vein, but viewed more positively, another student commented that there was a need to:

Extract 10.14

Acknowledge [that]we are students and that they [educators] are there to teach us. But not making us feel inferior to the therapists and giving us some space to work independently at the same time. **(OT-Mal32)**

Similarly, others referred to the need for practice educators to 'allow the student more responsibility to handle the clients themselves' (OT-Mal31), in turn allowing the student to 'develop their own identity' when tasks are delegated under 'adequate supervision' (OT-Ire43).

It seems then that the students came to see support as coming in various forms, and to varying extents. The notion of reassurance and affirmation featured either directly or indirectly in many experiential statements. Such experiential statements ranged from a simple call for 'more reassurance' (SLT-Ire1) to a desire not to be undermined or corrected in front of patients/clients (SLT-US25, PT-In29, SLT-SA45), and to be supported to become 'less afraid of being wrong – not put you down when you aren't fully sure of the answer to something' (OT-Ire41). One PT student summed up the need for reassurance and support in a critical way as follows (including reference to the 'imposter syndrome' discussed in Chapter 7):

Extract 10.15

I think it is a matter of experience and repetition in a clinical environment. More hands-on treatments with patients throughout the

> curriculum might help, but I think no matter what there will always be a time of uncertainty, lack of confidence, and feeling like an imposter. It is something that each student has to grow past on their way to becoming a clinician. **(PT-US10)**

The notion of 'growing past' these insecurities was seen by this student as just a part of the journey to 'becoming a clinician' (PT-US10).

The students also reflected upon the possibility of supervisors providing more encouragement to students while on placement and in the classroom. Being encouraged to ask questions 'as early as possible in your education at university' (SLT-Ire3) was seen as important by one student, while being allowed to 'make mistakes' was key for another (SLT-SA45). Providing encouragement to students was also referred to as embracing our 'differences as students' and providing 'more positivity' to students (SLT-SA45) in general.

Listening to the student (and allied healthcare professional) voice has been a core concern of the data discussed in this book. As can be concluded from the above discussion and from previous chapters, students have a lot to say as consumers of allied healthcare education and clinical practice. For the remaining sections of this book, we look to the future, being cognisant of a mandate from the students to pave the way forward with them, and alongside them, as they develop into the professionals they wish to become.

10.4 PAVING A WAY FORWARD

Thus far in this chapter, we have considered some ways forward for identity work through social interaction as proposed by the student respondents. We believe that hearing the collective student voice is important for educators so that the educational relationship can be one that is mutually beneficial and respectful to the contexts of teaching and learning through social interaction. While acknowledging that all contexts of teaching and learning, and the inherent teacher/learner relationships therein, are necessarily different and diverse, there remain core considerations for an improved educational experience, as described by the students. The main concerns of students for the *practical, collaborative, personalised* and *supportive* teaching and learning experiences outlined above are summarised in Figure 10.1.

Paving the way forward for identity development in allied healthcare education, therefore, includes a heightened focus on application of 'theory to practice', 'increased collaboration' through social interaction with other AHPs and students, enhanced attempts 'to personalise' the student experience, and finally, a more concerted effort to support students in becoming more 'autonomous' learners into their future. It is up to educators and students to work together to bring such realistic and practical goals into reality. We revisit these goals below in terms of what can be done to better support students on their learning journey to become a healthcare professional.

So, the question is posed then: what does all this information add up to? In the final paragraphs of this book, we avoid the overused analogy of a 'journey', preferring instead to talk of a student *trajectory* – that is, a route taken or a direction – dictated

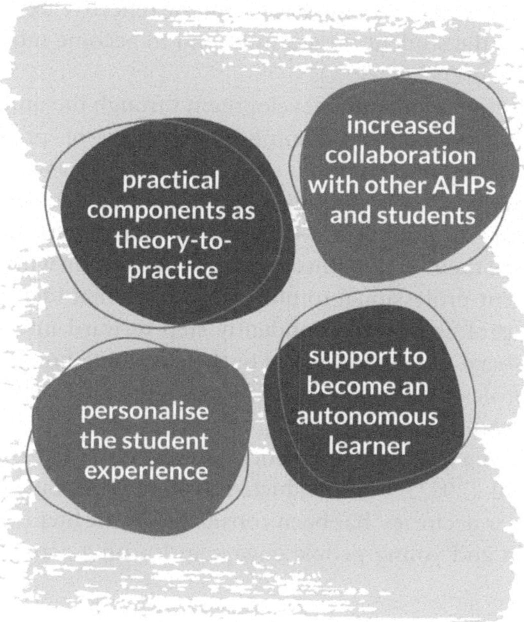

Figure 10.1 Key considerations in paving the way forward for student learning and identity development among AHP students

by the student experience and as articulated by them, and as influenced by their discipline's community of qualified professionals and supervisors.

10.4.1 A TRAJECTORY OF PROFESSIONAL IDENTITY FORMATION THROUGH SOCIAL INTERACTION IN EDUCATIONAL CONTEXTS

Despite our initial reservations about a limited yet diverse international, cross-discipline sample of respondents which informed the arguments in Chapters 7 to Chapter 10, the data captured a collective voice of those students surveyed as they navigated the final years of their allied healthcare education and as they readied themselves for the workplace. The similarities across their responses are striking and speak to the commonalities of the AHP student lived experience. Responding to a set of carefully adapted questions (from Sharpless et al. 2015; Table 6.5) offered the students a chance to reflect, to put words to their experiences that they may not have had the chance to do otherwise. It could be said that they were not only reflecting on their current 'self-as-student' (as they reflected on the many social interactions that they found themselves in while learning) but were also speaking to their 'future self' as a member of their chosen profession, their community of practice to come. From the quality and richness of the data discussed in this book, it seems that such opportunities for reflection are critical in professional identity formation. This finding is not new but is one that reinforces the need to allow reflective exercises to permeate curricula right across the student programme, and to become more interactive (see Wald et al. 2018, as referenced below).

Mapping the trajectory of identity development through the unfolding arguments in this book, we may suggest that coming from a place of 'pretending' in social interactions – or thinking oneself into a role – may be a necessary pre-requisite for the educational experience of becoming an AHP. Having the student acknowledge and occupy both their educational lifeworld and their socio-personal lifeworld, while communicating about their identity through social interaction with other professionals, equips the student professional to ultimately 'own' that identity. This 'owning' allows the student professional to confidently step forward into their community of practice, where social interaction is key to their ongoing honing of their identity as a fully-fledged professional upon graduation. Figure 10.2 shows that process, as discussed in the preceding chapters.

Our concern with the notion of 'trajectory', however, has also been recently taken up by Membrive et al. (2022), who conducted a recent systematic review of how the concept of 'learning trajectories' has been considered in the literature and as pertaining to how children and young people engage in learning across diverse contexts.

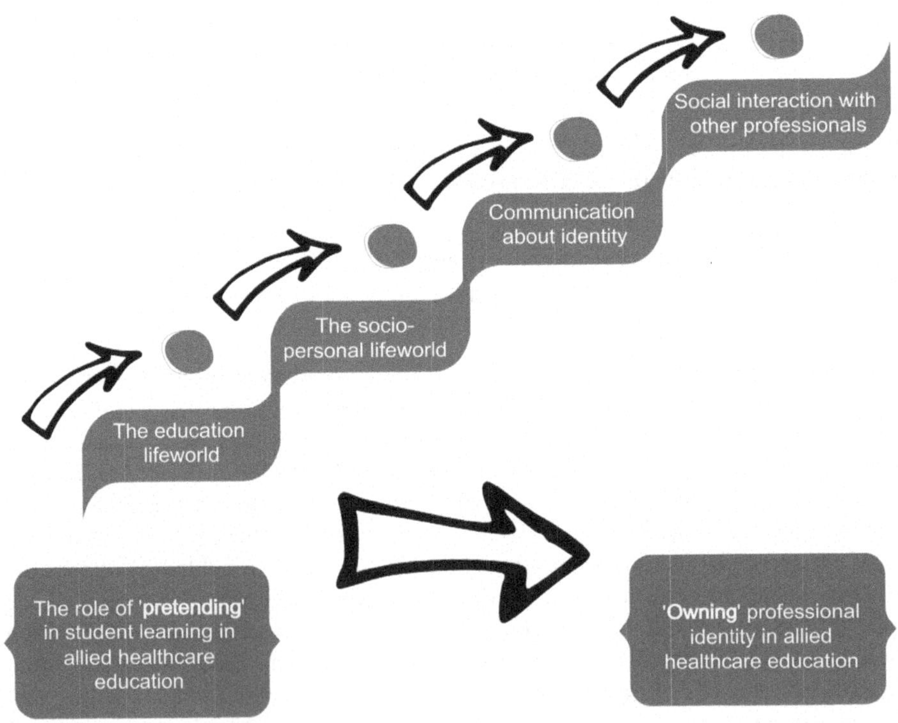

Figure 10.2 Visual representation of personal experiential themes by which social interaction may impact developing professional identity among students

Looking to both the empirical and theoretical content, they reviewed just under 60 articles and book chapters (dealing with the concept within primary, secondary, higher and career education contexts). Their review drew the following conclusions, calling for further consideration of the concept in research and teaching and learning practice (Membrive et al. 2022: 100658):

> One of the most salient ideas that emerges from the review is the consideration of personal learning trajectories as an integration of two different but interrelated levels of learning across contexts: the plane of participation and continuities across contexts and activities, and the plane of subjective learning experiences linked to that participation. In addition, learning trajectories are closely related to identity, agency, and interests. We can consider that identity and interest are phenomena that are constructed in the personal learning trajectory, both in people's participation in diverse activities and also in the subjective reconstruction of learning experiences. At the same time, they are phenomena that mediate the learner's agency and promote the construction of trajectories.

These conclusions are highly relevant to our own findings, especially in relation to the fusing or blending of what they propose are two 'planes', that of (i) participation across activities and contexts of learning, and (ii) the 'subjective reconstruction of those learning experiences', based on such participation experiences. Here we see both the importance of a range of diverse learning experiences and reflections on the same, both of which have been considered in our own arguments in this book thus far. Furthermore, and in keeping with our own socio-cultural stance, Membrive et al. (2022: 9) add that the 'role of other actors' (i.e. educators) is to help support and 'scaffold' those trajectories by 'increasing and promoting the flow of connections between activities and learning contexts and facilitating continuity across the learner's subjective experiences'. We return to the importance of this stance below, as we propose (like others to date) that making the implicit explicit is highly relevant in teaching and learning contexts. Furthermore, affording more credence to students' experiences of teaching and learning contexts is supported by the findings we have discussed in this book. The students' call for a personalised, practical, collaborative experience to facilitate autonomous learning must be heard when building upon existing curricular activities and designing new and innovative professional education initiatives. In the following sections we look at ways to honour their call, discussed against some recent developments in the area of healthcare education.

10.5 PERSONALISED, PRACTICAL, COLLABORATIVE EXPERIENCE TO FACILITATE AUTONOMOUS LEARNING

To deliver or at least to facilitate a personalised, practical, collaborative experience to facilitate autonomous learning is no mean task, but one that, as educators, we can strive to do by adapting or developing our teaching and learning practices while proactively considering student needs.

10.5.1 MAKING THE IMPLICIT EXPLICIT IN ALLIED HEALTHCARE EDUCATION

There are many practical ways of supporting students on their learning trajectory. In this section, we argue that students need to be encouraged to take (more) notice of social interaction for the valuable contribution it makes to their learning and professional development; in practice, taking notice of it can then be accounted for in classroom discussions or recorded in reflections (e.g. reflective logs, diaries, online discussion groups or fora via their institutional virtual learning environment (VLE)). As we have demonstrated in this book, common to many of the arguments presented is the place of social interaction; professionals and students alike acknowledge how much they learn about themselves and others from interacting with their peers and colleagues and seem to want more of just that to help integrate into and support themselves within their larger communities of practice. It seems then that identity work and social interaction are necessary bedfellows in allied healthcare education: each concept – or active process – cannot be discussed without the other; they are dynamically, even symbiotically related. However, the awareness of the relationship between identity and social interaction can be overlooked and missed due to lack of recognition of the centrality of social interaction to allied healthcare practice and education.

It seems then that educators and supervising clinicians are best placed to highlight and name the tacit learning and identity development that takes place in learning and clinical interactions. 'Making the implicit explicit' here is of the greatest importance. This idea is not new, its principles having been applied to many domains of teaching and learning, including as relevant to ethnic cultures in US elementary schools (Rothstein-Fisch, Trumbull and Garcia 2009), to morals and values in teacher education (e.g. Mergler 2008), literacy instruction (e.g. Brevit 2014; Didau 2014), to online teaching and learning experiences (Cassidy 2021) and to role modelling in medical education (Sternszus and Cruess 2016). Making the implicit explicit, and as relevant to just some of these targets (e.g. ethnicity, morals and values, and role modelling) echoes an argument we touched on in Chapter 2 (Section 2.2) of this book, where issues of diversity and inclusion were briefly considered. In paving any path forward in allied healthcare education and practice, diversity and inclusion must become embedded in practice and in the makeup of the student and AHP bodies. The question must be posed: what is the authenticity of 'role modelling' or any discussions of morals or values in allied healthcare if those roles and values are largely portrayed by a largely homogeneous – white, female and middle-class – demographic? Explicit attention to the richness, value and worth of diversity in race and ethnicity of the student cohort and AHP population is key to the educational experience for all, and not least to fully reflect and authentically represent the client/patient body that AHPs will ultimately serve. This need has not gone unnoticed across recent decades (e.g. Baldwin, Woods and Copeland Simmons 2006; Yeowell 2013; Knettle et al. 2021); however, progress is slow to address such needs. Universities and healthcare programmes have a duty to widen their student-intake demographic, while professional bodies must become more inclusive in their membership and training. Critically, the professions must move beyond 'a discourse of race neutrality that is ideologically consistent with colour-blind racism' (Yu et al. 2022: 578) and explicitly tackle the roots of the homogeneity in AHPs. Nancarrow and Borthwick (2021: 57) discuss the importance of 'intersectionality' in this context, that is, the recognition that 'social differences and divisions do not operate separately, but rather intersect', making for diverse, rich systems where, for example, gender, socio-economic status and ethnicity are integrative and part of the whole, as opposed to singular and separate. Wilbur et al. (2020: 222), among others in their review of relevant literature, conclude that in order to promote an environment of 'culturally responsive education and training', it seems that 'the most promising practices tended to be comprehensive programmes that include a combination of social support, academic support and financial support' – practical and 'do-able' solutions surely, within properly funded healthcare education and practice institutions.

Yet another concept relevant to the invisibility or implicit nature of processes in allied healthcare education and practice is the idea of the 'hidden curriculum'. The work of Hafferty and O'Donnell (2014) highlights the role of the hidden curriculum in in this context – an idea that has been discussed and debated since curricular formats, contexts and content have gained increasing attention from researchers and educators alike. The hidden curriculum can refer to the organised culture of the environment, that is, the implicit understandings and standards of the environment as contained and maintained. The hidden curriculum has been discussed in many spheres of healthcare and most often in medical education (Mulder et al. 2019: 42), where it is described as being 'generated by a professional microculture resulting from a process of group coping in which professional values are prioritised and interpreted in a specific way'. The notion of 'group coping' is relevant here and resonates with the idea of how group interactions have been described by Thomas, McGarty and Mavor (2016) as the 'crucible' of social identity formation. Hafferty and O'Donnell (2014) note the social and interactional nature of the hidden curriculum environment, while acknowledging that it too can be evident outside of the scope of social interactions.

Efforts have been made to expose – or make more explicit – the hidden curriculum through its assessment in medical education (Haidet and Teal 2014) and through approaching it in the medical workplace 'as a reflection of the professional microculture of a clinical team' (Mulder et al. 2019: 36). Traditionally, the hidden curriculum is intertwined and interlinked with other types of curricula, for example, the formal and informal curriculum. From the findings of our research, formal and informal curricular contexts were understood as not only referring to the physical environments (e.g. college, clinic or workplace) where social interaction takes place, but to the nature of those social interactions in a diverse range of milieus (e.g. in interactions with supervisors, professors, managers, family and peers). In allied healthcare practice and education, however, social interaction is one of the processes that AHPs often take for granted. In other words, it is just something that happens and is implicit to the modus operandi of the healthcare clinician, being the conduit for the delivery of healthcare across many disciplines. However, making this fact explicit to the student learner is often overlooked, and possibly relegated to a by-product of other more foregrounded teaching and learning activities. It is ironic that despite the often 'hidden' nature of such aspects of the curriculum, students and professionals talk about his aspect of their educational and work experience (as demonstrated in this book), affording salience to their experiences of social interaction aiding their professional identity formation. Karnieli-Miller et al. (2010) consider the idea that medical students' accounts can provide 'a window' on the nature and experience of the hidden curriculum, thus reinforcing the strength of the student voice in this context.

The above discussion also resonates with reflective practice, as previously discussed. The reflective practitioner will make explicit their learning in the workplace as they articulate to self, peers and/or supervisors what the challenges are in their daily practice and what they would like to do about them. Reflective practice is proactive. It is not hard to see from the many accounts shared by student AHPs that through reflection in their written accounts (in response to our survey) the students were already considering action into the future based on their learning from social interactions in the academic and clinical programmes (e.g. 'It [programme]challenges us to learn more about our profession and become advocates for our profession so that we can be active participants in the growth of the profession', PT-US11).

Moving forward, we would suggest that healthcare educators and supervising clinicians pay more attention to naming and highlighting social interaction as a core practical activity necessary for professional identity development in the many contexts that student professionals find themselves in. The value of the process of social interaction needs to be more obviously articulated. There are plenty of opportunities for this explicit reference, for example, in course handbooks and included in learning outcomes and module objectives, especially (but not only) in relation to clinical practice modules which are fundamental to healthcare programmes.

10.5.2 REFLECTIVE PRACTICE: PRACTICAL, PERSONAL AND COLLABORATIVE DIMENSIONS

We discussed in some detail the nature and value of reflection in Chapter 6 and indeed it is students' reflections that form the substantive data that have driven the many arguments put forward in this book. However, it can be the case that sometimes the more formal nature of some of these platforms – and written products – preclude students from more honestly or authentically expressing their worries and concerns in relation to clinical practicum, out of fear of being 'judged' or being 'marked down' in clinical assessments; students may just complete the task to 'get the job done' without putting the requisite time and thought into the (written) task. Mann and Walsh (2017: 132) warn against this tendency when engaging in written reflection tasks:

> Very often, writing entails the completion of checklist or pro-forma, a kind of 'tickbox' exercise which may not actually promote much reflection at all. Indeed, the repeated use of such instruments is likely to result in a mechanical, unthinking approach to reflection where the main concern is to get the task one rather than

> provide evidence of critical reflection. And of course, where reflective pieces form part of the assessment course work of a programme, they are subjected to the institutional assessment criteria of that course.

Nevertheless, there are ways of combatting the risk of reflective writing tasks being completed in an inauthentic or prosaic way and treated as 'pedestrian' by students. Mann and Walsh (2017: 133) argue that both 'audience' and 'purpose' are important considerations in reflective writing tasks, that is, 'reflective practitioners need to know why they are writing and who they are writing for'. Of relevance here is the fact that student respondents to our own survey, though not explicitly instructed to write 'their reflections' or 'in a reflective manner', ended up doing just that in response to the survey probes. The anonymous nature of this engagement most probably helped rather than hindered the authenticity of their responses. Moreover, the fact that their responses were not tethered to an assessment of sorts was probably an additional benefit.

To prevent some of the above factors getting in the way of authentic or veracious reflective writing and to nurture that task along, reflective writing can also become interactive. Wald et al. (2018: 7) discuss the notion of 'interactive reflective writing' (IRW) where healthcare educators:

> facilitate development of reflective capacity with crafting individualised written feedback to students' reflective writings. Such feedback includes supportive challenging of assumptions, exploring emotional responses (of patient and student), encouraging consideration of new perspectives as relevant, and highlighting lessons learned as well as sharing of relevant personal and/or clinical anecdotal experiences.

Indeed, echoing our own arguments in this book is Wald et al.'s reference to 'exploring emotional responses' and 'sharing of relevant personal and/or clinical anecdotal experiences', (the like of which were present in the students' accounts discussed in the latter chapters of this book), which seem fertile ground for these explorations and reflective work. Moreover, such interactive reflective writing could be extended to peer-to-peer contexts where perhaps a more relaxed interaction may prove conducive to authentic and honest reflections. The act of reflective writing, then, can become more personal, collaborative and interactive.

It seems then that there may be scope for a more open, relaxed forum where students can share information about their teaching and learning experiences in academic and clinical contexts. We live in an age of 'online being' – that is, we use our phones, tablets and computers to 'interact' with people in the virtual world, away from the face-to-face happenstance of meeting on the street or in the workplace corridor. People use online fora for all sorts of sharing activities (e.g. informing, instructing, chatting, gossiping, etc.). Given phones, tablets and such like are often the 'go-to' instruments for communicating, it seems that opportunities abound for exploitation of their use in student learning. For example, the establishment of a dedicated 'mobile app group' or other online platform may provide that environment for students to share aspects of their clinical and academic learning experiences. Most groups of third-level students already form such social online groups, not always for the sharing of content that has an educational component (but for arranging leisure or entertainment pursuits, for example). Nevertheless, before embarking on such an initiative, there are some important factors that would have to be considered, not least to ensure that such a forum can be a 'safe' place for expression of educational or clinical concerns while in training. Both the terms and conditions of involvement would need to be collectively drawn up and explicitly shared among potential members (similar to Mann and Walsh's (2017) consideration of 'audience' and 'purpose' referred to above). *Who* may be the administrator of such groups would be a starting point. It is not unusual in educational contexts to invite more senior or advanced students to mentor those in lower years, and something akin to this model might work in setting up such an online group. *What* content may be posted would also need to be considered to avoid, for example, confidentiality measures being breached (e.g. no mention or naming of medical sites, personnel or reference to patient details in messages while discussing clinical experiences) or inappropriate content being shared or posted. The *how*, then, of online sharing is also important. Given healthcare students are future professionals this should not be a concern, but online (over) sharing can occur and may not always be conducted in a professional or respectful manner. Over ten years ago, the risks of cyberbullying were discussed by Peebles (2014) in relation to children and adolescents, and unfortunately university students are not immune to such risks. Hence, close monitoring of such contexts remains necessary, even within the apparent safe environment of healthcare professional communities.

Gregory, Clegg and Cameron (2021: 150) describe 'case examples of practice' made available online to support speech and language therapy students during the recent pandemic. They also describe the development and uptake of a number of initiatives, including:

> a central, online student query document [which] was set up and provided a shared space for anonymised student queries from undergraduate and postgraduate programmes across all levels of study ... Staff were able to monitor this online forum and provide open, honest and timely responses.

A key component of the success of this 'student query document' could have been related to the 'anonymised' posting of concerns by students who viewed the document as a 'safe space' (as referred to above) to post queries and concerns about their 'learning, teaching, placement, and wellbeing' (Gregory et al. 2021: 150). Another initiative described by Gregory et al., with mixed success, was the setting up of online peer support groups, where students could share among themselves issues related to their courses, with the benefits reported as being predominantly in the realm of emotional support for each other in the absence of in-person social interaction in hallways and classrooms. Finally, Gregory and colleagues also share ideas around the development and operation of 'practice-based communities' (p. 151) and 'enhancing broader communities' (p. 152) within the context of the reduced attendance in 'live' clinical placements due to Covid-19 restrictions, ideas which once again can be easily extended to the post-Covid world of live social interaction. Being aware of the threats to developing a sense of professional identity divorced from the class- or clinic room was the catalyst for the above ideas outlined by the authors, recognising 'a collective responsibility to approach this crisis [Covid-19] as an opportunity for transformation and growth' (p. 153).

Recognising the opportunity for transformation and growth beyond the pandemic, there are many other online fora that may be exploited and which can be more typically used to support academic content or classroom discussions. For example, the development of Wikis, where students can essentially interact with a bespoke webpage to make changes, edit, add and correct information as part of their learning group, have been known to be integral to module learning and design in some programmes where students' participation is monitored. However, Zheng, Niiya and Warschauer (2015) warn of the need for firm pedagogical supports underpinning the implementation of this format to ensure optimal learning for the online learning community and its instructors.

It seems then that there are lessons to be learnt from measures developed during the pandemic, with such online strategies easily honed, improved and extended for practical application with AHP students in training. Such measures can supplement the more usual and traditional methods used in clinical healthcare education where, for example, video feedback and evaluation are used extensively. There is, however, a growing body of work developing in the healthcare professions that tends to look outwards, away from their core disciplines in order to help support professionals' learning and practice in different ways. Below, in our closing paragraphs, we consider once such route, that of health humanities, and how this area has begun to show itself in teaching and learning practices.

10.5.3 ALLIED HEALTHCARE EDUCATION AND PRACTICE: A CASE FOR HEALTH HUMANITIES

Finally, this section on considering personalised, practical and collaborative experiences to facilitate autonomous learning among AHP students would not be complete without touching on a relatively new development in this area of teaching and learning. More often discussed with regard to medicine (e.g. Macnaughton 2011; Bates, Bleakley and Goodman 2014; Guy 2024), the introduction of the arts and humanities as a stimulating forum to reflect on integrating theory and practice, and indeed attending to all aspects of healthcare and healthcare interaction across professional disciplines, is gaining momentum. For example, using the arts and humanities as a springboard for the teaching and learning of key clinical skills is becoming popular as educators reference the use of popular media, such as film and television, along with prose and poetry, to discuss skills-based learning and skill implementation (e.g. rapport building, case history taking, diagnostic interviews, ethical decision-making practice). Medical humanities – or the preferred term 'health humanities' (Crawford et al. 2010; O'Neill et al. 2016) – has the potential to render many other contexts as avenues to explore in allied healthcare education and practice, not least in the areas of professional identity and social interaction which have been the focus of this book.

In fact, Hooper at al. (2005: 131) review some films useful for what they term 'the professional and personal self of the physician', including exploration of doctor–patient interaction. Moreover, Waxman et al. (2005) provide a review of some films that may be used to discuss aspects of social interaction, for example, 'active listening', 'awkward moments' and 'interruptions' in clinical interaction.

The potential for the creative contribution of health humanities to other disciplines outside of medicine has not been overlooked. Walsh (2020) and Walsh and Mallinson (2022) consider healthcare humanities with regard to understanding communication disorder and within the context of an SLT curriculum. Other disciplines have long-recognised the potential of humanities in practice. Murray et al. (2000) discuss its relevance to 'practising reflection' in occupational therapy and Thow and Murray (1991) discuss the area's potential contribution to physiotherapy; Smith et al. (2006) discuss its value to education in both of these disciplines. Who knows where such creative leaps will take allied healthcare education, to ultimately qualify professionals who are well-informed, autonomous, critical thinkers and 'professional' to their core.

10.6 FINAL WORDS

This book started out with an objective to explore how social interaction impacts a developing professional identity among students in AHP education, with reference to speech and language therapy, physiotherapy, and occupational therapy. The writing of this book mostly took place during the pandemic (2020–3) and as the writing ends, we are emerging from the early responses to that pandemic while learning to live in its shadow.

Universities, including with regard to the education of allied health professionals, adapted to the disruption, and the pandemic has changed the way we behave, socially and educationally. Some of these changes are positive but there have also been casualties. As referred to in various chapters throughout this book, some students welcomed the move to online teaching and learning and the new learning experience of conducting 'telehealth' while on clinical placements. Others, however, significantly missed the in-person daily social interaction that is so much a part of education in the allied healthcare domains of practice. The following question arises: where do the experiences of the Covid-19 pandemic leave allied healthcare education now and what does the current landscape mean for the development of professional identity in these and future students?

The nature of allied healthcare education has in many cases incorporated the new learning and innovation resulting from the pandemic experiences. This new learning does not just extend to students but to their educators also. What started out for many as a 'steep learning curve' has become routine practice as they incorporate online innovations to enhance and enrich their teaching and learning. However, educators too have missed the 'buzz' of the in-person classroom interaction to stimulate engagement.

This book has highlighted the almost omnipresent nature of social interaction in healthcare education and practice. Students and healthcare professionals' accounts demonstrate the ubiquitous nature of social interaction in the context of healthcare and healthcare education, reinforced by the voices of those in the healthcare workplace; by professional discipline members as they recall the impact of their work with clients; and finally, by the collective student voice across disciplines and programmes. The evidence for the pivotal role of social interaction in allied healthcare and education and practice is there, waiting to be excavated, just as we have attempted to do in this volume, thereby earning its rightful place in dynamic contexts of teaching, learning and professional development in allied healthcare.

REFERENCES

Abrahams, K. and C. Brady (2013), 'Graduate reflective practice programme: Were long-term objectives achieved?', *Journal of Medical Imaging and Radiation Sciences*, 44(4), 203–8. https://doi.org/10.1016/j.jmir.2013.07.003

Adshead, G. and E. Horne (2021), *The Devil You Know: Stories of Human Cruelty and Compassion*. London: Faber & Faber.

Alhasan, M. and Q. Al-Horani (2021), 'Students' perspective on the online delivery of radiography and medical imaging program during COVID-19 pandemic', *Journal of Medical Imaging and Radiation Sciences*, 52(4S), S68–S77. https://doi.org/10.1016/j.jmir.2021.07.009

American Speech and Hearing Association (2019), 'Role ambiguity and speech-language pathology', *The ASHA Leader*, 14(16), 12–15. https://doi.org/10.1044/leader.FTR1.14162009.12

Artioli, G., L. Deiana, F. De Vincenzo, M. Raucci, G. Amaducci, M.C. Bassi, S. Di Leo, M. Hayter and L. Ghirotto (2021), 'Health professionals and students' experiences of reflective writing in learning: A qualitative meta-synthesis', *BMC Medical Education*, 21, 394. https://doi.org/10.1186/s12909-021-02831-4

Ashby, S.E., J. Adler and L. Herbert (2016), 'An exploratory study into occupational therapy students' perspectives of professional identity', *Australian Occupational Therapy Journal*, 63, 233–43. https://doi.org/10.1111/1440-1630.12271

Association of Occupational Therapists of Ireland (AOTI) (n.d.), 'What is occupational Therapy?' *AOTI*, www.aoti.ie/what-is-ot (accessed 23 February 2023).

Bailey, J.R. and S. Rehman (2022), 'Don't underestimate the power of self-reflection', https://hbr.org/2022/03/dont-underestimate-the-power-of-self-reflection (accessed 14 February 2024).

Baird, M. (2008), 'Towards the development of a reflective radiographer: Challenges and constraints', *Biomedical Imaging and Intervention Journal*, 4(1), e9. https://doi.org/10.2349/biij.4.1.e9

Baldwin, A., K. Woods and M. Copeland Simmons (2006), 'Diversity of the allied health workforce: The unmet challenge', *Journal of Allied Health*, 35(2), 116–20.

Banks, T.M. (2022), 'Leading the OT profession toward diversity, equity, and inclusion: Let's talk academia', *American Journal of Occupational Therapy*, 76(S1), 7610505071p1. https://doi.org/10.5014/ajot.2022.76S1-PO71

Bar, M.A., M. Pade, T. Jarus, S. Gat, Y. Kaufman Cohen and L. Lipskaya-Velikovsky (2018), 'Problem-based learning in occupational therapy curriculum – implications and challenges', *Disability and Rehabilitation*, 40(17), 2098–104. https://doi.org/10.1080/09638288.2017.1325942

Barrows, H.S. and R.M. Tamblyn (1980), *Problem-Based Learning: An Approach to Medical Education*. New York: Springer.

Bassir, S.H., P. Sadr-Eshkevari, S. Amirikhorheh and N.Y. Karimbux (2014), 'Problem-based learning in dental education: A systematic review of the literature', *Journal of Dental Education*, 78, 98–109. https://doi.org/10.1002/j.0022-0337.2014.78.1.tb05661.x

Bates, V., A. Bleakley and S. Goodman (eds.) (2014), *Medicine, Health and the Arts: Approaches to the Medical Humanities*. London: Routledge.

Bazrafkan, L., A.A. Hayat, S.Z. Tabei and L. Amirsalari (2019), 'Clinical teachers as positive and negative role models: An explanatory sequential mixed method design', *Journal of Medical Ethics and History of Medicine*, 12, 11. https://doi.org/10.18502/jmehm.v12i11.1448

Berger, P.L. and T. Luckmann (1967), *The Social Construction of Reality*. Harmondsworth: Penguin.

Binyamin, G. (2018), 'Growing from dilemmas: Developing a professional identity through collaborative reflections on relational dilemmas', *Advances in Health Science Education*, 23, 43–60. https://doi.org/10.1007/s10459-017-9773-2

Birney, M.E. (2023), *Self and Identity: The Basics*. Abingdon: Routledge.

Boniface, G. (2002), 'Understanding reflective practice in occupational therapy', *British Journal of Therapy and Rehabilitation*, 9(8), 294–98. https://doi.org/10.12968/bjtr.2002.9.8.13656

Bouayed, H., S. Dost and T. Hussian (2018), 'Medical students' reflective writings about challenging patient encounters: A final year medical student's perspective', *Medical Teacher*, 41(2), 235. https://doi.org/10.1080/0142159X.2018.1513643

Brackenridge, S.A. (2007), 'Perceptions of reflective practice among recent Australian radiation therapy graduates', *Radiographer: The Official Journal of the Australian Institute of Radiography*, 54, 18–23. https://doi.org/10.1002/j.2051-3909.2007.tb00068.x

Brevit, L.M. (2014), 'Making implicit practice explicit: How do upper secondary teachers describe their reading comprehension strategies instruction?', *International Journal of Educational Research*, 67, 52–66. https://doi.org/10.1016/j.ijer.2014.05.002

Bridges, S.J. (2018), 'Professional identity development: Learning and journeying together', *Research in Social and Administrative Pharmacy*, 14(3), 290–4. https://doi.org/10.1016/j.sapharm.2017.03.054

Brown, J.S. and P. Duguid (1991), 'Organisational learning and communities-of-practice: Toward a unified view of working, learning, and innovation', *Organisation Science*, 2(1), 40–57. https://doi.org/10.1287/orsc.2.1.40

Brown, S. and J. Everson (2019), 'Belonging, becoming, owning: The interplay between identity and self-esteem in trainee teachers in post-compulsory education and training', *Research in Post-Compulsory Education*, 24(2–3), 231–50. https://doi.org/10.1080/13596748.2019.1596419

Browne, C., P. Wall, S. Batt and R. Bennett (2018), 'Understanding perceptions of nursing professional identity in students entering an Australian undergraduate nursing degree', *Nurse Education in Practice*, 32, 90–6. https://doi.org/10.1016/j.nepr.2018.07.006

Burges Watson, D.L., R. Sanoff, J.E. Mackintosh, J.L. Saver, G.A. Ford, C. Price, S. Starkman, M. Eckstein, R. Conwit, A. Grace and M.J. Murtagh (2012), 'Evidence from the scene: Paramedic perspectives on involvement in out-of-hospital research', *Annals of Emergency Medicine*, 60(5), 641–50. https://doi.org/10.1016/j.annemergmed.2011.12.002

Byng, S. and J. Felson Duchan (2005), 'Social model philosophies and principles: Their applications to therapies for aphasia', *Aphasiology*, 19(10–11), 906–22. https://doi.org/10.1080/02687030544000128

Caeiro, C., E.B. Cruz and C. Pereira (2014), 'Arts, literature and reflective writing as educational strategies to promote narrative reasoning capabilities among physiotherapy students', *Physiotherapy Theory and Practice*, 30(8), 572–80. https://doi.org/10.3109/09593985.2014.928919

Cameron, A., S.M. McPhail, K. Hudson, J. Fleming, J. Lethlean and E. Finch (2015), 'Increasing the confidence and knowledge of occupational therapy and physiotherapy students when communicating with people with aphasia: A pre–post intervention study', *Speech, Language and Hearing*, 18(3), 148–55. https://doi.org/10.1179/2050572814Y.0000000062

Cameron, A., S.M. McPhail, K. Hudson, J. Fleming, J. Lethlean and E. Finch (2017), 'A pre–post intervention study investigating the confidence and knowledge of health professionals communicating with people with aphasia in a metropolitan hospital', *Aphasiology*, 31(3), 359–74. https://doi.org/10.1080/02687038.2016.1225277

Carroll, M. (2009), 'Supervision: Critical reflection for transformational learning, Part 1', *The Clinical Supervisor*, 28(2), 210–20. https://doi.org/10.1080/07325220903344015

Cassidy, D. (2021), 'Making the implicit explicit: Improve online learning through presence', *Times Higher Education*, www.timeshighereducation.com/campus/making-implicit-explicit-improve-online-learning-through-presence (accessed 10 November 2023).

Caty, M.È., E.A. Kinsella and P.C. Doyle (2015), 'Reflective practice in speech-language pathology: A scoping review', *International Journal of Speech and Language Pathology*, 17(4), 411–20. https://doi.org/10.3109/17549507.2014.979870

Clarke, M, A. Hyde and J. Drennan (2013), 'Professional identity in higher education', in Kehm, B.M and U. Teichler (eds.), *The Academic Profession in Europe: New Tasks and New Challenges, The Changing Academy*. The Changing Academic Profession in International Comparative Perspective 5. Dordrecht: Springer Science Business Media, pp. 7–21.

Clouder, L. (2000), 'Reflective practice in physiotherapy education: A critical conversation', *Studies in Higher Education*, 25(2), 211–23. https://doi.org/10.1080/713696142

Clouston, T.J., L. Westcott, S.W. Whitcombe, J. Riley and R. Matheson (eds.) (2010), *Problem-Based Learning in Health and Social Care*. London: Blackwell.

Colaianni, D., G. Tovar, D. Wilson and H. Zapanta (2022), 'Factors influencing the diversity of occupational therapy students', *Journal of Occupational Therapy Education*, 6(1). https://doi.org/10.26681/jote.2022.060102

Collins Dictionary (2023), 'Allied health professions', www.collinsdictionary.com/dictionary/english/allied-health- (accessed 5 August 2020).

Connect – The Communication Disability Network (2023), 'Living with aphasia: UK Connect', www.aphasia.org/stories/living-with-aphasia-uk-connect/ (accessed 23 February 2023).

Cook, K.J., C. Messick and M.J. McAuliffe (2023), 'Written reflective practice abilities of SLT students across the degree programme', *International Journal of Language and Communication Disorders*, 58(4), 994–1016. https://doi.org/10.1111/1460-6984.12815

Cooper, H. and E. Spencer-Dawe (2006), 'Involving service users in interprofessional education: Narrowing the gap between theory and practice', *Journal of Interprofessional Care*, 20, 603–17. https://doi.org/10.1080/13561820601029767

Coster, S., I. Norman, T. Murrells, S. Kitchen, E. Meerabeau, E. Sooboodoo and L. d'Avray (2008), 'Interprofessional attitudes amongst undergraduate students in the health professions: A longitudinal questionnaire survey', *International Journal of Nursing Studies*, 45(11), 1667–81. https://doi.org/10.1016/j.ijnurstu.2008.02.008

Crawford, P., B. Brown, V. Tischler and C. Baker (2010), 'Health humanities: The future of medical humanities?' *Mental Health Review Journal*, 1(3), 4–10. https://doi.org/10.5042/mhrj.2010.0654

Crawford, J., S. Kippax, J. Onyx, U. Gault and P. Benton (1992), *Emotion and Gender*. London: Sage.

Cross, V., C. Liles, J. Conduit and J. Price (2004), 'Linking reflective practice to evidence of competence: A workshop for allied health professionals', *Reflective Practice*, 5(1), 3–31. https://doi.org/10.1080/1462394032000169938

Cruess, S.R., R.L. Cruess and Y. Steinert (2019), 'Supporting the development of a professional identity: General principles', *Medical Teacher*, 41(6), 641–9. https://doi.org/10.1080/0142159X.2018.1536260

de Visser, E. (2021), *That One Patient: Doctors and Nurses' Stories of the Patients Who Changed Their Lives Forever*. London: Fourth Estate.

Deisseroth, K. (2021), *Connections: A Story of Human Feeling*. London: Penguin Random House.

Department of Health (2020), *Sharing the Vision: A Mental Health Policy for Everyone*. Dublin: Stationery Office Government of Ireland.

Department of Health and Children (2006), *A Vision for Change: Report on the ExpertGroup on Mental Health Policy*. Dublin: Stationery Office, Government of Ireland.

Dewey, J. (1933), *How We Think*. Chelmsford, MA: Courier Corporation.

Didau, D. (2014), *The Secret of Literacy: Making the Implicit, Explicit*. Carmarthen, Wales: Independent Thinking Press.

Dijk, S.W, E.J. Duijzer and M. Wienold (2020), 'Role of active patient involvement in undergraduate medical education: A systematic review', *British Medical Journal Open*, 10: e037217. https://doi.org/10.1136/bmjopen-2020-037217

Dring, J.C. (2019), 'Problem-based learning – Experiencing and understanding the prominence during medical school: Perspective', *Annals of Medicine and Surgery*, 47, 27–8. https://doi.org/10.1016/j.amsu.2019.09.004

Eatough, V. and K. Shaw (2019), '"It's like having an evil twin": An interpretative phenomenological analysis of the lifeworld of a person with Parkinson's disease', *Journal of Research in Nursing*, 24(1–2), 49–58. https://doi.org/10.1177/1744987118821396

Edwards, H. and D. Dirette (2010), 'The relationship between professional identity and burnout among occupational therapists', *Occupational Therapy in Health Care*, 24(2), 119–29. https://doi.org/10.3109/07380570903329610

Ellis, R. and E. Hogard (2021), 'Professional identity: Issues and approaches', in Ellis, R. and E. Hogard (eds.), *Professional Identity in the Caring Professions: Meaning, Measurement and Mastery*. London: Routledge, pp. 1–16.

Erickson, S. and T. Serry (2016), 'Comparing alternate learning pathways within a problem-based learning speech-language pathology curriculum', *International Journal of Speech-Language Pathology*, 18(1), 97–107. https://doi.org/10.3109/17549507.2015.1089936

Erickson, S. and T. Serry (2020), 'Graduate perspectives of a Problem-Based Learning (PBL) speech language pathology curriculum', *Speech, Language and Hearing*, 23(2), 101–9. https://doi.org/10.1080/2050571X.2019.1650429

Evans, J.R. and A. Mathur (2005), 'The value of online surveys', *Internet Research*, 15, 196–219. https://doi.org/10.1108/10662240510590360

Evans, J.R. and A. Mathur (2018), 'The value of online surveys: A look back and a look ahead', *Internet Research*, 28(4), 854–87. https://doi.org/10.1108/IntR-03-2018-0089

Farr, F. (2005), 'Reflecting on reflections: The spoken word as a professional development tool in language teacher education', https://hdl.handle.net/10344/4588 (accessed 12 February 2024).

Finch, E., A. Cameron, J. Fleming, J. Lethlean, K. Hudson and S. McPhail (2017), 'Does communication partner training improve the conversation skills of speech-language pathology students when interacting with people with aphasia?', *Journal of Communication Disorders*, 68, 1–9. https://doi.org/10.1016/j.jcomdis.2017.05.004

Fincham, A.G. and C.F. Shuler (2001), 'The changing face of dental education: The impact of PBL', *Journal of Dental Education*, 65, 406–21. https://doi.org/10.1002/j.0022-0337.2001.65.5.tb03410.x

Gibbs, G. (1988), *Learning by Doing: A Guide to Teaching and Learning Methods*. Oxford: Further Education Unit at Oxford Polytechnic.

Giddens, A. (1991), *Modernity and Self-identity: Self and Society in the Late Modern Age*. Cambridge: Polity Press.

Glen, S. and K. Wilkie (eds.) (2000), *Problem Based Learning in Nursing: A New Model for a New Context?* London: Macmillan Press.

Goffman, E. (1959), *The Presentation of Self in Everyday Life*. New York: Doubleday.

Goffman, E. (1967), *Interaction Ritual*. New York: Doubleday.

Gray, H., K. Colthorpe, H. Ernst and L. Ainscough (2020), 'Professional identity of undergraduate occupational therapy students', *Journal of Occupational Therapy Education*, 4(1). https://doi.org/10.26681/jote.2020.040102

Gray, J. and T. Morton (2018), *Social Interaction and English Language Teacher Identity*. Edinburgh: Edinburgh University Press.

Gregory, E., J. Clegg and H. Cameron (2021), 'Supporting speech and language therapy students in uncertain times', *Advances in Communication and Swallowing*, 24(2), 147–55. https://doi.org/10.3233/ACS-210030

Guillemin, M., J. Archer, S. Nunn and S. Regan de Bere (2014), 'Revalidation: Patients or process? Analysis using visual data', *Health Policy*, 114(2–3), 128–38. https://doi.org/10.1016/j.healthpol.2013.12.006

Guinan, E. M., E. Barrett, F. Neill, T. Grimes, D. Sullivan, M. O'Sullivan, A. Patterson, T. Stapleton, I.P. Walsh, J.J. Walsh and K.C. Conlon (2018), 'Attitudes to interprofessional education among health science students engaging in a multidisciplinary workshop series', *International Journal of Health Sciences Education*, 5(1). https://dc.etsu.edu/ijhse/vol5/iss1/2

Gunn, H., H. Hunter and B. Haas (2012), 'Problem based learning in physiotherapy education: A practice perspective', *Physiotherapy*, 98(4), 330–5. https://doi.org/10.1016/j.physio.2011.05.005

Guy, C. (2024), *The Art of Medical Communication: Bringing the Humanities into Clinical Practice*. London: CRC Press, Taylor & Francis.

Guy, L., K. Cranwell, D. Hitch and C. McKinstry (2020), 'Reflective practice facilitation within occupational therapy supervision processes: A mixed method study', *Australian Occupational Therapy*, 67(4), 320–9.

Hafferty, F.W. and J.F. O'Donnell (2014), 'Working within the framework: Some personal and system-level journeys into the field', in Hafferty, F.W. and J.F. O'Donnell (eds.), *The Hidden Curriculum in Health Professional Education*. Hanover, NH: Dartmouth College Press, pp. 21–2.

Haidet, P. and C.R. Teal (2014), 'Organising chaos: A conceptual framework for assessing hidden curricula in medical education', in Hafferty, F.W. and J.F. O'Donnell (eds.), *The Hidden Curriculum in Health Professional Education*. Hanover, NH: Dartmouth College Press, pp. 84–95.

Hallinger, P. (2021), 'Tracking the evolution of the knowledge base on problem-based learning: A bibliometric review, 1972–2019', *The Interdisciplinary Journal of Problem-Based Learning*, 15(1). https://doi.org/10.14434/ijpbl.v15i1.28984

Hammond, R., V. Cross and A. Moore (2016), 'The construction of professional identity by physiotherapists: A qualitative study', *Physiotherapy*, 102(1), 71–7. https://doi.org/10.1016/j.physio.2015.04.002

Hayes, C., A. Fox, J. Scott-Thomas and Y. Graham (2018), 'The relevance of tacit knowledge to healthcare assistant practice', *British Journal of Healthcare Assistants*, 12(2), 84–90. https://doi.org/10.12968/bjha.2018.12.2.84

Health Services Executive (HSE) (2019), *A Guide to the Health and Social Care Professions.* Galway, Ireland: National HSCP Office.

Higgins, E.T. (1987), 'Self-discrepancy: A theory relating self and affect', *Psychological Review,* 94(3), 319–40. https://doi.org/10.1037/0033-295X.94.3.319

Hmelo-Silver, C.E. (2004), 'Problem-based learning: What and how do students learn?' *Educational Psychology Review,* 16(3), 235–66. https://doi.org/10.1023/B:EDPR.0000034022.16470.f3

Holtz, B.E. (2021), 'Patients' perceptions of telemedicine visits before and after the coronavirus disease 2019 pandemic', *Telemedicine and E-Health,* 27(1), 107–12. https://doi.org/10.1089/tmj.2020.0168

Hooper, S.P., M. Alexander, T.A. Albright, C. Wan, J.K. Burks and P. Lenahan (2005), 'The professional and personal self of the physician', in Alexander, M., P. Lenahan and A. Pavlov (eds.), *Cinemeducation: A Comprehensive Guide to Using Film in Medical Education.* Oxford: Radcliffe Publishing, pp. 131–6.

Hoppler, S.S., R. Segerer and J. Nikitin (2022), 'The six components of social interactions: Actor, Partner, Relation, Activities, Context, and Evaluation', *Frontiers in Psychology,* 12. https://doi.org/10.3389/fpsyg.2021.743074

Howatson-Jones, L. (2016), *Reflective Practice in Nursing.* London: Sage.

Hsieh, J-G., L-C. Kuo and Y-W. Wang (2019), 'Learning medical professionalism: The application of appreciative enquiry and social media', *Medical Education Online,* 24, 1586507. https://doi.org/10.1080/10872981.2019.1586507

Hutchins, E. (1995), *Cognition in the Wild.* Cambridge, MA: MIT Press.

Ikiugu, M.N. and H.M. Rosso (2003), 'Facilitating professional identity in occupational therapy students', *Occupational Therapy International,* 10(3), 206–25. https://doi.org/10.1002/oti.186

Irish Association of Speech and Language Therapy (IASLT) (2022), 'Considering a career in speech and language therapy?' *IASLT,* www.iaslt.ie/a-career-in-speech-language-therapy/ (accessed 23 February 2023).

Jagoe, C. and R. Roseingrave (2011), '"If this is what I'm meant to be...": The journeys of students participating in a conversation partner scheme for people with aphasia', *Journal of Academic Ethics,* 9(2), 127–48. https://doi.org/10.1007/s10805-011-9140-5

Jagoe, C. and I.P. Walsh (2016), '"Dear Fabulous!" Personal and professional identities evolving in the interactional context of self-reflection', *Journal of Interactional Research in Communication Disorders,* 7(2), 169–89. https://doi.org/10.1558/jircd.v7i2.29883

Joyce-McCoach, J. and K. Smith (2016), 'A teaching model for health professionals learning reflective practice', *Procedia – Social and Behavioral Sciences,* 228, 265–71. https://doi.org/10.1016/j.sbspro.2016.07.039

Karnieli-Miller, O., T.R. Vu, M.C. Holtman, S.G. Clyman and T.S. Inui (2010), 'Medical students' professionalism narratives: A window on the informal and hidden curriculum', *Academic Medicine,* 85, 124–33. https://doi.org/10.1097/ACM.0b013e3181c42896

Kemp, N. and R. Grieve (2014), 'Face-to-face or face-to-screen? Undergraduates' opinions and test performance in classroom vs. online learning', *Frontiers in Psychology,* 5, 1278. https://doi.org/10.3389/fpsyg.2014.01278

Killion, J. and G. Todnem (1991), 'A process of personal theory building', *Educational Leadership,* 48(6), 14–17.

Kinsella, E.A., È. Caty, S. Ng and K. Jenkins (2012), 'Reflective practices for allied health: Theory and applications', in English, L.M. (ed.), *Adult Education and Health.* London: University of Toronto Press, pp. 210–28.

Knettle, M., R.S. King, A.S. Nowacki, J.K. Stoller, P. Patel and N.R. Barbor (2021), 'Representing diversity or lack-thereof: An analysis of college/university health science education programme websites', *Journal of Best Practices in Health Professions Diversity*, 14(2), 113–24. www.jstor.org/stable/27203545

Knightbridge, L. (2019), 'Reflection-in-practice: A survey of Australian occupational therapists', *Australian Occupational Therapy Journal*, 66, 337–46. https://doi.org/10.1111/1440-1630.12559

Kolb, D.A. (1984), *Experiential Learning: Experience as the Source of Learning and Development* (Vol. 1). Englewood Cliffs, NJ: Prentice-Hall.

Korpi, H., L. Peltokallio and A. Piirainen (2014), 'The story models of physiotherapy students' professional development: Narrative research', *European Journal of Physiotherapy*, 16(4), 219–29. https://doi.org/10.3109/21679169.2014.934279

Koshy, K., C. Limb, B. Gundogan, K. Whitehurst and D.J. Jafree (2017), 'Reflective practice in health care and how to reflect effectively', *International Journal of Surgery Oncology*, 2(6), e20. https://doi.org/10.1097/IJ9.0000000000000020

Kovalcikiene. K. and L. Buksnyte-Marmiene (2015), 'Towards an understanding of doctoral students' professional identity complexity', *Procedia – Social and Behavioural Sciences*, 191, 2693–8. https://doi.org/10.1016/j.sbspro.2015.04.603

Kovarsky, D. and I.P. Walsh (2018), 'Issue editor foreword', *Topics in Language Disorders*, 38(2), 91–5. https://doi.org/10.1097/TLD.0000000000000152

Kyle, M.A., R.J. Blendon, M.G. Findling and J.M Benson (2021), 'Telehealth use and satisfaction among U.S. households: Results of a national survey', *Journal of Patient Experience*, 8, 23743735211052737. https://doi.org/10.1177/23743735211052737

Kyte, R., H. Frank and Y. Thomas (2018), 'Physiotherapy students' experiences of role-emerging placements: A qualitative study', *International Journal of Practice-based Learning in Health and Social Care*, 6(2), 1–13. https://doi.org/10.18552/ijpblhsc.v6i2.505

Lau, D.C. and J.K. Murnighan (1998), 'Demographic diversity and fault lines: The compositional dynamics of organisational groups', *Academy of Management Review*, 23(2), 325–40. https://doi.org/10.2307/259377

Launer, J. (2022), *Reflective Practice in Medicine and Multi-Professional Healthcare*. London: CRC Press, Taylor & Francis.

Lavie-Ajayi, M., N. Almog and M. Krumer-Nevo (2012), 'Chronic pain as a narratological distress: A phenomenological study', *Chronic Illness*, 8(3), 192–200. https://doi.org/10.1177/1742395312449665

Lindquist, I., M. Engardt, L. Garnham, F. Poland and B. Richardson (2006), 'Physiotherapy students' professional identity on the edge of working life', *Medical Teacher*, 28(3), 270–6. https://doi.org/10.1080/01421590600605272

Little, W. (2016), *Introduction to Sociology*. 2nd Canadian edition. Victoria, BC: BCcampus. https://opentextbc.ca/introductiontosociology2ndedition/

Liu, C., P. Wan, G-J. Hwang, Y-F. Tu and Y. Wang (2023), 'From competition to social interaction: A mobile team-based competition approach to promoting students' professional identity and perceptions', *Interactive Learning Environments*, 31(2), 1158–72. https://doi.org/10.1080/10494820.2020.1823855

Loughran, J. (1996), *Developing Reflective Practice: Learning about Teaching and Learning Through Modelling*. London: Falmer Press.

Lucey, J. (2014), *In My Room: The Recovery Journey as Encountered by a Psychiatrist*. Dublin: Gill & Macmillan Ltd.

MacAskill, W., W.J. Chua, H. Woodall and J. Pinidiyapathirage (2023), 'Beyond the written reflection: A systematic review and qualitative synthesis of creative approaches to reflective learning amongst medical students', *Perspectives on Medical Education*, 12(1), 361–71. https://doi.org/10.5334/pme.914

Machost, H. and M. Stains (2023), 'Reflective practices in education: A primer for practitioners', *CBE Life Sciences Education*, 22(2), es2. https://doi.org/10.1187/cbe.22-07-0148

Macnaughton, J. (2011), 'Medical humanities' challenge to medicine', *Journal of Evaluation in Clinical Practice*, 17(5), 927–32. https://doi.org/10.1111/j.1365-2753.2011.01728.x

MacRae, D., M.R. Jara, J. Tyerman and M. Luctkar-Flude (2021), 'Investing in engagement: Integrating virtual learning experiences across an undergraduate nursing programme', *Clinical Simulation in Nursing*, 52, 17–32. https://doi.org/10.1016/j.ecns.2020.12.005

Malik, M. (2023), *A Vision from the Margin: Intersectional Insights on Navigating Diversity in Speech and Language Therapy*. Guildford: J&R Press.

Malthouse, R. and J. Roffey-Barensten (2020), *Reflective Practice in Education and Training*, London: Learning Matters, Sage.

Mann, S. and S. Walsh (2013), '"RP" or "RIP": A critical perspective on reflective practice', *Applied Linguistics Review*, 4(2), 291–315. https://doi.org/10.1515/applirev-2013-0013

Mann, S. and S. Walsh (2017), *Reflective Practice in English Language Teaching: Research-Based Principles and Practice*. London: Routledge.

Mantzourani, E., S. Desselle, J. Le, J.M. Lonie and C. Lucas (2019), 'The role of reflective practice in healthcare professions: Next steps for pharmacy education and practice', *Research in Social and Administrative Pharmacy*, 15(12), 1476–9. https://doi.org/10.1016/j.sapharm.2019.03.011

Matthews, J., A. Bialocerkowski and M. Molineux (2019), 'Professional identity measures for student health professionals: A systematic review of psychometric properties', *BMC Medical Education*, 19, 308. https://doi.org/10.1186/s12909-019-1660-5

McCartney, J. and S.A. Boschmans (2018), 'South African pharmacy student perspectives of a hospital-based experiential learning programme', *Pharmacy Education*, 18(1), 29–40.

McCluskey, J., A.L. Gallagher and C.A. Murphy (2022), 'Reflective practice across speech and language therapy and education: A protocol for an integrative review', *HRB Open Research*, 4, 29. https://doi.org/10.12688/hrbopenres.13234.2

McDermott, F. (2020), *Inside Group Work: A Guide to Reflective Practice*. Abingdon: Routledge.

McHale, C.T and J.E. Cecil (2021), 'Observing identity: Measuring professional identity empirically in the healthcare professions', in Ellis, R. and E. Hogard (eds.), *Professional Identity in the Caring Professions*. London: Routledge, pp. 354–72.

McNeil, K.A., R.J. Mitchell and V. Parker (2013), 'Interprofessional practice and professional identity threat', *Health Sociology Review*, 22(3), 291–307. https://doi.org/10.5172/hesr.2013.22.3.291

Membrive, A., N. Silva, M.J. Rochera and I. Merino (2022), 'Advancing the conceptualization of learning trajectories: A review of learning across contexts', *Learning, Culture and Social Interaction*, 37, 100658. https://doi.org/10.1016/j.lcsi.2022.100658

Mergler, A. (2008), 'Making the implicit explicit: Values and morals in Queensland teacher education', *Australian Journal of Teacher Education*, 33(4), 1–10. http://dx.doi.org/10.14221/ajte.2008v33n4.1

Merriam-Webster Collegiate Dictionary (n.d.), 'Pretending', www.merriam-webster.com/dictionary/pretend (accessed 8 October 2023).

Mileder, L.P., A. Schmidt and H.P. Dimai (2014), 'Clinicians should be aware of their responsibilities as role models: A case report on the impact of poor role modelling', *Medical Education Online*, 19(1). https://doi.org/10.3402/meo.v19.23479

Miles-Tapping, C., G.A. Rennie, M. Duffy, L. Rooke and S. Holstein (1992), 'Canadian physiotherapists' professional identity: An exploratory survey', *Physiotherapy Canada*, 44(4), 31–5.

Miller, S. (2005), '"What it's like being the 'holder of the space'": A narrative on working with reflective practice in groups', *Reflective Practice*, 6(3), 367–77. https://doi.org/10.1080/14623940500220129

Miraglia, R. and M.E. Asselin (2015), 'Reflection as an educational strategy in nursing professional development: An integrative review', *Journal for Nurses in Professional Development*, 31, 62–72. https://doi.org/10.1097/NND.0000000000000151

Mishler, E.G. (1984), *The Discourse of Medicine: The Dialectics of Medical Interviews*. Norwood, NJ: Ablex.

Mohammadi, E., H. Shahsavari, A. Mirzazadeh, A.A. Sohrabpour and S. Mortaz Hejri (2020), 'Improving role modeling in clinical teachers: A narrative literature review', *Journal of Advances in Medical Education and Professionalism*, 8(1), 1–9. https://doi.org/10.30476/jamp.2019.74929

Mulder, H., E. ter Braak, H. Carrie Chen and O. ten Cate (2019), 'Addressing the hidden curriculum in the clinical workplace: A practical tool for trainees and faculty', *Medical Teacher*, 41(1), 36–43. https://doi.org/10.1080/0142159X.2018.1436760

Murray, R., E. McKay, S. Thompson and M. Donald (2000), 'Practising reflection: A medical humanities approach to occupational therapist education', *Medical Teacher*, 22(3), 276–81. https://doi.org/10.1080/01421590050006250

Nancarrow, S. and A. Borthwick (2021), 'Diversity in the allied health professions', in Nancarrow, S. and A. Borthwick (eds.), *The Allied Health Professions: A Sociological Perspective*. Bristol: Policy Press, pp. 57–82.

National HSCP Office (2019), *A Guide to the Health and Social Care Professions by the National HSCP Office*. Galway, Ireland: Health Services Executive (HSE). https://acslm.ie/wp-content/uploads/2022/04/a-guide-to-the-health-and-social-care-professions.pdf

Nikas, I.P., D. Lamnisos, M. Meletiou-Mavrotheris, S.C. Themistocleous, C. Pieridi, D.G. Mytilinaios, C. Michaelides and E.O. Johnson (2022), 'Shift to emergency remote preclinical medical education amidst the Covid-19 pandemic: A single-institution study', *Anatomical Sciences Education*, 15(1), 27–41. https://doi.org/10.1002/ase.2159

Nikitin, J. and A.M. Freund (2018), 'Feeling loved and integrated or lonely and rejected in everyday life: The role of age and social motivation', *Developmental Psychology*, 54, 1186–1198. https://doi.org/10.1037/dev0000502

Nikkels, A., P. Berns and K. Neijenhuis (2023), 'Communication partner training for SLT students: Changes in communication skills, knowledge and confidence', *Journal of Communication Disorders*, 105, 106366, 1–12. https://doi.org/10.1016/j.jcomdis.2023.106366

Noble, C., I. Coombes, L. Nissen, P.N. Shaw and A. Clavarino (2015), 'Making the transition from pharmacy student to pharmacist: Australian interns' perceptions of professional identity formation', *International Journal of Pharmacy Practice*, 23(4), 292–304. https://doi.org/10.1111/ijpp.12155

Noble, C., L. McKauge and A. Clavarino (2019), 'Pharmacy student professional identity formation: A scoping review', *Integrated Pharmacy Research and Practice*, 8, 15–34. https://doi.org/10.2147/IPRP.S162799

O'Hare, A.J. (2021), 'Risking being yourself: Owning your identity within the academic framework', in Hall, M.P. and A.K. Brault (eds.), *Academia from the Inside*. Cham: Palgrave Macmillan, pp. 25–46.

O'Leary, N. and P. Cantillon (2020), 'Why shouldn't we do that on placement if we're doing it in the real world? Differences between undergraduate and graduate identities in speech and language therapy', *Advances in Health Sciences Education*, 25(4), 781–97. https://doi.org/10.1007/s10459-020-09955-0

O'Neill, D., E. Jenkins, R. Mawhinney, E. Cosgrave, S. O'Mahony, C. Guest and H. Moss (2016), 'Rethinking the medical in medical humanities', *Medical Humanities*, 42(2), 109–14. https://doi.org/10.1136/medhum-2015-010831

O'Rourke, K.C., P. Rooney and F. Boylan (2015), 'What's the use of a VLE?', *Irish Journal of Academic Practice*, 4(1), Article 10. http://arrow.dit.ie/ijap/vol4/iss1/1

Paice, E., S. Heard and F. Moss (2002), 'How important are role models in making good doctors?', *British Medical Journal*, 325, 707–10. https://doi.org/10.1136/bmj.325.7366.707

Pais Marden, M. and J. Herrington (2022), 'Encouraging reflective practice through learning portfolios in an authentic online foreign language learning environment', *Reflective Practice*, 23(2), 177–89. https://doi.org/10.1080/14623943.2021.2001321

Palacios, N., Y. Gao, E. Mourelatou and R. Rafique (2024), 'Engaging in online peer-led group reflective practice through the share your research ideas project: Students' and tutors' reflective accounts', *Reflective Practice*, 25(1), 27–39. https://doi.org/10.1080/14623943.2023.2284320

Peebles, E. (2014), 'Cyberbullying: Hiding behind the screen', *Paediatrics & Child Health*, 19(10), 527–8. https://doi.org/10.1093/pch/19.10.527

Philip, L. (2006), 'Encouraging reflective practice amongst students: A direct assessment approach', *Planet*, 17(1), 37–9. https://doi.org/10.11120/plan.2006.00170037

Porter, J. and A. Wilton (2019), 'Professional identity of allied health staff', *Journal of Allied Health*, 48(1), 11–17.

Porter, J. and A. Wilton (2020), 'Professional identity of allied health staff associated with a major health network organizational restructuring', *Nursing and Health Sciences*, 22(4), 1103–10. https://doi.org/10.1111/nhs.12777

Pratt, M.G., K.W. Rockman and J.B. Kaufmann (2006), 'Constructing professional identity: The role of work and identity learning cycles in the customisation of identity among medical residents', *Academy of Management Journal*, 40(2), 235–62. https://doi.org/10.5465/amj.2006.20786060

Préfontaine, C., I. Gaboury, H. Corriveau, J. Beauchamp, C. Lemire and M-J. April (2021), 'Assessment tools for reflection in healthcare learners: A scoping review', *Medical Teacher*, 44(4), 394–400. https://doi.org/10.1080/0142159X.2021.1998400

Pyrko, I., V. Dörfler and C. Eden (2019), 'Communities of practice in landscapes of practice', *Management Learning*, 50(4), 482–99. https://doi.org/10.1177/1350507619860854

Quigley, D. (2021), 'When I say...feedback literacy', *Medical Education*, 55(10), 1121–2. https://doi.org/10.1111/medu.14541

Rainford, L.A., M. Zanardo, C. Buissink, R. Decoster, W. Hennessy, K. Knapp, B. Kraus, L. Lanca, S. Lewis, T.B. Mahlaola, M. McEntee, D.O' Leary, H. Precht, T. Starc and J.P. McNulty (2021), 'The impact of Covid-19 upon student radiographers and clinical training', *Radiography*, 27, 464–74. https://doi.org/10.1016/j.radi.2020.10.015

Rappazzo, L., S. Seagrave and S. Gough (2022), 'Forming and shaping of professional identity within pre-registration physiotherapy curricular: A scoping review', *Nurse Education Today*, 109, 105250. https://doi.org/10.1016/j.nedt.2021.105250

Ravalier, J.M., P. Wegrzynek, A. Mitchell, J. McGowan, P. Mcfadden and C. Bald (2023), 'A rapid review of reflective supervision in social work', *The British Journal of Social Work*, 53(4), 1945–62. https://doi.org/10.1093/bjsw/bcac223

Richards, K. (2006), *Language and Professional Identity: Aspects of Collaborative Interaction*. Basingstoke: Palgrave Macmillan.

Rolfe, G., D. Freshwater and M. Jasper (2001), *Critical Reflection in Nursing and the Helping Professions: A User's Guide*. Basingstoke: Palgrave Macmillan.

Rose, G. (2001), *Visual Methodologies*. London: Sage.

Rothstein-Fisch, C., E. Trumbull and S.G Garcia (2009), 'Making the implicit explicit: Supporting teachers to bridge cultures', *Early Childhood Research Quarterly*, 24(4), 474–86. https://doi.org/10.1016/j.ecresq.2009.08.006

Rubin, H. and I. Rubin (2005), *Qualitative Interviewing: The Art of Hearing Data*. London: Sage.

Ryan, E. (2018), *"I Think Everybody's Finding It a Challenge to Be Honest": The Experience of Mental Health Professionals Working in Child and Adolescent Mental Health Services in Ireland*. Unpublished M.Litt Thesis, Trinity College Dublin, Ireland.

Sahin, I. and M. Shelley (eds.) (2020), *Educational Practices during the COVID-19 Viral Outbreak: International Perspectives*. Monument, CO: ISTES Organization.

Sarangi, S. and C. Roberts (1999), *Talk, Work and Institutional Order: Discourse in Medical, Mediation and Management Settings*. Berlin: Mouton de Gruyter.

Scaffa, M.E. and D.M. Wooster (2004), 'Effects of problem-based learning on clinical reasoning in occupational therapy', *American Journal of Occupational Therapy*, 58, 333–6. https://doi.org/10.5014/ajot.58.3.333

Schön, D.A. (1983), *The Reflective Practitioner: How Professionals Think in Action*. New York: Basic Books.

Sellars, M. (2017), *Reflective Practice for Teachers*. London: Sage.

Sert, O. (2015), *Social Interaction and L2 Classroom Discourse*. Edinburgh: Edinburgh University Press.

Shadden, B. (2005), 'Aphasia as identity theft: Theory and practice', *Aphasiology*, 19(3–5), 211–23. https://doi.org/10.1080/02687930444000697

Shadden, B.B and J.P. Agan (2004), 'Renegotiation of identity: The social context of aphasia support groups', *Topics in Language Disorders*, 24(3), 174–86. https://doi.org/10.1097/00011363-200407000-00005

Sharpless, J., N. Baldwin, R. Cooke, A. Kofman, A. Morley-Fletcher, R. Slotkin and H.S. Wald (2015), 'The becoming: Students' reflections on the process of professional identity formation in medical education', *Academic Medicine*, 90, 713–17. https://doi.org/10.1097/ACM.0000000000000729

Shaver, J. (2022), 'The state of telehealth before and after the COVID-19 pandemic', *Primary Care*, 49(4), 517–30. https://doi.org/10.1016/j.pop.2022.04.002

Simmons-Mackie, N. (1998), 'In support of supported conversation for adults with aphasia', *Aphasiology*, 12, 831–7. https://doi.org/10.1080/02687039808249576

Simmons-Mackie, N. (2000), 'Social approaches to management of aphasia', in Worrall, L. and C. Frattali (eds.), *Neurogenic Communication Disorders: A Functional Approach*. New York: Thieme, pp. 162–88.

Simmons-Mackie, N. (2001), 'Social approaches to aphasia intervention', in R. Chapey (ed.), *Language Intervention Strategies in Adult Aphasia*. Baltimore, MD: Williams & Wilkins, pp. 246–68.

Simmons-Mackie, N. and R.J. Elman (2011), 'Negotiation of identity in group therapy for aphasia: The Aphasia Café', *International Journal of Language & Communication Disorders*, 46(3), 312–23. https://doi.org/10.3109/13682822.2010.507616

Smith, J.A. and M. Fieldsend (2021), 'Interpretative phenomenological analysis', in Camic, P.M. (ed.), *Qualitative Research in Psychology: Expanding Perspectives in Methodology and Design*. Washington, DC: American Psychological Association, pp. 147–66.

Smith, J.A. and I. Nizza (2021), *Essentials of Interpretative Phenomenological Analysis*. Washington, DC: APA.

Smith, J.A. and M. Osborn (2003), 'Interpretative phenomenological analysis', in Smith, J.A. (ed.), *Qualitative Psychology: A Practical Guide to Methods*. London: Sage, pp. 51–80.

Smith, J.A. and M. Osborn (2015), 'Interpretative phenomenological analysis as a useful methodology for research on the lived experience of pain', *British Journal of Pain*, 9(1), 41–2. https://doi.org/10.1177/2049463714541642

Smith, J.A., P. Flowers and M. Larkin (2009), *Interpretative Phenomenological Analysis: Theory, Method and Research*. London: Sage.

Smith, J.A., P. Flowers and M. Larkin (2022), *Interpretative Phenomenological Analysis: Theory, Method, Research* (2nd ed.). London: Sage.

Smith, S., M. Molineux, N. Rowe and L. Larkinson (2006), 'Integrating medical humanities into physiotherapy and occupational therapy education', *International Journal of Therapy and Rehabilitation*, 13(9), 421–47. https://doi.org/10.12968/ijtr.2006.13.9.21787

Snell, R., S. Fyfe, G. Fyfe, D. Blackwood and C. Itsiopoulos (2020), 'Development of professional identity and professional socialisation in allied health students: A scoping review', *Focus on Health Professional Education: A Multi-Professional Journal*, 21(1), 29–56. https://doi.org/10.11157/fohpe.v21i1.322

Snowdon, D.A., M. Sargent, C.M. Williams, S. Maloney, K. Caspers and N.F. Nicholas (2020), 'Effective clinical supervision of allied health professionals: A mixed methods study', *BMC Health Services Research*, 20(2). https://doi.org/10.1186/s12913-019-4873-8

Snyder, C.R., B.K. Frogner and S.M. Skillman (2018), 'Facilitating racial and ethnic diversity in the health workforce', *Journal of Allied Health*, 47(1), 58–65.

Solomon, P. (2005), 'Problem-based learning: A review of current issues relevant to physiotherapy education', *Physiotherapy Theory and Practice*, 21(1), 37–49. https://doi.org/10.1080/09593980590911499

Sravanti, L., J.V.S. Kommu, S.C. Girimaji and S. Seshadri (2022), 'Lived experiences of children and adolescents with obsessive-compulsive disorder: Interpretative phenomenological analysis', *Child and Adolescent Psychiatry and Mental Health*, 16(1), 44. https://doi.org/10.1186/s13034-022-00478-7

Sternszus, R. and S. Cruess (2016), 'Learning from role modelling: Making the implicit explicit', *Lancet*, 387(10025), 1257–8. https://doi.org/10.1016/S0140-6736(16)00381-0

Stillman, R., R. Snow and K. Warren (1999), '"I used to be good with kids": Encounters between speech-language pathology students and children with pervasive developmental disorders (PDD)', in Kovarsky, D., M. Maxwell and J.F Duchan (eds.), *Constructing (In)competence: Disabling Evaluations in Clinical and Social Interaction* (1st ed.). New York: Psychology Press, pp. 29–48.

Stokes, J. and M. McCormick (2015), *Speech and Language Therapy and Professional Identity: Challenging Received Wisdom*. Guildford: J&R Press.

Strudwick, R.M., N. Cushen-Brewster, C. Doolan and P. Driscoll-Evans (2021), 'An evaluation of the experiences of academics and practice educators who supported radiography students working on the temporary HCPC register during the COVID-pandemic', *Radiography*, 27, 1179–84. https://doi.org/10.1016/j.radi.2021.07.001

Tajfel, H. and Turner, J.C. (1979), 'An integrative theory of intergroup conflict', in Austin, W.G. and S. Worchel (eds.), *The Social Psychology of Intergroup Relations*. Monterey, CA: Brooks/Cole, pp. 33–48.

Taubner, H., M. Hallén and Å. Wengelin (2020), 'Still the same? Self-identity dilemmas when living with post-stroke aphasia in a digitalised society', *Aphasiology*, 34(3), 300–18. https://doi.org/10.1080/02687038.2019.1594151

Taylor, B. (1993), 'Phenomenology: One way to understand nursing practice', *International Journal of Nursing Studies*, 30(2), 171–9. https://doi.org/10.1016/0020-7489(93)90066-4

Teskereci, G. and I. Boz (2019), '"I try to act like a nurse": A phenomenological qualitative study', *Nurse Education in Practice*, 37, 39–44. https://doi.org/10.1016/j.nepr.2019.03.009

Thomas, E.F., C. McGarty and K. Mavor (2016), 'Group interaction as the crucible of social identity formation: A glimpse at the foundations of social identities for collective action', *Group Processes and Intergroup Relations*, 19(2), 137–51. https://doi.org/10.1177/1368430215612217

Thow, M. and R. Murray (1991), 'Medical humanities in physiotherapy: Education and practice', *Physiotherapy*, 77(11), 733–6. https://doi.org/10.1016/S0031-9406(10)62042-1

Towle, A. and W. Godolphin (2013), 'Patients as educators: Interprofessional learning for patient-centred care', *Medical Teacher*, 35, 219–25. https://doi.org/10.3109/0142159X.2012.737966

Tracy, K. and J.S. Robles (2013), *Everyday Talk: Building and Reflecting Identities* (2nd ed.). London: Guildford Press.

Trede, F., R. Macklin and D. Bridges (2012), 'Professional identity development: A review of the higher education literature', *Studies in Higher Education*, 37(3), 365–84. https://doi.org/10.1080/03075079.2010.521237

Turner, A. and J. Knight (2015), 'A debate on the professional identity of occupational therapists', *British Journal of Occupational Therapy*, 78(11), 664–73. https://doi.org/10.1177/0308022615601439

Turner, S. and A. Whitworth (2006), 'Conversational partner training programmes in aphasia: A review of key themes and participants' roles', *Aphasiology*, 20(6), 483–510. https://doi.org/10.1080/02687030600589991

Urban, E. (2013), 'Reflections on research and learning from the patient: The art and science of what we do', *Journal of Analytical Psychology*, 58(4), 510–29. https://doi.org/10.1111/1468-5922.12030

van Manen, M. (2014), *Phenomenology of Practice: Meaning-giving Methods in Phenomenological Research and Writing*. Walnut Creek, CA: Left Coast Press.

van Manen, M. (2017), 'But is it phenomenology?', *Qualitative Health Research*, 27(6), 775–9. https://doi.org/10.1177/1049732317699570

Volpe, R.L., M. Hopkins, P. Haidet, D.R. Wolpaw and N.E. Adams (2019), 'Is research on professional identity formation biased? Early insights from a scoping review and metasynthesis', *Medical Education*, 5(2), 119–32. https://doi.org/10.1111/medu.13781

Wald, H., J. White, S. Reis, A. Esquibel and D. Anthony (2018), 'Grappling with complexity: Medical students' reflective writings about challenging patient encounters as a window into professional identity formation', *Medical Teacher*, 41(2), 152–60. https://doi.org/10.1080/0142159X.2018.1475727

Walder, K., M. Bissett, M. Molineux and G. Whiteford (2022), 'Understanding professional identity in occupational therapy: A scoping review', *Scandinavian Journal of Occupational Therapy*, 29(3), 175–97. https://doi.org/10.1080/11038128.2021.1974548

Walsh, I.P. (2020), 'Medical humanities and the constructions of "self": Invoking literary autobiography to educate healthcare students in communication and mental health disorder', in Jagoe, C. and I.P. Walsh (eds.), *Communication and Mental Health Disorders: Developing Theory, Growing Practice*. Guildford: J R Press Ltd, pp. 151–76.

Walsh, I.P. and A. Mallinson (2022), 'Spotlight on: Humanities in speech and language therapy', *Advances in Communication and Swallowing*, 25(1), 53–7. https://doi.org/10.3233/ACS-210040

Walsh, I.P., P. Delmar and C. Jagoe (2018), '"It's not the Asperger's that causes the anxiety, it's the communication": Person-centred outcomes of hope and recovery in a cultural–clinical borderland', *Topics in Language Disorders*, 38(2), 108–25. https://doi.org/10.1097/TLD.0000000000000149

Waxman D., M. Alexander, H.A. Kirkpatrick and P. Blasco (2005), 'Interviewing skills', in Alexander, M., P. Lenahan and A. Pavlov (eds.), *Cinemeducation: A Comprehensive Guide to Using Film in Medical Education*. London: Routledge, pp. 125–9.

Wenger, E. (1998), *Communities of Practice: Learning, Meaning and Identity*. Cambridge: Cambridge University Press.

Wenger-Trayner E, M. Fenton-O'Creevy, S. Hutchison, C. Kubiak and B. Wenger-Trayner (2014), *Learning in Landscapes of Practice: Boundaries, Identity, and Knowledgeability in Practice-Based Learning*. New York: Routledge.

Whalen, S., J. Goldstein, R. Urquhart and A.J.E. Carter (2018), 'The novel role of paramedics in collaborative emergency centres aligns with their professional identity: A qualitative analysis', *Canadian Journal of Emergency Medicine*, 20(4), 518–22. https://doi.org/10.1017/cem.2018.401

Whitehill, T.L., S. Bridges and K. Chan (2014), 'Problem-based learning (PBL) and speech-language pathology: A tutorial', *Clinical Linguistics and Phonetics*, 28(1–2), 5–23. https://doi.org/10.3109/02699206.2013.821524

Wilbur, K., C. Snyder, A.C. Essary, S. Reddy, K.K. Will and M. Saxon (2020), 'Developing workforce diversity in the health professions: A social justice perspective', *Health Professions Education*, 6(2), 222–9. https://doi.org/10.1016/j.hpe.2020.01.002

Wilding, P.M (2008), 'Reflective practice: A learning tool for student nurses', *British Journal of Nursing*, 17(11), 720–4. https://doi.org/10.12968/bjon.2008.17.11.29644

Winkel, A.F., S. Yingling, A.A. Jones and J. Nicholson (2017), 'Reflection as a learning tool in graduate medical education: A systematic review', *Journal of Graduate Medical Education*, 9(4), 430–9. https://doi.org/10.4300/JGME-D-16-00500.1

Wong, A. and K. Trollope-Kumar (2014), 'Reflections: An inquiry into medical students' professional identity formation', *Medical Education*, 48(5), 489–501. https://doi.org/10.1111/medu.12382

Wortham, S. (2006), *Learning Identity: The Joint Emergence of Social Identification and Academic Learning*. Cambridge: Cambridge University Press.

Yeowell, G. (2013), '"Isn't it all Whites?" Ethnic diversity and the physiotherapy profession', *Physiotherapy*, 99(4), 341–6. https://doi.org/10.1016/j.physio.2013.01.004

Yu, B., R. Horton, B. Munson, B.L. Newkirk-Turner, V.E. Johnson, R. Khamis-Dakwar, M.L. Muñoz and Y.D. Hyter (2022), 'Making race visible in the speech, language, and hearing sciences: A critical discourse analysis', *American Journal of Speech-Language Pathology*, 31(2), 578–600. https://doi.org/10.1044/2021_AJSLP-20-00384

Zheng, B., M. Niiya and M. Warschauer (2015), 'Wikis and collaborative learning in higher education', *Technology, Pedagogy and Education*, 24(3), 357–74. https://doi.org/10.1080/1475939X.2014.948041

Ziebart, C. and J.C. MacDermid (2019), 'Reflective practice in physical therapy: A scoping review', *Physical Therapy*, 99(8), 1056–68. https://doi.org/10.1093/ptj/pzz049

INDEX